Men of Integrity

Men of Integrity

A Daily Guide to the Bible and Prayer

W PUBLISHING GROUP™

www.wpublishinggroup.com

A Division of Thomas Nelson, Inc.
www.ThomasNelson.com

Scripture quotations used in this book are from the *Holy Bible, New
International Version* (NIV). Copyright © 1973, 1978, 1984, International Bible
Society. Used by permission of Zondervan Bible Publishers.

Editors: Harry Genet, Ashley Nearn, Linda Gehrs.
Art Director, Interior: Doug Johnson.

*With special thanks to Linda Gehrs,
who went above and beyond the call of duty
to bring this book together.*

Library of Congress Cataloging-in-Publication Data

Men of Integrity : a daily guide to the Bible and prayer /
by Christianity Today, Inc.
p.   cm.
ISBN 0-8499-3774-4 (tp)
1. Christian men Prayer-books and devotions—English.
2. Devotional calendars. I. Christianity Today, Inc.
BV4843.M46   1999
242'.642—dc21
99-38049
CIP

Printed in the United States of America
9 RRD 05 04 03 02

Preface

This book fulfills a dream.

People told us, "You·can't do a devotional for men. There are hardly any devotionals for men because men don't use devotionals."

We said, "Maybe men don't use devotionals because they haven't had ones created just for them. What would happen if we created from scratch a devotional by men for men?"

So we started meeting with men's groups, most of which meet at six o'clock in the morning. We talked to men in suburban churches, small-town churches, urban churches. These men told us with gut-level honesty about what they really wanted and would use in a devotional:

- The Bible verses should be printed in full inside the guide, because often men are in their cars or trucks or on a plane and don't have a Bible available.

- The topics needed to address real-life issues men face—work, anger, sexual purity, courage, listening to God.

- Each day's reading needed to be short enough so men could finish it in the limited time they had.

- The devotional should be written by well-known Christian leaders and also by ordinary Christian men who are trying to live out their faith.

We listened and then went to work with our friends at Promise Keepers to create *Men of Integrity*. We've already tested these devotional readings with more than thirty thousand men, and we've found they love and use them. In fact, men using *Men of Integrity* read it almost every single day!

Since *Men of Integrity* was created by men like you, for men like you, I'm confident it will help you read the Bible and learn from it. It will help you pray and to live a life pleasing to God. My prayer is that as you read *Men of Integrity,* you will hear God speak to you.

—*Kevin A. Miller*
Vice President, Editorial Development
Christianity Today, Inc.

Reading My Wife's Face

Key Bible Verses: Husbands, love your wives, just as Christ loved the church and gave himself up for her to make her holy … without stain or wrinkle or any other blemish, but holy and blameless *(Ephesians 5:25–27)*. *Bonus Reading: 1 Peter 3:7; Proverbs 15:13*

Not long ago, God showed me I had been blind to the pain of my wife, Lyndi. It's a humbling admission. Imagine, the founder of a men's movement dedicated to honoring Jesus and family didn't have his own act together at home!

My wake-up call came when a preacher said, "Do you want to know the character of a man? Look into the face of his wife. Whatever he has invested in her or withheld from her will be reflected in her countenance."

That preacher went through Scripture, showing me God has *mandated* that every man draw his wife to splendor in Jesus Christ.

I looked at Lyndi, and instead of splendor, I saw pain.

I knew then, for the sake of our marriage and the testimony of Jesus Christ in my life, that I had to choose. I resigned as football coach at the University of Colorado to devote myself to Lyndi. I wanted to do my part as a husband so God could bring Lyndi back to her glory, and I have not regretted it.

—Bill McCartney, founder of Promise Keepers

Personal Challenge:
• *Look at your wife's face. Does it reflect your love?*
• *Pray to love your wife as Christ loved the church.*

Thought to Apply: The face is the mirror of the mind; and eyes, without speaking, confess the secrets of the heart.   —JEROME (Bible translator, 4th century)

The Power of Listening

Key Bible Verse: Everyone should be quick to listen, slow to speak and slow to become angry… *(James 1:19).*
Bonus Reading: Proverbs 17:27–28

Not long ago, my wife, Norma, and I went on a short trip with our good friends the Brawners. In the driveway before we left, Suzette said to Jim, "I feel so nervous about leaving Travis (their 17-year-old) home alone the first week of two-a-day football practices. Who's going to make his breakfast? Who's going to have his sandwiches ready? Isn't Travis going to feel he's been abandoned?"

Without thinking, Jim said, "Come on, Suzette, will you relax? We've got to take vacations once in a while. Let the kids grow up."

Then he realized what he was doing, and he stopped attacking his wife's feelings. He hugged her and said, "I see you're really hurting. That's OK. Should we cancel the trip?"

"No, I want to go. It's just hard," she said.

We men need to understand that in healthy homes, everyone feels free to express feelings without fear of hearing "That's stupid!" "Only an idiot would feel like that," or "Why don't you grow up?" Maybe the feelings are immature, but they're real nonetheless. It's not our job to analyze; it *is* our duty to love, value, and understand our families.

—*Gary Smalley, co-author of* The Language of Love

Personal Challenge:

• *Ask a family member, "How was your day?" Listen well.*
• *Thank God that he listens to you.*

Thought to Apply: He who can no longer listen to his brother will soon no longer be listening to God, either.
—DIETRICH BONHOEFFER (pastor martyred by Hitler's regime)

Me and My Big Mouth

Key Bible Verse: Honor your father and your mother, so that you may live long in the land the Lord your God is giving you *(Exodus 20:12). Bonus Reading: Ephesians 6:1–3; Colossians 3:20*

When I became a Christian at 19, I was excited and tried to tell my parents.

But I was clueless about tact. I came across as pious and judgmental, like Mom and Dad had failed me in my religious upbringing. I criticized the "dead" church I'd grown up in. I challenged my parents' faith. I did everything but literally whack them over the head with my Bible.

That was the beginning of many years of tension between me and my parents. It reached the point where we couldn't discuss religion without a big argument.

But over the years, I've learned a few things about diplomacy and relationships, especially with my parents. It all boils down to this:

Do the things I say and do *honor* my parents?

Today's Key Bible Verse applies not just to young children, but adults as well. No matter how right I think I am, God always calls me to honor Mom and Dad.

—*Mark Moring, editor of Men of Integrity*

Personal Challenge:
• *Think about your relationship with your parents. In what ways do you show honor and respect? In what ways might you have to improve?*
• *Ask God to show you practical ways to show honor to your parents.*

Thought to Apply: "Reverence for parents" stands written among the three laws of most revered righteousness.
—AESCHYLUS (ancient Greek playwright)

"I'm So Sorry"

Key Bible Verse: Confess your sins to each other and pray for each other so that you may be healed *(James 5:16). Bonus Readings: Psalm 51:1–12; Proverbs 28:13*

Kim and I had been married just a few months when we took a week-long vacation to a Caribbean island. No phones, no TVs, just peace and relaxation ... but I had a confession to make.

"Kim," I said, "all the time we were dating, when you thought I was being true to you, I wasn't."

She stared at me, her eyes filling. "You mean ... ?" she said.

I nodded.

"You were with other girls?"

I nodded miserably. "I'm so sorry."

Kim's trust faded and her pain built right before my eyes. I told her I was starting over and that I would be the man God wanted me to be from then on.

It's taken months and years of pain, but slowly, I began to earn Kim's trust.

Our marriage today is deeper and happier and more honest than ever. But it all started with that confession.

God began working in me because I had emptied myself. God filled the void in me that had so long been filled by my ego, my sin.

I was finished running from God. I was running to him.

—Mike Singletary, former Chicago Bears linebacker

Personal Challenge:
* *Do you have a confession to make to a family member?*
* *Pray that God will help you to honestly share your struggles.*

Thought to Apply: We need not "sin that grace may abound." We are sinners and need only to confess that grace may abound. — C. FITZSIMONS ALLISON (Christian leader)

The Ultimate Protection Plan

Key Bible Verses: Pray continually; give thanks in all circumstances, for this is God's will for you in Christ Jesus *(1 Thessalonians 5:17–18). Bonus Reading: John 17:6–19*

Without a doubt, the most important protection we can offer our wives and children is in our prayers.

That may sound like something right out of a sermon, but it's true. In fact, surveys illustrate the power of prayer.

We've all seen the alarming statistics for the divorce rate in the United States. Sadly, the rate isn't much better for people who say they're evangelical Christians.

But a Gallup Poll also revealed an amazing stat: For couples who pray together every night, the divorce rate is an incredible 1 in 1,052!

I mention this not because God's Word needs independent verification, but because it amazes me how science always eventually catches up to the Scriptures.

The way Jesus prayed for protection for his followers gives a model of how we can put a spiritual hedge around ourselves and our families. God may still allow us to encounter times of severe testing, but he remains faithful to us and our families when we are committed to prayer.

—John Trent, president of Encouraging Words

Personal Challenge:
• *What family needs can you consistently pray for?*
• *Ask God to help you faithfully pray for your family.*

Thought to Apply: A man prayed, and at first he thought that prayer was talking. But he became more and more quiet until in the end he realized that prayer is listening. —SOREN KIERKEGAARD (theologian, 19th century)

Up Close & Personal with Rod Cooper

What DO Wives Want?

Q What do wives want from their husbands?

A I've counseled hundreds of men and their wives, and the wife raises the same lament: over and over "Why won't he let me into his life? Why won't he share with me? Why can't we have the intimacy that I long to have in this relationship?"

But that can be scary.
I confess that I've found this to be true in my own life. I've been married for fourteen years. I have a wonderful wife who loves me beyond words. But whenever we get close—you know what I mean: a "soul" closeness—I get nervous and scared and want to pull away. It's as if this wall goes up in me, and alarms go off: "Red alert, red alert!"

By God's grace and the patience of my wife, I've been slowly tearing down the bricks in the wall and have started to come out of hiding—but it has not been easy.

Give us an example.
I remember coming back from a trip for Promise Keepers. I'd given my message, and God had blessed the time. I couldn't wait to tell Nancy about how well it had gone, but that meant also telling her how scared I'd been.

When I entered the door, Nancy hugged me and asked me those four key words, "How did it go?" I then responded with my one key word, "Fine." Inside, it seemed a wall had gone up. I, for some irrational reason, felt that if I told Nancy about my fears, I would be judged for not trusting God enough and consequently be abandoned for not being a good spiritual leader.

Nancy did continue to ask me, and finally I told

her about my fear. She only affirmed me and told me how much faith it took to get in front of all those men and be God's spokesman. Nancy didn't abandon me—she blessed me. We men miss tremendous blessings from those around us, due to our belief that if we share our inadequacies, we'll be abandoned. In fact, by being silent, we end up being abandoned, which is the very thing we fear.

Dr. Rodney L. Cooper is director of the Robert B. Pamplin Institute for Leadership, Education Development, and Research at Western Seminary in Portland, Oregon.

Family — Sunday, Week 1

For Personal Study or Group Discusssion

Real Life Application

Key Bible Verse: Be kind and compassionate to one another, forgiving each other, just as in Christ God forgave you *(Ephesians 4:32). Bonus Reading: Ephesians 4:25-31*

Think and pray about these sentence starters.

☐ To me, a good family is …

☐ As I've been thinking about my family this week, I've realized …

☐ One way I'd like God to help me and my family is …

To order *Men of Integrity* **for your men's group, call 1-800-806-7796. Credits:** Adapted from—Monday: *Go the Distance: The Making of a Promise Keeper* (Focus on the Family, 1996); Tuesday: *Seven Promises of a Promise Keeper* (Focus on the Family, 1994); Thursday: *Singletary on Singletary* by Mike Singletary and Jerry B. Jenkins (Thomas Nelson Publishers, Inc., 1991); Friday: *The Making of a Godly Man* (Focus on the Family, 1997); Saturday: *Shoulder to Shoulder* by Rodney L. Cooper (Copyright © 1997 by Rodney L. Cooper. Used by permission of Zondervan Publishing House).

Pouring a Foundation

Key Bible Verse: Everyone who hears these words of mine and puts them into practice is like a wise man who built his house on the rock *(Matthew 7:24).*
Bonus Reading: Isaiah 33:6; 1 Corinthians 3:10–15

When our church organized a work team for a short-term missions trip to Spain, they wanted "skilled" workers, but were willing to take a few non-handy guys like me.

Fortunately, we had enough guys like Art, who knew everything there was to know about pouring concrete. We were building foundations for buildings at a Christian camp for kids.

Another church team had worked at the site the week before we arrived. Unfortunately, the foundations they'd poured were already beginning to crumble at the edges.

But Art knew how to do it right, using forms around the edges and reinforcing rods to hold things together.

Jesus tells us to take the same care with our spiritual foundations, to build our "house upon the rock."

How do we do that? Through a promise keeper's first promise—honoring Christ through worship, prayer and obedience to God's Word.
—*Mark Moring, editor of Men of Integrity*

Personal Challenge:
• *In what ways do you honor Christ?*
• *Praise God today that he is worthy to obey.*

Thought to Apply: You become stronger only when you become weaker. When you surrender your will to God, you discover the resources to do what God requires.
—ERWIN LUTZER (pastor and author)

No Thanks, Playmates

Key Bible Verses: Put off your old self, which is being corrupted by its deceitful desires ... and put on the new self, created to be like God in true righteousness and holiness *(Ephesians 4:22, 24). Bonus Reading: Ephesians 4:17–32*

Florida State University's sports information department had big news for Clay Shiver a few years ago: *Playboy* magazine had selected him for its preseason All-America football team.

But the 6-foot-2, 280-pound center said, "No thanks."

"I couldn't see any good coming from being in the magazine," says Shiver.

Although Shiver realized this "honor" is one of the highest preseason awards a college football player can receive from sportswriters, it also meant an endorsement of *Playboy*. Clay didn't want to embarrass his mother and grandmother by appearing in the magazine or give old high school friends an excuse to buy that issue.

"Clay really gave up being named 'the best player in the country' at his position. It was a witness to people in the football program," says Purvis.

Shiver adds, "I don't want to let anyone down, and number one on that list is God."

—*Ken Walker in* Christian Reader

Personal Challenge:
• *Are you willing to give up honor for yourself in order to honor Christ?*
• *In prayer, give God honor today.*

Thought to Apply: There is only one way to achieve happiness on this terrestrial ball. And that is to have either a clear conscience or none at all.

—OGDEN NASH (poet and humorist)

Barefoot before God

Key Bible Verses: God called to him from within the bush, "Moses! Moses!…Take off your sandals, for the place where you are standing is holy ground" *(Exodus 3:4–5). Bonus Reading: Psalm 100; Revelation 4:1–11*

The incredible story of Moses leading Israel out of Egypt began when Moses fell at God's feet in worship. Walk through it with him:

1. God calls a man into his fiery presence (Exodus 3:1–4). The man who avoids the flame of God's Spirit will never experience a complete burning away of fear and pride.

2. God calls a man to remove his shoes (Exodus 3:5). The issue wasn't bare feet but the removal of one's own self-fashioned support.

3. God calls a man to know God's heart (Exodus 3:7–8). Only in God's presence did Moses learn of God's gentle heart, compassionate nature, and desire to heal and deliver.

4. God calls a man to leadership (Exodus 3:9–10). For Moses, the call was to lead a nation. Your call and mine will likely be less visible, but we are leaders!

Our response to God's call should mirror Moses' response: "Who am I to do these things?" To which God always replies, "I will be with you."
—Jack Hayford, pastor in Van Nuys, California

Personal Challenge:

• *Moses responded to God's call by saying, "Who, me?" When have you felt like that?*
• *Ask God to give you the willingness to do whatever he asks.*

Thought to Apply: We pay God honor and reverence, not for his sake (because he is of himself full of glory to which no creature can add anything), but for our own sake.
—THOMAS AQUINAS (medieval theologian)

Really Big Prayer Requests

Key Bible Verse: The prayer of a righteous man is powerful and effective *(James 5:16b). Bonus Reading: Matthew 6:9–13; Ephesians 6:18*

We live in a culture in decline, with its high rates of violent crime, illegitimate births, teen pregnancy, abortion—I could go on and on. What can we men do to make a difference?

We can pray for revival.

Consider the case of Howell Harris. In 1735, Wales was in decline politically and spiritually, with an upsurge of the occult and black magic. Harris, a new Christian, started to pray, and God met him in a powerful way. Harris traveled around the country, preaching and praying, until all of South Wales was awakened. Even notorious criminals changed their ways.

The secret to Harris's influence was prayer. He understood that nothing could be accomplished—either in himself or throughout his nation—without prayer.

God still needs men who, like Howell Harris, will give themselves to prayer and then go and do whatever the Holy Spirit tells them—men who will fall on their knees and cry out to God. That's where we begin the journey of being transformed into the image of Christ. And as men are transformed, the course of a nation can be changed.

—Wellington Boone, bishop and author in Atlanta

Personal Challenge:
• *Pray for your area and country today.*

Thought to Apply: As it is the business of tailors to make clothes and of cobblers to mend shoes, so it is the business of Christians to pray.

—MARTIN LUTHER (reformer, 16th century)

The Word on THE Word

Key Bible Verse: For those God foreknew he also predestined to be conformed to the likeness of his Son, that he might be the firstborn among many brothers. *(Romans 8:29). Bonus Reading: Psalm 119:97–106; 2 Timothy 3:16–17*

A major sign of manhood is a man's word. To be conformed to the image of Christ, our words must conform to God's Word.

Here are five vital truths concerning God's Word:

1. God's Word is his bond. When God made a promise to Abraham, he swore by himself, because he could swear by nothing greater.

2. God's Word is the expression of his nature. Jesus said, "Anyone who has seen me has seen the Father" (John 14:9).

3. God's Word is the measure of his character. As the Alpha and Omega, there is no end to God's character, and thus no end to his Word.

4. God's Word is magnified above his name. God's name is as good as His Word. When we pray in Jesus' name, we're using His authority.

5. God's Word is the sole source of faith and the absolute rule of conduct. "There is no other name . . . by which we must be saved" (Acts 4:12).

—Edwin Louis Cole, founder of the Christian Men's Network

Personal Challenge

• *What Bible passage has helped you become more like Christ?*
• *Ask God to use His Word to transform your life.*

Thought to Apply: A Bible that's falling apart probably belongs to someone who isn't.

—CHRISTIAN JOHNSON

Up Close & Personal with Randy Phillips

Q. What's it mean to be a man who honors Christ?

A. Ron Brown, assistant football coach at the University of Nebraska, once said, "As a coach, I'm not interested in 'part-time' players. I'm looking for full-time players who will show up ready to play every day, every play. Men who are willing to do what it takes in practice also have what it takes to win in a game. God is looking for full-time players too!"

What's it mean to be a full-time player for God?
They're men who will pay the price of godliness every day. Will there be spiritual mediocrity, or will there be a dynamic, intimate relationship with Jesus Christ?

Randy Phillips is president of Promise Keepers.

For Personal Study or Group Discussion

Key Bible Verse: I will praise you, O Lord, with all my heart; I will tell of all your wonders *(Psalm 9:1). Bonus Reading: Mark 12:30*

Think and pray about these sentence starters on your own. Or, discuss them with other men.

☐ To me, "honoring Christ" means …

☐ Some practical ways I have honored Christ include …

Credits: Tuesday: From *Christian Reader* (Sept./Oct., 1995); Wednesday, Thursday and Friday: Adapted from *Seven Promises of a Promise Keeper* (Focus on the Family, 1994); Saturday: Adapted from *Go the Distance* (Focus on the Family, 1996).

Why I Resist Accountability

Key Bible Verse: As iron sharpens iron, so one man sharpens another *(Proverbs 27:17). Bonus Reading: Ecclesiastes 4:9–12*

Doug Self, with whom I've been meeting weekly since 1976, and I were enjoying our early cup of coffee as usual. We filled each other in on our week's events as usual.

Then, out of the blue, Doug said, "Louis, I have something for you from the Lord."

Not as usual.

Doug proceeded to point out some ungodly attitudes in me that he'd been noticing. He had been hearing me be critical and unloving.

Ouch! I knew what he was referring to. The encounter reminded me why I need accountability—and why I sometimes resist it. I find accountability difficult for at least four reasons:

1. I fear rejection.
2. I feel embarrassed.
3. I fear giving up control.
4. I don't like facing my negative feelings.

Fortunately, my accountability group got my attention. I had some long, painful talks with the Lord. I was reminded of God's grace toward me. I had to deal with the speck in my eye, which turned out to be a two-by-four.

—Louis McBurney, psychiatrist in Marble, Colorado

Personal Challenge:
• *If you're already in an accountability group, thank God for each of the other men. If you're not, ask God if he's leading you to join one.*

Thought to Apply: A single arrow is easily broken, but not ten in a bundle.   —JAPANESE PROVERB

"He Knows Everything about My Life"

Key Bible Verse: If one falls down, his friend can help him up. But pity the man who falls and has no one to help him up! *(Ecclesiastes 4:10). Bonus Reading: 1 Samuel 20*

When Justin Armour was a rookie wide receiver with the Buffalo Bills, some veteran teammates invited him to a preseason party. Justin went, and couldn't believe what he saw: Gorgeous women everywhere, offering free sex to any of the guys who wanted it.

"It was the most eye-opening experience I've ever had," Justin says. "I had heard about things like this, but I was so naive. I got out of there as fast as I could!"

As a single Christian guy, Justin had committed to saving sex for marriage. To do so, he knows he's got to run from temptation.

"I'd rather not have my mind polluted by those things. Once you've been in a couple situations where's there's temptation, you learn how to avoid them and you don't go back."

Justin also calls his best friend and accountability partner, Steve Stenstrom.

"You need someone to hold you accountable for walking with Christ," says Justin. "Steve does that for me. He knows everything about my life, good and bad, and there's nothing he won't hold me accountable for."
—*Mark Moring, editor of* Men of Integrity

Personal Challenge:
• *Is there someone you can call when you struggle with temptation? If so, thank God for him and pray for God to strengthen him.*

Thought to Apply: Flee temptation and don't leave a forwarding address. —Anonymous

Paul, Barnabas, and Timothy

Key Bible Verses: Timothy, my son, I give you this instruction in keeping with the prophecies once made about you, so that by following them you may fight the good fight, holding on to faith and a good conscience *(1 Timothy 1:18–19). Bonus Reading: Acts 11:22–29*

Every man should seek to have three individuals in his life: a Paul, a Barnabas, and a Timothy.

A Paul is an older man who is willing to mentor you, to build into your life. Not someone who's smarter or more gifted than you, but somebody who's been down the road. Somebody willing to share his strengths and weaknesses—everything he's learned in the laboratory of life. Somebody whose faith you'll want to imitate.

A Barnabas is a soul brother, somebody who loves you but is not impressed by you. Somebody to whom you can be accountable. Somebody who's willing to keep you honest, who's willing to say, "Hey, man, you're neglecting your wife, and don't give me any guff!"

A Timothy is a younger man into whose life you are building. For a model, read 1 and 2 Timothy. Here was Paul, the quintessential mentor, building into the life of his protégé—affirming, encouraging, teaching, correcting, directing, praying.

Do you have these three guys in your life?

—*Howard Hendricks, professor at Dallas Theological Seminary*

Personal Challenge:
• *Can you be a Paul—a spiritual mentor—to someone else? Ask God to keep you open to this.*

Thought to Apply: A friend is one who makes me do my best.   —OSWALD CHAMBERS (devotional writer)

"That's Hard for Me"

Key Bible Verse: The sacrifices of God are a broken spirit; a broken and contrite heart, O God, you will not despise *(Psalm 51:17). Bonus Reading: Matthew 5:3–10; James 5:13–18*

The guys who make up the popular Christian singing group 4Him have had their share of spats.

"Put a bunch of people together on a packed tour bus, and you've got a situation that's ripe for conflict," says group member Marty Magehee.

To resolve those conflicts, 4Him meets regularly with an "accountability board" of friends and pastors, where they're free to vent their feelings.

Says the group's Mark Harris, "One of the most important things we're learning is to say, 'I'm wrong! I'm wrong!'"

"That's hard for me," says the group's Andy Chrisman. "But I'm learning to let go of my need to always be right."

Says Mark, "Our love for one another grows stronger because we deal with our conflicts more openly and in a way the Bible commands us to."

Are you willing to admit to your friends when you're wrong? If you are, your friends likely will be too.
        —*Chris Lutes, editor of* Campus Life *magazine*

Personal Challenge:
• *How do you usually handle conflict with friends?*
• *Ask God to help you confess when you've been wrong.*

Thought to Apply: Friends, if we be honest with ourselves, we shall be honest with each other.
        —GEORGE MACDONALD (Scottish writer, 19th century)

The Buddy System

Key Bible Verse: A man of many companions may come to ruin, but there is a friend who sticks closer than a brother *(Proverbs 18:24)*. *Bonus Reading: Amos 3:3*

We were at war with Vietnam. And there I was, at the U.S. Army Ranger School at Fort Benning, Georgia. It was brutal.

I can still hear the raspy voice of the sergeant: "We are here to save your lives. We're going to see to it that you overcome all your natural fears. We're going to show you just how much incredible stress the human mind and body can endure. And when we're finished with you, you will be the U.S. Army's best!"

Then, before he dismissed the formation, he announced our first assignment. We'd steeled ourselves for something really tough—like running 10 miles in full battle gear or rappelling down a sheer cliff.

Instead, he told us to— find a buddy.

"Find yourself a Ranger buddy," he growled. "You will stick together. You will never leave each other. You will encourage each other, and, as necessary, you will carry each other."

It was the army's way of saying, "Difficult assignments require a friend. Together is better."

Who's your "Ranger buddy"?
—*Stu Weber, pastor of Good Shepherd Community Church in Boring, Oregon*

Personal Challenge:
• *Think of some of the tough spots in your life. What difference have friends made during those times? What difference might they have made?*
• *Thank God for the "Ranger buddies" in your life.*

Thought to Apply: No problem is ever as dark when you have a friend to face it with you.   —ANONYMOUS

Up Close & Personal with Spencer Perkins

When Friends Disappoint Each Other

Spencer Perkins was a national leader in the area of racial reconciliation and community development until his death, at age 43, this year. In his final public address, Spencer talked about a difficult time in his friendship with Chris Rice, his ministry partner of 10 years:

Q. What happened between Chris and you?

A. Chris and I came to what seemed like insurmountable obstacles in our relationship. By summer's end, both of us held tightly to a long list of ways that each had been hurt or disappointed by the other. We were close to settling for irreconcilable differences and going our separate ways.

What did you do?
We sought the counsel of some dear friends. In my mind, we were just going through the motions. The damage was already done. The pain was too great.

These friends rambled on about grace. "Yeah, yeah, I know all about grace," I thought.

What happened?
Through that conversation, though, Chris and I saw, as clearly as anything we had ever seen before, that only by giving each other grace could we find healing and restoration. We could either hold on to our grievances and demand that all of our hurts be redressed, or we ▶

could follow God's example, give each other grace, and trust God for the

lack. We chose grace.

*Chris Rice (left) and
the late Spencer Perkins,
co-authors of*
More Than Equals.

For Personal Study or Group Discussion

Real Life Application

Key Bible Verse: For we are taking pains to do what is right, not only in the eyes of the Lord but also in the eyes of men *(2 Corinthians 8:21). Bonus Reading: 1 Peter 3:8–9*

Think and pray about these sentence starters on your own. Or, if you meet with other men, use them to trigger your discussion.

☐ To me, accountability means ...

☐ It's difficult to be accountable to someone because ...

☐ If I could ask God for one thing to help me in the area of friendship and accountability, it would be ...

Credits: Monday: Adapted from *Leadership* (Summer 1996); Tuesday and Thursday: Adapted from *Campus Life* (September/October 1996); Wednesday: Adapted from *Seven Promises of a Promise Keeper* (Focus on the Family, 1994); Friday: Adapted from *Go the Distance* (Focus on the Family, 1996); Saturday: Adapted from *Reconcilers* (Spring 1998).

Conquering Cable TV

Key Bible Verses: Who may ascend the hill of the Lord? … He who has clean hands and a pure heart *(Psalm 24:3–4). Bonus Reading: Psalm 101:2–4; Ephesians 6:10*

I travel alone a lot in my job, and I stay in a lot of hotels with cable TV. I sometimes struggle whether to watch pornography while in the room.

One time, I was flipping through the channels to find the World Series. While flipping, I came across a channel with half-nude women. I flipped over to the baseball game. Ten minutes later, I flipped back to the movie, and then quickly back to the World Series. I did that four or five times before I shut off the TV.

I was unnerved at the power of temptation, especially since I've given my life to combat pornography. I've had to come face to face with the Lord and plead for mercy: "Lord, how is this possible?" I began to lose confidence in my prayers.

God reminded me, "Jerry, I'm not surprised by your sin. I've known all along you were a sinner. I've known all along that you were weak. I needed you to know that you were weak. And I need you to know that I alone will make you strong."

—Jerry Kirk, founder of the National Coalition for the Protection of Children & Families

Personal Challenge:
• *What's your strategy for avoiding images you know you should avoid?*
• *Thank God that he knows your weaknesses, and that he promises to make you strong.*

Thought to Apply: Of all the inventions of our time, TV is likely to prove the most destructive.
—MALCOLM MUGGERIDGE (late British journalist)

Confessions of a Sex Addict

Key Bible Verse: Confess your sins to each other and pray for each other so that you may be healed *(James 5:16a). Bonus Reading: Psalm 51:1–12; Proverbs 28:13*

Married for 16 years and with two great kids, Kurt Stansell seems to have it all together. He has a successful investment counseling business, and he's a founding elder at his church.

And he's a sex addict. Kurt's the first to admit it.

For years, Kurt struggled with pornography. It started with magazines, but eventually turned into visits to Triple-X theaters and strip joints. Kurt kept repeating a cycle of guilt and remorse, then prayer and repentance, only to find himself back at it again.

Eventually, Kurt found an accountability partner named Stan. At first, Kurt held back, being less than honest about his problem. But when he finally confessed, telling Stan the whole truth, Kurt immediately felt a weight lifted from his shoulders. He was on the road to victory.

"I began to understand what shame does," Kurt says. "When we Christians try to hide something in the darkness, we give Satan incredible license to work in our lives. So, the more open I could be, the less of a hold Satan seemed to have."

—Gregg Lewis, author of The Power of a Promise Kept

Personal Challenge:
• *Do you have a friend with whom you can share your failures? If so, how has that helped? If not, where might you find such a person?*

Thought to Apply: For him who confesses, shams are over, and realities have begun.

—WILLIAM JAMES (19th century philosopher)

Real Men Don't

Key Bible Verse: You shall not commit adultery *(Exodus 20:14). Bonus Reading: Proverbs 5; Matthew 5:27–28*

Remember the book *Real Men Don't Eat Quiche,* and all those funny one-liners on the definitive characteristics of a real man?

I've got a one-liner, but it's not meant to be funny:

Real men don't commit adultery.

Adultery in America is an epidemic of staggering proportions. And not just outside the body of Christ. This epidemic has not only found its way into the church, but has wormed its way up to the highest echelons of church leadership.

I remember some years ago watching Phyllis George interview Dallas Cowboys quarterback Roger Staubach. It was a dull interview until Phyllis asked, "Roger, how do you feel when you compare yourself with Joe Namath, who is so sexually active and has a different woman on his arm every time we see him?"

"Phyllis," Roger answered, "I'm sure I'm just as sexually active as Joe. The difference is that all of mine is with one woman."

Touchdown! Roger hit the end zone with that comeback. Real men don't commit adultery. A real man sticks with one woman. Period.

—Steve Farrar, president of Strategic Living Ministries in Dallas

Personal Challenge:
• *What can help you remain sexually faithful?*

Thought to Apply: It is as absurd to say that a man can't love one woman all the time as it is to say that a violinist needs several violins to play the same piece of music.
—HONORE DE BALZAC (19th century French novelist)

An Amazing Streak

Key Bible Verse: Marriage should be honored by all, and the marriage bed kept pure, for God will judge the adulterer and all the sexually immoral *(Hebrews 13:4). Bonus Reading: 1 Corinthians 6:18–20; Romans 6:11–14*

A. C. Green of the Dallas Mavericks set a remarkable record last season, playing in his 907th consecutive game, an NBA record.

A. C. is proud of that mark. But he's even prouder of this: He's almost 35 years old, and still a virgin.

During his rookie year with the Los Angeles Lakers, A. C.'s teammates said he'd never be able to keep his vow to save sex for marriage.

"We're going to give you six weeks," they told A. C., according to a *Sports Illustrated* article. "You'll see this girl come into the Forum. You'll start getting your paychecks."

A. C. has seen plenty of girls and paychecks—and remained abstinent all along.

"Abstinence before marriage is something I very much believe in," A. C. says. "Responsibility is the main issue, being responsible for the decisions that you make, realizing that every decision has a consequence."

The abstinence streak? It's up to 12,702 days today . . . and counting.

Personal Challenge:
• *A. C. says "responsibility is the main issue." Why do you think he says that?*
• *Thank God that he gives you power to be holy.*

Thought to Apply: There is no getting away from it: the old Christian rule is "Either marriage, with complete faithfulness to your partner, or else total abstinence." Chastity is the most unpopular of our Christian virtues.

—C. S. LEWIS (20th century Christian author)

Start on the Inside

Key Bible Verse: Nothing outside a man can make him "unclean" by going into him. Rather, it is what comes out of a man that makes him "unclean" *(Mark 7:15).* *Bonus Reading: Mark 7:20–23*

I t's not easy to be pure in an impure world. Even if you become a cultural ostrich and avoid all movies, listen only to Christian radio, and read only Christian books and magazines, you're still going to struggle.

You will never become a godly man by negation. A pure, pollution-free environment doesn't make pure people. In today's Key Verse, Jesus makes it clear that what's inside a man defiles him. That's where we need to start.

If a farmer doesn't plant seeds, he will never harvest a crop. It doesn't matter how weed-free his ground is; he must also plant and cultivate good seed.

In the same way, we can only reap a harvest of purity and integrity by planting the good seed of God's Word into our lives. I'm not talking about merely reading the Bible. I'm talking about allowing the Holy Spirit to plant the truths of Scripture deep into our hearts and minds through consistent Bible reading and memorization, meditation and prayer.

—Dr. Gary Oliver, clinical director of Southwest Counseling Associates in Littleton, Colorado

Personal Challenge:
• *What are you planting in your heart?*
• *Ask God to plant the truths of Scripture deep into you.*

Thought to Apply: A heart in every thought renewed/And full of love divine/Perfect and right and pure and good/A copy, Lord, of thine
—CHARLES WESLEY (18th century Methodist hymnwriter)

Up Close & Personal with Jerry Kirk

Winning the TV Battle

Q. How do you minimize the temptations of TV when you're alone in a hotel?

A. I no longer flip through the channels, because I may run across Showtime and HBO, which sometimes show explicit sex. Instead, I choose a channel and punch in that number. Also, when I arrive at a hotel, I ask the front desk to disconnect any sex channels before I get to my room, putting the hardcore stuff out of reach. Then, I have a time of prayer before I even turn on the TV.

How do those prayers go?
I recall several Scripture passages that I've memorized for this occasion. For instance, I'll quote John 17:19, where Jesus prays, "And for their sake I consecrate myself that they also may be consecrated in truth." I'll use that prayer for my family: "For my wife's sake, I consecrate myself. For my five children and their five spouses' sake, I consecrate myself. For my 16 grandchildren's sake, I consecrate myself. For my pastor friends who look to me for strength and protection, I consecrate myself." And so on.

What other strategies help?
I also carry with me at all times a picture of my family and put it on top of the TV. I believe men are to be a protection, for their family.

So, when arriving at a hotel, the key thing is to move immediately on the offensive—in prayer, in worship, in taking authority over the Evil One. The best preparation for defense is a good offense.

Jerry Kirk is the founder of the National Coalition for the Protection of Children & Families.

For Personal Study or Group Discussion

Real Life Application

Key Bible Verse: Our old self was crucified with him so that the body of sin may be done away with, that we should no longer be slaves to sin *(Romans 6:6). Bonus Reading: Galatians 5:16–18*

☐ Some situations that test my sexual purity are …

☐ Some practical ways I can keep sexual purity include …

☐ If I were honest with God, I would tell him …

Credits: Monday and Saturday: Adapted from *Leadership* (Summer 1995); Tuesday: Adapted from *The Power of a Promise Kept* (Focus on the Family, 1995); Wednesday: Adapted from *What Makes A Man?* (NavPress, 1992; For copies of the book call 800-366-7788); Friday: Adapted from *Seven Promises of a Promise Keeper* (Focus on the Family, 1994).

Keep Your Head in the Game

Key Bible Verse: A time . . . has now come when the true worshipers will worship the Father in spirit and truth, for they are the kind of worshipers the Father seeks *(John 4:23)*. *Bonus Reading: Exodus 34:13; Psalm 95:6*

When I was the coach at Colorado, Sunday mornings were stressful. I'd be up and out of the house by 6 A.M., rushing to the office to break down the previous day's game film. It never failed to be a gut-wrenching experience, isolating and analyzing every mistake in minute detail.

After a couple hours of this, my blood pressure might be through the ceiling. And then I'd go pick up the family for church.

I was rarely in the right frame of mind for worship. Try as I might to stay focused on the sermon, I was often distracted. My mind kept drifting back to Saturday's game, and I'd start thinking about next week's opponent.

It was frustrating.

I rarely left church feeling deeply ministered to or satistfied that I'd received the full benefit of God's Word.

What about you? Are you so consumed by your work— or something else—that your head's not completely "in the game" at church?

—*Bill McCartney, founder & CEO of Promise Keepers*

Personal Challenge:

• *Do you find your mind drifting away while sitting in church? Where's it drifting? What can you do about it?*
• *Ask God to help you worship him fully in church.*

Thought to Apply: If we haven't learned to be worshipers, it doesn't really matter how well we do anything else.

—ERWIN LUTZER (pastor and author)

More Than Fast Food

Key Bible Verse: Now you are the body of Christ, and each one of you is a part of it *(1 Corinthians 12:27)*.
Bonus Reading: 1 Corinthians 12:12–27; Ephesians 4:11–13

Many Americans treat going to church much the same way they decide where to eat a fast-food lunch: "We went to McDonald's last week, so let's go to Burger King this week."

As Christian husbands and fathers, I'm convinced it's crucial that we keep our family's roots planted deeply in our home church. Otherwise, if you and I remain shallow in this important area of commitment, we'll lose out on the support of other Christians when the storms of life hit.

By neglecting to minister within our home church, we also cause other Christians to lose something. Jesus says he is the vine and we are his branches (John 15:5–8). We are literally connected to each other through the church.

Today's Key Verse shows us the importance of being connected to one another through the church. How you and I relate to the body of Christ directly affects other Christians.

We need each other! And the church is the best place tostart meeting one another's needs. *—Luis Palau, international evangelist*

Personal Challenge:
• How does your life show that church matters to you?
• Ask God to show you how you can be a "need-meeter" in your church.

Thought to Apply: We are members of one body. We are responsible for each other. And . . . the time will soon come when, if men will not learn that lesson, then they will be taught it in fire and blood and anguish.
—J. B. PRIESTLEY (18th century scientist)

Facing Foreclosure

Key Bible Verse: God will meet all your needs according to his glorious riches in Christ Jesus *(Philippians 4:19)*. *Bonus Reading: Proverbs 22:9; Romans 12:4–8*

When a friend of mine couldn't sell his home after a move, he decided to rent it out. Twice in three years, tenants broke the lease and skipped town after trashing the place, leaving my friend with thousands of dollars in repairs.

He tried to sell the house again, and it sat on the market for months while he made mortgage payments he couldn't afford. His credit cards maxed out, foreclosure became a possibility, and his stress was sky-high.

When he told friends at church about his problem, within 48 hours:

• His couples' Bible study gave him and his wife a check that more than covered their next mortgage payment, giving them more time to sell the house

• His Sunday school teacher—a realtor and financial adviser—prayed with him and his wife, encouraging them

• A church elder—an attorney my friend could never afford—spent 90 minutes on the phone, giving advice

My friend was striking out, and the church stepped up to the plate. But it never could have happened if he hadn't put his pride aside and made his needs known.

—*Mark Moring, editor of* Men of Integrity

Personal Challenge:
• *What's harder for you—helping someone in need, or asking for help? Why?*

Thought to Apply: Church-goers are like coals in a fire. When they cling together, they keep the flame aglow; when they separate, they die out. —BILLY GRAHAM (evangelist)

I Can't Outgive God

Key Bible Verse: Each man should give what he has decided in his heart to give, not reluctantly or under compulsion, for God loves a cheerful giver *(2 Corinthians 9:7). Bonus Reading: Proverbs 11:25; Luke 6:38*

I'm a dollars-and-cents guy. I like to know what I'm going to get for how much I shell out. I like to know why I'm spending what I'm spending, and how it's going to improve my life.

Whether it's a mutual fund or a vacation, I calculate the minimum cost for the maximum benefit. After all, we have a limited supply of money, and an unlimited supply of choices to spend it on.

So what do I do about giving to God's work, to the church? How do I make the calculations? How do I figure the payoff?

I've discovered there's no way to figure it. How many times has God prevented a flat tire on my car? Why has my furnace lasted so long? Why don't I have health problems? Why did my property taxes go down?

I'll never know until heaven how much God has spared me, financially or emotionally, but I do know God loves a cheerful giver. That's what I want to be. After all, no matter what I give, I can't outgive God!
—*John VanDyke, corporate product development manager at Independent Bank Corp. in Ionia, Michigan*

Personal Challenge:
• *What's going through your mind when you write a check to your church?*
• *Ask God to help you be a "cheerful giver" as you make your decisions about giving.*

Thought to Apply: If you haven't got any charity in your heart, you have the worst kind of heart trouble.
—BOB HOPE (comedian)

Deep Weeds

Key Bible Verse: Brothers, pray for us that the message of the Lord may spread rapidly and be honored, just as it was with you *(2 Thessalonians 3:1). Bonus Reading: Ephesians 6:18–20; Hebrews 13:17*

In one of the "Peanuts" cartoons, poor Linus, surrounded by tall weeds in right field, says, "I don't mind standing out here, if this is where I can do the team the most good. The only thing that bothers me is that I don't know if I'm facing the right way."

Many pastors find themselves in the same situation. Overworked, sometimes underpaid, under constant spiritual attack, many feel they're in over their heads. They're unable to discern if they're even facing the right way.

Pastors are expected to be all things to all people—expert counselors, deft mediators, eloquent preachers, gifted financiers, noble visionaries.

In the face of these expectations, many pastors wonder if they're really making a difference for you and me.

As men of God, we must come alongside our pastors with our service and daily prayers for their families, their marriages, and, most importantly, their continued growth in their relationship with Jesus.

—Jesse Miranda, associate dean of the School of Theology at Azusa Pacific University

Personal Challenge:
• *Think of something encouraging you can do or say for your pastor this week.*
• *Pray for your pastor.*

Thought to Apply: A pastor needs the tact of a diplomat, the strength of Samson, the patience of Job, the wisdom of Solomon—and a cast-iron stomach.

—JAMES STREET (Christian leader, 1903–1954)

Up Close & Personal with Jesse Miranda

Honoring Your Pastor

Q. Where did you learn the importance of honoring pastors?

A. From my mother. As a teenager, I came home from work one day to find that the first car I had ever owned was gone. I asked Mother about it, and she said, "I noticed you've bought another car, so I gave your old one to the pastor. You're a single man and had two cars. The pastor has a wife and five children and only one car."

I asked, "Why do you do so much for the pastors?"

"Son," she said, "I do for my pastors what I wish people will do for you some day, should the Lord call you into ministry."

How can we honor our pastors?
I see five critical ways:

1. Start a relationship without an agenda. Make an appointment with your pastor to say, "I just want to know how I could pray for you and encourage you."

2. Provide opportunities for your pastor to bless his family. Take your pastor and his son to a ballgame. Give his family a restaurant gift certificate. Babysit his kids so he can take his wife out for a date.

3. Be specific in praising his ministry in your life. Don't just say, "Nice sermon." Tell him why it was good.

4. Be a churchman, not a spectator. Pitch in and help in some way, attend services ▶

regularly, support the church financially.

5. Pray for your pastor and his family regularly. Your prayers not only support and protect him, but empower him to live out his high calling.

Jesse Miranda is associate dean of the School of Theology at Azusa Pacific University and a board member of Promise Keepers.

For Personal Study or Group Discussion

Real Life Application

Key Bible Verse: You are a chosen people, a royal priesthood, a holy nation, a people belonging to God, that you may declare the praises of him who called you out of darkness into his wonderful light *(1 Peter 2:9)*. *Bonus Reading: Acts 2:42–47*

☐ On a scale of 1 (low) to 5 (high), this is how important church is to me …

☐ One way church really has helped me is …

☐ I am going to honor my pastor this week by …

Credits: Monday: Adapted from *Sold Out* (Word, 1997); Tuesday: Adapted from *What Makes a Man?* (NavPress, 1992; For copies of the book call 800-366-7788); Friday and Saturday: Adapted from *Go the Distance* (Focus on the Family, 1996).

"Daddy, I'm Pregnant"

Key Bible Verse: Love always protects, always trusts, always hopes, always perseveres *(1 Corinthians 13:7)*. *Bonus Reading: Ephesians 4:26–32; 1 Thessalonians 3:12*

"I'm pregnant."

After Cori, my 21-year-old, unwed daughter, said those words, I went through all kinds of emotions.

Yes, it would be embarrassing. I wrote the book *Sanctified Sex.* I had crisscrossed the country telling thousands of young adults like my daughter to "just say no."

Yes, it broke my heart. I stayed awake many nights listening to my wife's muffled sobs. I came home many days to referee a family feud.

My wife, Roberta, and I have always wanted our home to be a place where no-strings-attached love could grow.

Throughout the crisis, I have asked God, "How do I model sensitivity and strength when my family is falling apart?"

God replied with several questions: "Will you quit, Haman? Will you quit loving your daughter? Will you quit investing in her life? Will you quit forgiving her as you have been forgiven?"

My answer continues to be: "No, I won't quit, Lord. With your help, my family will make it."

—*Haman Cross, Jr., pastor of Rosedale Park Baptist Church in Detroit*

Personal Challenge:
• *Which of your family members are you finding it most difficult to love right now?*
• *Ask God for his strength to not quit loving that person.*

Thought to Apply: It's always too soon to quit.

—V. RAYMOND EDMAN (former Wheaton College president)

Hoping Your Spouse Reads Minds

Key Bible Verse: I hope to see you soon, and we will talk face to face. *(3 John 14). Bonus Reading: Ephesians 4:29–32; Philippians 2:1–4*

When Christian musician Michael Card got married in 1982, he and Susan expected smooth sailing. But it wasn't long before they started running into selfishness and communication problems.

"I was shocked to realize there were some things we couldn't talk through," Susan says.

Their struggles intensified as Michael began to spend more time on the road, doing up to 150 concerts a year.

The Cards' pastor suggested they get some counseling before small problems turned into large ones. They say it took humility to admit they were as needy as everyone else. But through the counseling sessions, the Cards built some communication skills they use to this day.

"I still can get quiet and distant, hoping Susan will read my mind," Michael says. "After all, it's a lot easier to hope your spouse is a psychic than to work through how you feel about an issue and then present your feelings in a graceful, Christlike manner. A creeping separateness comes between Susan and me when we don't rely on God's tools to keep our marriage solid."

—*Louise Ferrebee*
in Marriage Partnership

Personal Challenge:
• *What can you do to improve communication with family?*
• *Ask God to give you tact as you communicate.*

Thought to Apply: Be humble and gentle in your conversation; and of few words, I charge you; but always pertinent when you speak. —WILLIAM PENN (founder of Pennsylvania)

Descending into Greatness

Key Bible Verse: Submit to one another out of reverence for Christ *(Ephesians 5:21). Bonus Reading: Colossians 3:19; 1 Peter 3:7*

I'd just finished mowing the lawn, and it seemed like the perfect time to spray Weed & Feed on the grass. Except I didn't have any Weed & Feed.

"I'm going to the store," I told Karen.

"But the kids and I are waiting for you to go to the pool with us," she said.

"That can wait," I said.

"Honey," she said, "we promised the kids we'd all go."

Next thing I knew, we were having a heated argument. I knew what I wanted; what she wanted could wait.

Most of us stumble over the words of today's Key Bible Verse because we're concentrating on what's fair. But if we insist on playing out our marriage that way, we only bring pain to our spouses and ourselves. To paraphrase Tevye in "Fiddler on the Roof," "If you insist on an eye for an eye and a tooth for a tooth, you'll both end up blind and toothless." God wants to spare us that pain, so he gives us a better way: "Submit to one another."

That doesn't come naturally. Scripture has to remind me: Exaltation comes after humility. You have to descend into greatness.

— Kevin A. Miller, an editor in suburban Chicago

Personal Challenge:

• *What do you think it means to submit to another person, as the Bible commands?*

• *Ask God to help you put others' needs before your own.*

Thought to Apply: Wisdom is oftentimes nearer when we stoop than when we soar.

—WILLIAM WORDSWORTH (19th century English poet)

Withdrawal Symptoms

Key Bible Verses: "In your anger, do not sin": Do not let the sun go down while you are still angry, and do not give the devil a foothold *(Ephesians 4:26–27). Bonus Reading: Colossians 3:12–14; James 1:19–20*

Early in our marriage, I specialized in withdrawal. I'd respond to conflict by clamming up, building a wall, and shutting out my wife, Norma. I did it to punish her.

I remember when our family took a three-week vacation to the Colorado mountains in our mobile home. After two miserable weeks, Norma and our daughter, Kari, urged me to take them back home. I got so angry that I didn't speak to Norma most of the way home.

As we approached home, my son Greg confronted me: "Dad, is this the example you want to give Michael, Kari and me? Mom is really hurting, and she needs you. It also hurts me when you won't talk to us. I love you, and I feel alone when you shut us out."

Greg's words stung me and made me realize how wrong I'd been. I hadn't realized how much damage I was inflicting. I confessed my sin to Norma and promised her I'd never withdraw again and close her out of any kind of conflict. It's the only way to go.

—Gary Smalley, president of Today's Family

Personal Challenge:
• *How do you react to conflict in your marriage?*
• *Ask God for wisdom to constructively deal with conflicts in your family.*

Thought to Apply: A house divided against itself cannot stand.

—ABRAHAM LINCOLN, quoting Jesus

A Promise to Pray

Key Bible Verse: I will . . . call on the name of the Lord *(Psalm 116:17). Bonus Reading: Matthew 6:9–13; Philippians 4:6*

On my wedding day, I made a promise: To pray with my wife every night at bedtime. Marriage is intended by God to be a partnership between three persons—husband, wife, and God. A brief daily meeting of the three, where sincere and honest communication takes place, goes a long way toward strengthening a successful, productive and happy partnership for life.

Your prayer together need not be long nor formal nor "religious." The two need not both pray aloud; just one is enough. All areas of need or concern needn't be covered. What matters most is that you as the husband see that it happens every night:

To be still before God.

To be reconciled if anything has come between you.

To bring to God the things you know you need him to help you handle, to thank him, and to recommit yourselves to his care and his way.

Many nights I have been tempted to turn away from my wife into my own selfishness or anger, but my promise to pray every night has forced me to come back to her—and to God.

—John Yates, co-author (with wife Susan) of What Really Matters at Home

Personal Challenge:
• *If you're married, what makes praying with your wife difficult?*
• *Ask God to help you pray for and with the ones you love.*

Thought to Apply: The Christian on his knees sees more than the philosopher on tiptoe.
—DWIGHT L. MOODY (19th century evangelist)

Up Close & Personal with Gary Smalley

How to Invest in Your Marriage

Q. You've been married 33 years, but not all of them were smooth.

A. In the first five years of our marriage, Norma and I experienced severe trials, big-time disappointment, and deep dissatisfaction with each other.

What was causing the problems?
In premarital sessions, our pastor asked me if I loved Norma. How could I say anything but yes? When he asked if I would lay down my life for her, I had no idea what that meant. I thought it meant I'd be willing to take a bullet for her, so again, I said yes. But no one really ever explained to me how to love a woman sacrificially day by day or how to communicate meaningfully.

What helped you learn how?
A lot of prayer and education. But the countless ways of love can be summed up in one equation we learned from John Gottman, whose research into thousands of marriages concludes: The husband and wife must average five positive deposits into each other's emotional bank accounts for every one negative withdrawal.

Gottman's material lists a ton of "positive deposits" and "negative withdrawals," but I'll only mention a few here. The "positives" include: praise for contributions and ideas; showing affection; actively listening; being understanding; and showing honor. "Negatives" are the opposite: criticizing contributions and ideas; withholding affection; showing disdain; being argumentative, defensive; and disgracing or shaming. For every negative you're guilty of, you need to make sure you've made at least five positive deposits into your wife's account.

Gary Smalley is president of Today's Family in Branson, Missouri. He is the author of Making Love Last Forever *(Word, 1996). Book cited is* John Gottman's Why Marriages Succeed or Fail *(Simon & Schuster, 1994)*

Marriage & Family   Sunday, Week 6

For Personal Study or Group Discussion

Real Life Application

Key Bible Verse: Do everything without complaining or arguing, so that you may become faultless and pure ... *(Philippians 2:14–15). Bonus Reading: Proverbs 5:18–19*

☐ **Loving my family sacrificially means ...**

☐ **When there are conflicts in our family, we usually resolve it by ...**

☐ **In my family life, I need God's help to ...**

Credits: Monday: Adapted from *Urban Family* (Spring 1995); Tuesday: Adapted from "House of Cards," *Marriage Partnership* (Summer 1996); Wednesday: Adapted from "Coming in Second," *Marriage Partnership* (Fall 1996); Thursday and Saturday: Adapted from *Go the Distance* (Focus on the Family, 1996); Friday: Adapted from *What Makes a Man?* (NavPress, 1992; For copies of the book call 800-366-7788).

On the Night Shift

Key Bible Verses: For it is by grace you have been saved, through faith—and this not from yourselves, it is the gift of God—not by works, so that no one can boast *(Ephesians 2:8–9). Bonus Reading: Romans 6:23; 1 John 5:11–12*

The *San Diego Union-Tribune* reported the story of Nicholas Zenns. On his night job at Taco Bell, 17-year-old Nicholas was taking orders at the drive-up window. He heard a woman scream, turned, and saw a very pregnant Devorah Anderson standing in front of him.

The high-school student pulled off his headset, called the paramedics, and tried to make the woman comfortable. But the baby wouldn't wait.

"The baby's head just popped out into my hands," Nicholas said.

Paramedics finally arrived and took baby and parents to the hospital. Nicholas cleaned up, "sterilized my hands about a thousand times," and finished his shift.

Nicholas says the event changed his perspective. "Things have been pretty bad in my life lately, and then I got to do this. I'm really glad."

Likewise, even in your normal routine, God brings people in your life to take part in their birth as Christians. Are you ready and willing to help?

Personal Challenge:
• *Who would you most like to see become a Christian? Pray for that person today.*

Thought to Apply: Angels cannot preach the gospel, only beings such as Paul and you and I can preach the gospel.

—OSWALD CHAMBERS (devotional writer)

If You Don't Have the Gift

Key Bible Verses: Jesus came to them and said, "All authority in heaven and on earth has been given to me. Therefore go and make disciples of all nations …" *(Matthew 28:18–19). Bonus Reading: Mark 16:15–16; Acts 1:8*

You might read today's Key Bible Verses (also known as the Great Commission) and say to me, "Well, Luis, I agree that God wants us to share our faith. It's just that, um, I suspect he's thinking more of using you than using me. After all, I certainly don't have the gift of evangelism."

Cut!

I don't see anything in the Great Commission about gifts or talent or personality or even opportunity.

The Lord is clear: "You … and you … and you, I'm calling all of you men to go, make disciples."

It's not a matter of gift. It's a matter of obedience.

So, will you pray these words: "Lord, I promise to help fulfill your Great Commission."

Will you?

It's not a matter of gift. It's a matter of heart—a heart for Jesus Christ that has a passion for lost souls, a heart that strives for holiness, a heart that is bold about reaching out and taking risks, a heart that is faithful to the end.

Sounds a lot like a promise keeper, doesn't it?

— *Luis Palau, international evangelist*

Personal Challenge:

• *What things keep you from effectively sharing your faith with others?*

• *Ask God to give you more of his compassion for people.*

Thought to Apply: Being an extrovert isn't essential to evangelism—obedience and love are.

—REBECCA MANLEY PIPPERT (Christian author)

"I Could Never Do That!"

Key Bible Verse: Do not seek revenge or bear a grudge against one of your people, but love your neighbor as yourself. I am the Lord *(Leviticus 19:18). Bonus Reading: Romans 12:9–10; 1 Corinthians 13:4–8*

I know two law partners who used to hate each other. When one became a Christian, he asked me, "Now that I'm a Christian, what should I do?"

I said, "Why not ask him to forgive you and tell him you love him?"

"I could never do that!" he said, "because I don't love him."

That lawyer had put his finger squarely on one of the great challenges of the Christian life: to learn to love as Christ loves —unconditionally.

We can't manufacture that kind of love. It comes only from God; and it's a love that draws people to Christ.

I prayed with that attorney. The next morning, he told his partner, "I've become a Christian, and I want to ask you to forgive me for all I've done to hurt you, and to tell you that I love you."

The partner was so surprised and convicted that he, too, asked for forgiveness and said, "I would like to become a Christian. Would you tell me how?"

See what love can do?

—Bill Bright, founder and president, Campus Crusade for Christ

Personal Challenge:

• *Think of someone you don't like. How can you show love to that person?*

Thought to Apply: Love is the only force capable of transforming an enemy into a friend.

—MARTIN LUTHER KING, JR.

What a Christian Looks Like

Key Bible Verse: By this all men will know that you are my disciples, if you love one another *(John 13:35).* *Bonus Reading: John 15:13; 1 John 4:7–8*

When I led a Young Life group, I did my best to round up kids who really needed to hear the gospel when we went to summer camp. Mark was one of those kids.

Bob Mitchell, the main speaker that week, called most of the shots—including when meals would be served. So "Mitch" was always talking with the cook.

The cook loved her work, but it was exhausting. She always looked tired. Whenever she talked to Mitch, he got up and gave her his chair—and a moment's rest—while they discussed meal plans.

Nobody noticed Mitch doing this ... except Mark.

Mark hadn't come to hear about Jesus. But when he saw Jesus' love lived out in that simple act of kindness by the camp speaker, he began to listen to his talks. Later that week, Mark asked Jesus to be his Savior.

It wasn't because of the messages, Mark said, but because of the love he saw in Mitch.

"If that's what it means to be a Christian," Mark said, "I want to be one."

—John Trent, co-author of The Hidden Value of a Man

Personal Challenge:
• *What can you do today that might prompt someone to say, "If that's what it means to be a Christian, I want to be one"?*

Thought to Apply: Preach the gospel at all times. If necessary, use words.

—FRANCIS OF ASSISI (medieval founder of the Franciscans)

Monday Night for Eternity

Key Bible Verses: These commandments that I give you today are to be upon your hearts. Impress them on your children. Talk about them when you sit at home and when you walk along the road, when you lie down and when you get up *(Deuteronomy 6:6–7).*
Bonus Reading: Matthew 18:1–10

In *Christian Parenting Today*, Douglas R. Sword told this story:

"As I was giving my 4-year-old son a bath, I was trying to hurry because Monday Night Football would be on soon. He began telling me that Christmas was coming and that we needed to have a birthday party for Jesus. We talked a little more, and then he asked, "What does it mean to have Jesus in your heart?"

On the outside I was calm, but inwardly my heart was doing flips. I explained that sometimes we do bad things and that God sent His son Jesus to die on the cross to pay the penalty for when we disobey. We need to ask God to forgive us and for Jesus to come into our heart to help us to obey God.

He said, "Can I pray and ask Jesus to come into my heart?"

It was the greatest pleasure a father can have. I do not remember who won the football game that night, but I will never forget leading my son to Christ.

Personal Challenge:
• *Pray for the children in your life, that they will come to know God, or grow in their faith.*
• *Thank God that He welcomes all who come to Him in faith.*

Thought to Apply: Now, as always, God discloses Himself to "babes" and hides Himself in thick darkness from the wise and the prudent. —A. W. TOZER (20th century Christian writer)

Up Close & Personal with John Trent

Q. I want to share my faith, but where do I start?

A. With love. When asked by the teachers of the Law which commandment was the most important, Jesus responded with what we now call the Great Commandment (Mark 12:28–31): Each of us is to love God "with all your heart and with all your soul and with all your mind and with all your strength." But there was more, said Jesus: "Love your neighbor as yourself. There are no commandments greater than these."

Dr. John Trent is a marriage and family counselor, and co-author of The Blessing.

For Personal Study or Group Discussion

Key Bible Verse: I am not ashamed of the gospel, because it is the power of God for the salvation of everyone who believes *(Romans 1:16). Bonus Reading: 2 Timothy 4:5; 1 Peter 3:15–16*

Think and pray about these sentence starters.

☐ The last time I tried to share my faith with someone ...

☐ When it comes to sharing my faith, I'm asking God to ...

Credits: Monday: From *Fresh Illustrations* (CTi/Baker, 1997). Tuesday and Wednesday: Adapted from *Seven Promises of a Promise Keeper* (Focus on the Family, 1994); Thursday and Saturday: Adapted from *The Making of a Godly Man* (Focus on the Family, 1997); Friday: From *Christian Parenting Today* (May/June 1998).

My Brother's Keeper

Key Bible Verses: If anyone says, "I love God," yet hates his brother, he is a liar. … Whoever loves God must also love his brother *(1 John 4:20–21). Bonus Reading: 1 John 2:9–11; 1 John 3:10–16*

Perhaps you look at the issue of racism and say, "That's not me! I don't hate anybody!" Or, "I can't be responsible for what happened many years ago. I wasn't there."

If that's you, let me ask you to rethink the issue.

Take the time to prayerfully examine your heart. In God's presence, ask yourself questions like these: "Do I truly not consider myself better than people of other races—more intelligent, creative, honest, hard-working, moral, trustworthy? How would I feel if a family of another race sat next to me in church, invited my family to a picnic in a public park, or moved in next door? What if my boss were someone of another race? How would I respond if my child married someone of a different race?"

As you ask yourself such questions, keep in mind the words of today's Key Bible Verses. Then, as you lay your heart open to God, deal with any traces of racism you find there, asking God to begin the process of changing your mind and heart.

—*Bill McCartney, founder & CEO of Promise Keepers*

Personal Challenge:
• *Follow Coach Mac's suggestions and before God, ask the questions above.*

Thought to Apply: There is no more evil thing in this world than race prejudice. … It justifies and holds together more baseness, cruelty, and abomination than any other sort of error in the world.   —H. G. WELLS (British author, 1866–1946)

When the Sun Broke Through

Key Bible Verse: For he himself is our peace, who has made the two one and has destroyed the barrier, the dividing wall of hostility *(Ephesians 2:14). Bonus Reading: 1 Corinthians 12:12–13; Galatians 3:26–29*

I was at a Promise Keepers conference in Washington when one of the speakers delivered a powerful message on the sin of racism.

The speaker called for men who still had feelings of racial superiority, and those who had harbored anger about being victims of racism, to come forward to the stage to confess their sin.

About 1,000 men came down the aisles and stood before the stage. Men of different colors were talking to each other, many embracing.

Meanwhile, the praise band was playing as we sang, "Lord, cause Your face to shine upon us again." At that very moment, the sky, which had been dark and full of clouds, opened up, and the late afternoon sun shone through. Incredibly, the bowl of the stadium cut a shadow on everyone in attendance—except those men at the stage in reconciliation and confession, who were suddenly bathed in God's brilliant sunlight.

It was an amazing sight, one I'll never forget.

—Dave Endrody, an American Express account executive in Wheaton, Illinois

Personal Challenge:

• *Think of someone in your life of a different race. What can you do this week to encourage him?*

Thought to Apply: Skin color does not matter to God, for he is looking upon the heart . . . When men are standing at the foot of the cross, there are no racial barriers.

—BILLY GRAHAM (evangelist)

Friendship Breaks Stereotypes

Key Bible Verse: Be devoted to one another in brotherly love. Honor one another above yourselves *(Romans 12:10). Bonus Reading: Romans 12:16; 15:5-7*

I minister in a racially mixed church on the west side of Chicago. I attended a wedding not long ago of a family that lives in Nebraska. I remember standing on this farmer's front lawn and seeing only one road, no other people, and corn in every direction. The scene couldn't have been farther from the west side of Chicago. Yet, this farmer has developed one of the closest relationships with the people of our community.

It began the day he arrived with a work crew some years ago. During that week, he got connected with people in the neighborhood, and all his stereotypes began to break down.

When he returned for a second visit, he told me: "The Monday after I came home from my first work trip to Chicago, I met with the same fellas I've been having coffee and a roll with for twenty-five years. But this time, I had to get up and leave, because the same jokes, the same conversation, the same prejudices that never bothered me before now got to me."

His daughter is now a staff member at our church.
—*Glen Kehrein in* Leadership

Personal Challenge:
• *Pray for wisdom how to respond to the racial comments that happen around you.*

Thought to Apply: When a person of one race treats with contempt a person of another race, he is revealing weaknesses in his own character.

—WELLINGTON BOONE (bishop and author)

"We'll Hang You, Boy"

Key Bible Verses: When they came to the place called the Skull, there they crucified him.... Jesus said, "Father, forgive them, for they do not know what they are doing" *(Luke 23:33–34). Bonus Reading: Matthew 18:21–22; Luke 10:25–37*

Recently I went with four of my friends to the Smoky Mountains to do some rock climbing. We came to this little town just outside of Knoxville and pulled into a country store.

I walked in and there were three guys sitting there giving me looks I've never seen before. The older of the three said, "You don't belong around here—boy."

At first I thought, *Is he talking to me?* I couldn't believe my ears when he said, "You stick around here after dark and we'll hang you." I was thinking, *Man, we're sending rockets to Mars and there are still people living in this kind of blind ignorance.* Suddenly I was experiencing hatred, the kind of bigotry I'd only read about or seen on TV. I'll never forget how I felt in that little country store. For just a split second I felt less than human. I felt alone.

Fortunately, I didn't lash out; I knew Jesus wouldn't have. I calmly explained to that man that racism is a thing of the past. I even surprised myself at the restraint I showed.

—Michael Tait, member of Christian music group dcTalk

Personal Challenge:
• *How would you have reacted in Michael's situation?*

Thought to Apply: Doing an injury puts you below your enemy; revenging one makes you even with him; forgiving it sets you above him.　　　—Anonymous

Six Steps to Healing

Key Bible Verse: This is what the Lord Almighty says: "Administer true justice; show mercy and compassion to one another" *(Zechariah 7:9). Bonus Reading: Micah 6:6–8; Colossians 3:12*

As Christians, we should feel compelled to do what we can to help bring healing between the races. To that end, here are six things I've tried to practice in my own life:

1. Acknowledge the existence of the problem. If you're ready to admit there's a problem, you've taken a big first step toward eliminating it.

2. Confess your own guilt. Most of us have sinned by perpetuating racial division. But even if you haven't, it's appropriate to confess the guilt of our fathers.

3. Seek God's guidance. Ask God what he wants you to do. Ask him to show you areas in your community where you can help bring about reconciliation.

4. Be willing to take risks. Be willing to be rejected or humiliated in order to build a bridge to someone of another race.

5. Discover opportunities for action. Talk to people in your community and you'll begin to find out what the needs are.

6. Move beyond saying hello. Engage in serious dialogue. It may take a lot of love and patience, but it will be worth it.

—John Perkins, founder of the Christian Community Development Association

Personal Challenge:
• *Which of the six steps do you need to start with?*

Thought to Apply: Integration forced some people to change their behavior. Reconciliation invites the changing of hearts. —Spencer Perkins (late Christian leader)

Up Close & Personal with John Perkins

Why Reconciliation Won't Come Automatically

Q. **You grew up in Mississippi in the 1930s and '40s. What was that like?**

A. Well, all my major experiences with white people gave me reason to get as far away from them as I could.

One Saturday afternoon in 1946, my brother Clyde and I were waiting in line to see a movie. Too many people were jammed into the small, hot alley leading to the theater's "colored" entrance.

When some pushing broke out, a deputy yelled, "You niggers quiet down!" He didn't appreciate Clyde's defiant posture, and tried to hit Clyde with his nightstick.

Instinctively, Clyde grabbed the stick to protect himself.

What happened next?

The deputy took a couple steps back, shot Clyde twice in the stomach, then turned around and left. A few hours later, Clyde was dead. And for what?

For many of us blacks, the wounds seem much too deep, and the least little scrape can peel off the scab and expose the painful sore. But that's not why I tell stories from my past.

For me, they demonstrate the power of the gospel to reconcile people, no matter how much they've been alienated from each other. ▶

These stories are also a reminder that we should not take reconciliation for granted. It won't come auto- matically just because we say we want it. We'll have to work for it.

John Perkins is founder of the Christian Community Development Association and author of numerous books.

For Personal Study or Group Discussion

Real Life Application

Key Bible Verse: All this is from God, who reconciled us to himself through Christ and gave us the ministry of reconciliation *(2 Corinthians 5:18). Bonus Reading: Matthew 5:23–24; Romans 5:10–11*

Think and pray about these sentence starters on your own. Or, discuss them with other men.

☐ When I think about racism and racial reconciliation, I feel ...

☐ Some things that make racial reconciliation difficult in my life are ...

☐ Some ways to overcome those difficulties might be ...

Credits: Monday: Adapted from *Seven Promises of a Promise Keeper* (Focus on the Family, 1994); Wednesday: From *Leadership* (Winter 1995); Thursday: Adapted from *WWJD Interactive Devotional,* compiled by Dana Key (Zondervan, 1997); Friday and Saturday: Adapted from *Go the Distance* (Focus on the Family, 1996).

Courage on Crutches

Key Bible Verse: I can do everything through him who gives me strength *(Philippians 4:13). Bonus Reading: (2 Corinthians 1:8–11)*

I once received this online message: "Christianity is a crutch for the weak."

I had recently been on crutches for six weeks after a soccer injury.

From my point of view, crutches are not for the weak. For the last month and a half, my arms and especially my underarms had gotten quite a workout. And they were feeling much stronger, thank you.

And crutches are definitely not for the faint of heart. For sheer tension, crossing an icy parking lot on crutches rivals rappelling down a cliff.

Who are crutches for? For those who are broken, who admit something is wrong and want to get better. For people who want to continue being active—not sitting around with their feet up.

Likewise, Christianity is for broken people. But it's definitely not for the weak or faint of heart. Any Christian virtue demands strength of character, not atrophied spiritual muscle. Faith is no easy out from reality. It's an invitation to walk again after reality breaks you.

—*Marshall Shelley
in* Leadership

Personal Challenge:

• *Where are you broken and in need of God? Admit that to God in prayer.*

• *Pray that God will give you the courage to walk in complete dependence on Christ.*

Thought to Apply: Success is never final; failure is never fatal; it is courage that counts.
—Winston Churchill (English Prime Minister during World War II)

The Guts to Lead

Key Bible Verse: Follow my example, as I follow the example of Christ *(1 Corinthians 11:1). Bonus Reading: 1 Thessalonians 2:1–12*

Scott Turow begins his novel *Presumed Innocent* with the words of a prosecuting attorney named Rusty. Rusty is explaining his approach to the jury when he is in court. Rusty says:

"This is how I always start:
'I am the prosecutor.

'I represent the state. I am here to present to you the evidence of a crime. Together you will weigh the evidence. You will deliberate upon it. You will decide if it proves the defendant's guilt.

'This man—' and here I point . . .

If you don't have the courage to point . . . you can't expect them to have the courage to convict.

And so I point. I extend my hand across the courtroom. I hold one finger straight. I seek the defendant's eye. I say:

'This man has been accused . . .' "

Scott Turow shows in the courtroom a principle that holds true in all of life. People need leaders to galvanize their courage. People need leaders to point, to take a stand, to say what they believe.
—*Craig Brian Larson, pastor in Chicago*

Personal Challenge:
• *In what situations do others need you to point the way? Who needs your courage?*
• *Pray for God to empower you to be a leader in what is right.*

Thought to Apply: The great need for anyone in authority is courage. —ALISTAIR COOKE (actor)

Saying What You Feel

Key Bible Verse: Now that you have purified yourselves by obeying the truth so that you have sincere love for your brothers, love one another deeply, from the heart *(1 Peter 1:22). Bonus Reading: 1 Thessalonians 4:9–10*

Gale Sayers and Brian Piccolo, both running backs for the Chicago Bears, began rooming together in 1967.

During the 1969 season, Piccolo was cut down with cancer.

They had planned, with their wives, to sit together at the Professional Football Writers annual dinner in New York, where Sayers was to be given the George S. Halas Award as the most courageous player in pro football. But instead, "Pick" was confined to his bed at home. At the dinner, Sayers stood to receive the award, tears in his eyes. The ordinarily terse athlete had this to say as he took the trophy: "You flatter me by giving me this award, but I tell you here and now that I accept it for Brian Piccolo. Brian Piccolo is the man of courage who should receive the George S. Halas Award. I love Brian Piccolo, and I'd like you to love him."

"*I love Brian Piccolo.*" How many times have you heard a man say something like that? Not very often. Yet how much richer would our lives be if we had the courage to declare our affection as Sayers did that night in New York.

—Rodney L. Cooper, institute director at Western Seminary in Portland

Personal Challenge:
• *In the next week tell someone how much you care about him or her.*

Thought to Apply: Courage is being scared to death but saddling up anyway. —JOHN WAYNE (movie star)

No Compromise

Key Bible Verse: I eagerly expect and hope that I will in no way be ashamed, but will have sufficient courage so that now as always Christ will be exalted in my body, whether by life or by death *(Philippians 1:20)*. *Bonus Reading: Daniel 3*

On a recent trip to the former Soviet Union, an aged pastor told me, "Stalin's reign was the worst time. I had two KGB agents come to me and say, 'We'll take care of you. You stay the pastor of that church, but once a week give us a report on every one of these Christians. Work for us.'

"I can't do that to God, and I can't do that to this flock," he replied.

So they sent him to a prison camp in Siberia. He endured the forced labor and the cold for ten years. But he did find other Christians in the camp, and God used these believers to fulfill his purposes.

"I was a carpenter building towns for Stalin," said the pastor. "We'd go out in sixty-mile radiuses, and there we would fellowship together. Today there are hundreds of churches in Siberia as a result of these small prisoner fellowship groups."

When men refuse to compromise, they may lose much, but through them God will fulfill his higher eternal purpose.

—Joe Stowell, president of Moody Bible Institute

Personal Challenge:
• *Tempted to compromise what you know is right? Trust God and stand firm.*

Thought to Apply: The hottest places in hell are reserved for those who, in a period of moral crisis, maintain their neutrality.   —DANTE (13th century writer)

Tough Choices

Key Bible Verse: If your right hand causes you to sin, cut it off and throw it away. It is better for you to lose one part of your body than for your whole body to go into hell *(Matthew 5:30). Bonus Reading: Matthew 7:13–27*

On July 20, 1993, while cutting oaks in a Pennsylvania forest, Don Wyman got his leg pinned beneath a fallen tree.

No one could hear his yells for help. After digging for more than an hour to try to free his bleeding, shattered leg, he hit stone. He would bleed to death unless he did something drastic.

Wyman made his decision. Using a wrench and the starter cord from his chain saw as a tourniquet, he cut off the flow of blood to his shin. Somehow he had the fortitude to amputate his own leg below the knee with his pocket knife. He crawled to his vehicle and drove to a farmer's home. The farmer got him the help that saved his life.

Like Don Wyman, men who want to follow Christ face tough choices. We have something we want to keep as badly as our leg—sinful habits. We also have a Lord and Savior who calls us to repent. It takes strength to cut off our wickedness.

—Craig Brian Larson, pastor in Chicago

Personal Challenge:
• Do you have a sinful habit that is as dear to you as your right hand? Cut it off—today!

Thought to Apply: He who loses wealth loses much; he who loses a friend loses more; but he who loses his courage loses all. —Miguel de Cervantes (Spanish author, 16th century)

Up Close & Personal with Firefighter Steve Ruda

Giving Our Lives for Others

Q. Why did you choose firefighting as a career?

A. I wanted a job where I would think of others before myself. With that in mind, I once studied to be a Catholic priest. But I later realized that firefighting was my exact call.

What about your job gives you the most satisfaction?
Helping people at the most critical moment in their lives. I was once part of a search and rescue team that went into a burning building and saved a father and his 9-year-old son. When we brought the boy out, he wasn't breathing, but I brought him back by doing CPR. Thank God, the little boy lived—both the father and son survived the fire.

What is the greatest challenge you have faced?
I was in a structure fire where the roof of a building collapsed as my men and I ran for the edge. I was as good as dead—and I was sure I had killed all my crew. We were left hanging onto the wall, but everyone survived.

How has Promise Keepers influenced you?
It brought me to my knees. I saw 50,000 men who were not ashamed to promote Christ in their lives. Never before had I taken up Christ on his challenge when he said, "If you do not acknowledge me before men, neither will I acknowledge you before my father."

Steve Ruda is a firefighter in Southern California and a Promise Keepers Covenant Partner.

For Personal Study or Group Discussion

Real Life Application

Key Bible Verse: Have I not commanded you? Be strong and courageous. Do not be terrified; do not be discouraged, for the Lord your God will be with you wherever you go *(Joshua 1:9). Bonus Reading: Joshua 1:1–18.*

Think and pray about these sentence starters on your own. Or, if you meet with other men, use them to trigger your discussion.

☐ I have learned that following Jesus takes courage, because ...

☐ Fear is something that I ...

☐ At work I need courage from God to ...

☐ The most courageous Christian I know is ...

☐ The area of my life where I most need courage is ...

Men of Integrity is published in association with Promise Keepers by Christianity Today, Inc., 465 Gundersen Drive, Carol Stream, IL 60188. Printed in U.S.A. Canada Post International Publications Mail Sales Agreement No. 546526. GST R126028836. **Staff:** Editors: Mark Moring, Craig Brian Larson; Design Director: Doug Johnson. **Advisory Board**: Ed Barron, Kevin A. Miller. **Subscriptions:** A one-year subscription to *Men of Integrity* is available for a suggested donation of $20 to Promise Keepers, P.O. Box 103001, Denver, CO 80250-3001. **Credits:** Monday: Adapted from *Leadership* (summer 1995); Tuesday and Friday: From *Contemporary Illustrations: For Preachers, Teachers, & Writers* (Baker, 1996); Wednesday: Adapted from *Shoulder to Shoulder* (Zondervan, 1997); Thursday: Adapted from *Preaching Today* (#178); Saturday: Adapted from PK's "Covenant Partner Profile."

Sounds Great—on Paper

Key Bible Verse: Husbands, love your wives, just as Christ loved the church and gave himself up for her ... *(Ephesians 5:25). Bonus Reading: Ephesians 5:28–33; Romans 5:5–8*

Sacrificial love sounds great—on paper. But every married person knows how tough it is to put into practice. Too bad the Bible doesn't say, "Love your wife as Christ loved the church, and here are ten easy steps for accomplishing that."

Christ set the example for sacrificial love when he left heaven's glory to live 33 years of grime, dust, humanness and rejection, all without sinning, just so he could give Himself up for the people he loved. For Christ, love was a motive, not a duty.

I admit that too many times I have served my wife, Jane, out of a sense of duty or to keep peace, without the motive of love. Reality is messy, and I'm still learning what it means to love as Christ loved when my desires and Jane's conflict. For instance, she'll ask me to "come in and talk" while she prepares dinner. But I'm an introvert who just wants some peace and quiet while I read the paper.

Times like these teach me the practical aspects of "giving myself up" as Christ would.
　　　—Jerry Bridges, author of
　　　　The Pursuit of Holiness

Personal Challenge:
• *Who in your life especially needs to feel your love right now?*
• *Pray for the unselfishness to show sacrificial love.*

Thought to Apply: The love of a man and woman gains immeasurably in power when placed under divine restraint. —ELISABETH ELLIOT (Christian author)

He Walked Away Crushed

Key Bible Verse: Therefore, I urge you, brothers, in view of God's mercy, to offer your bodies as living sacrifices, holy and pleasing to God—which is your spiritual act of worship *(Romans 12:1). Bonus Reading: 2 Corinthians 8:9*

Several years ago, my second son, Steve, tried out for the high school football team. One day he walked into my office and proclaimed with great excitement, "Dad, I made the team!"

I turned and said, "Yeah, but are you starting?" Steve walked away crushed. At the time, Steve was a junior in high school, and I just assumed that he would make the team. I was so preoccupied that I didn't take the time to understand what was important to Steve.

As fathers, we need to find out what's important to our children and then make those things our priority.

The apostle Paul compares his ministry to fatherhood: "We dealt with each of you as a father deals with his own children, encouraging, comforting and urging you to live lives worthy of God" (1 Thess. 2:11-12). None of this will transpire unless the father is in the house. Attend their sporting events or drama presentations—whatever is important to them—even though it may mean giving up something else you would like to do.

—Phillip H. Porter, Jr.
chairman, board of directors
Promise Keepers

Personal Challenge:
• *Ask the Holy Spirit to help you make sacrifices you need to make.*

Thought to Apply: When we come to the end of life, the question will be, "How much have you given?" not "How much have you gotten?"

—GEORGE SWEETING (former president, Moody Bible Institute)

Worth Fighting For

Key Bible Verse: Marriage should be honored by all …
*(Hebrews 13:4). Bonus Reading: Proberbs 5:18–19;
Proverbs 18:22*

Steven Curtis Chapman is one of Christian music's most popular stars. His love song, "I Will Be Here," written for wife Mary Beth, is often sung at weddings.

In *Marriage Partnership* magazine, writer Joan Brasher explains that the Chapmans have a strong marriage, but they're the first to admit that it isn't perfect.

Steven grew up in a family where everybody talked about everything; they just put it all on the table. Mary Beth's family was just the opposite: They shut down communication whenever things got tense.

So how have Steven and Mary Beth, married for 14 years, worked things out? They've worked hard at it.

They've been to their pastor for counseling. They've recruited friends who aren't afraid to step in and mediate when the Chapmans reach a stand-off.

Steven, who was shocked by his parents' divorce after 28 years of marriage, says his marriage is worth every sacrifice: "We're not just beating the air, wrestling for the sake of wrestling. We are fighting for a cause, for a relationship that is second only to our relationship with God. And God has been faithful to us."

Personal Challenge:

• *How hard are you willing to work to make things better in your marriage or family?*
• *Pray that God will increase your desire to do what it takes to keep your close relationships healthy.*

Thought to Apply: Never, never, never, never give up.

—WINSTON CHURCHILL (British Prime Minister during World War II)

Riptide in Alaska

Key Bible Verse: Christ loved us and gave Himself up for us as a fragrant offering and sacrifice to God *(Ephesians 5:2). Bonus Reading: 1 Peter 4:7-11*

In *Man in the Mirror*, Patrick Morley tells of a group of fishermen who landed in a secluded bay in Alaska and had a great day fishing for salmon. But when they returned to their sea plane, they found it aground because of the fluctuating tides. They waited until the next morning for the tides to come in, but when they took off, they only got a few feet into the air before crashing back into the sea. Being aground the day before had punctured one of the pontoons, and it had filled up with water.

The sea plane slowly began to sink. The passengers, three men and a 12-year-old son of one of the men, prayed and then jumped into the icy cold waters to swim to shore. The riptide was strong, but two of the men reached the shore exhausted. They looked back, and saw the father with his arms around his son being swept out to sea.

The boy had not been strong enough to make it. The father was a strong swimmer, but he had chosen to die with his son rather than to live without him.

—*Robert Russell*
minister and author

Personal Challenge:
• *Are you as willing to live for your child as you would be to die for your child?*

Thought to Apply: Those who give much without sacrifice are reckoned as having given little.

—ERWIN W. LUTZER (author and pastor)

The Few Survivors

Key Bible Verses: Your attitude should be the same as that of Christ Jesus: Who . . . made Himself nothing, taking the very nature of a servant *(Philippians 2:5-7).*
Bonus Reading: John 13:1-17

In the movie *The Poseidon Adventure*, the ocean liner *S.S. Poseidon* is on the open sea when it hits a huge storm. Lights go out, smoke pours into rooms and, amid all the confusion, the ship flips over.

Because of the air trapped inside the ocean liner, it floats upside down. But in the confusion, the passengers can't figure out what's going on. They scramble to get out, mostly by following the steps to the top deck. The problem is, the top deck is now 100 feet under water. In trying to get to the top of the ship, they drown.

The only survivors are the few who do what doesn't make sense. They do the opposite of what everyone else is doing and climb up into the dark belly of the ship until they reach the hull. Rescuers hear them banging and cut them free.

In life, it's as if God has turned the ship over and the only way for us to find freedom is to choose what does not make sense: lay down our lives by serving, supporting, and sacrificing for others.
—*Kevin A. Miller, an editor in suburban Chicago*

Personal Challenge:
• *How do you view serving others—as beneath you, or as work that makes you like Christ?*

Thought to Apply: One thing I know: The only ones among you who will be really happy are those who will have sought and found how to serve.
—ALBERT SCHWEITZER (missionary doctor, 1875-1965)

Up Close & Personal with Senator John Ashcroft

What It Takes to Serve Others

Q. People often discuss the importance of delayed gratification; what do you mean when you talk about "displaced gratification"?

A. In delayed gratification, we put off something so that we can enjoy something even better later on—avoiding a "sex life" before marriage, for instance, so that we can more fully enter into a deeper love of the marital union. In displaced gratification, we put off something so that the gratification can go to somebody else. Within marriage, for example, we put our spouse's needs ahead of our own.

When William Booth finally left the Salvation Army, he sent a one-word telegram to every member of his army. That one word embodied the guiding principle of Booth's life: "Others."

What is the reward of displaced gratification?
The man or woman who understands delayed and displaced gratification realizes that "others" are what it's all about. Instead of demanding our rights and satisfaction, we can work for the rights of others, we can find fulfillment in seeing other people satisfied, and we can serve instead of trying to conquer. Displaced gratification is the oil that keeps our society running smoothly.

Where do you draw inspiration to live this way?
Learning to put the needs of others above your own is the "displaced gratification" my father taught me about. The ultimate understanding of displaced gratification is reflected in the life of Christ, who gave up heaven for earth, ▶

who could have been crowned king, and who could have called ten thousand angels to rescue Him from the cross.

Instead He accepted brutal torture on our behalf.

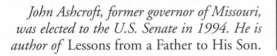

John Ashcroft, former governor of Missouri, was elected to the U.S. Senate in 1994. He is author of Lessons from a Father to His Son.

Sunday, Week 10   **Sacrifice**

For Personal Study or Group Discussion

Real Life Application

Key Bible Verse: This is how we know what love is: Jesus Christ laid down His life for us. And we ought to lay down our lives for our brothers *(1 John 3:16)*. *Bonus Reading: 1 John 4:7-21*

Think and pray about these sentence starters on your own. Or, if you meet with other men, use them to trigger your discussion.

☐ When I think of what Christ sacrificed for me, I feel ...

☐ When faced with making personal sacrifices, I ...

☐ The personal sacrifice that would make me a better follower of Christ is ...

Credits: Monday: Adapted from "How to Do the Undoable," by Jerry Bridges with Annette LaPlaca, *Marriage Partnership* (summer 1996) Copyright © 1998 Christianity Today, Inc.; Tuesday: *Better Men*, Phillip H. Porter, Jr., with W. Terry Whalin (Zondervan, 1998); Wednesday: *Marriage Partnership* (Spring 1997); Thursday: *Preaching Today* #176; Friday: *Marriage Partnership* (Fall 1996); Saturday: *Lessons from a Father to His Son* (Thomas Nelson, 1998).

Faith Is the Glue

Key Bible Verse: I tell you the truth, if you have faith as small as a mustard seed, you can say to this mountain, "Move from here to there" and it will move. Nothing will be impossible for you *(Matthew 17:20). Bonus Reading: Jeremiah 17:5-8*

The people who jest about faith don't realize how big a part it plays in everyday affairs.

It takes faith to get married because marriage vows are basically promises.

It takes faith to send children off to school.

It takes faith to get a prescription filled.

It takes faith to eat in a restaurant, deposit money in a bank, sign a contract, drive on the highway, or get on an airplane or an elevator.

Faith isn't some kind of religious experience for the elite; it's the glue that helps hold people's lives together.

But remember, faith is only as good as its object. If we trust people, we get what people can do; if we trust money, we get what money can do; if we trust ourselves, we get what we can do; if we trust God, we get what God can do.

—Warren Wiersbe
author and speaker
Lincoln, Nebraska

Personal Challenge:

• *For what area of your life do you need to put more trust in God?*
• *What is keeping you from trusting God? Pray honestly about that today.*

Thought to Apply: Faith is not belief without proof but trust without reservation.

—D. ELTON TRUEBLOOD (late Christian author)

Handling What You Don't Know

Key Bible Verse: We live by faith, not by sight
(2 Corinthians 5:7). Bonus Reading: Hebrews 11:1-16;
Philippians 2:12-13

I still don't understand, nearly 10 years later. At least I don't understand why the Lord allowed my sons to be afflicted with infantile bilateral striatal necrosis. I don't understand why Jonathan died or why Christopher lived. Today he's 16 and nearly totally recovered.

All I understand is this: life is a riddle, which God wants me to experience but not necessarily solve. When I was struggling to solve it, I found 1 Corinthians 13:12, which only makes sense in the original Greek: "For now we see (or understand) through a mirror, *in a riddle,*" the apostle Paul wrote, "but then face to face."

Modern Christians sometimes rush to put God's truth into little boxes, neatly systematized, categorized, organized, and principle-ized, when God's perspective on suffering is too big for any of that. While for some, "spirituality" is defined by what you know, God may be more concerned with how you handle what you cannot know.

A riddle loses its mystery and its power, even perhaps its significance, once it is solved. By keeping us in our riddle (every person's riddle is unique), God is helping us learn to walk by faith, and not by sight.

—*David Biebel, author*

Personal Challenge:
• *Let God be God. In prayer today, give up the idea that you can control everything.*

Thought to Apply: True faith goes into operation when there are no answers. —ELISABETH ELLIOT (missionary and author)

You Can't Keep Promises

Key Bible Verse: I have been crucified with Christ and I no longer live, but Christ lives in me. The life I live in the body, I live by faith in the Son of God, who loved me and gave Himself for me *(Galatians 2:20). Bonus Reading: 1 Thessalonians 5:24; Galatians 3:3-5*

Realize that you can't keep your promises. That may seem like a strange first step toward the goal of keeping promises, but it's true.

Consider this question: If we could keep our promises, wouldn't we have done it by now? How many times have we made the same promises?

Many of us have struggled with promise-keeping for one reason: We have focused on our performance more than on Jesus Christ. We have tried to keep our promises, but the Bible teaches that effective Christian living doesn't come by trying. It comes by trusting Christ to express His life through us. He is the only One who can successfully keep promises.

Before we can be effective promise keepers, we must become promise receivers. The Bible is clear about God's promise: the One who has given us His life will be the One who lives it for us. Only Jesus Christ can effectively live the perfect life. He lives inside believers today and wants to reveal His perfect life through us.

—Steve McVey, president
Grace Walk Ministries

Personal Challenge:
• *What promise do you need God's help to keep? Ask God to empower you.*

Thought to Apply: Faith does not operate in the realm of the possible. ... Faith begins where man's power ends.
—GEORGE MÜLLER (orphanage founder, 19th century)

Hardest Thing I've Done

Key Bible Verses: The God of all grace, who called you to His eternal glory in Christ, after you have suffered a little while, will Himself restore you and make you strong, firm and steadfast *(1 Peter 5:10)*. *Bonus Reading: 1 John 1:5-2:6; Psalm 56:3-4*

I went to Promise Keepers in Indianapolis, knowing God was going to deal with me in an area I had held on to for over a year. It's tragic to admit, but I had been unfaithful to my wife. Sure enough, God told me to tell her. I was frightened by the thought, yet I knew I had to tell her.

When I arrived home, after trying to ignore the conviction of the Holy Spirit, I acted upon God's promise, and I told my wife. It was the hardest thing I've ever had to do, but God has been faithful.

My wife was very hurt and is still going through the process of healing, but she is committed to our marriage. God truly forgives a repentant heart. God honored my honesty. I had to be anchored in Him to survive the storm that followed, but if I wanted to reach the full potential that a godly marriage has to offer, I had to confess, both to God and to my wife.

—A promise keeper in Tennessee

Personal Challenge:
• *Are you hiding some wrong for fear of the consequences?*

Thought to Apply: It is a man's business to do the will of God; God takes on Himself the special care of that man; therefore that man ought never to be afraid of anything. —GEORGE MACDONALD (19th century Scottish writer)

The Day I Got Cut

Key Bible Verses: The Lord's unfailing love surrounds the man who trusts in Him. Rejoice in the Lord and be glad, you righteous; sing, all you who are upright in heart *(Psalm 32:10-11)*.
Bonus Reading: Daniel 6:1-23; Isaiah 26:3-4

Seattle Seahawks' head coach Mike Holmgren looks back at a heart-breaking moment—when he was cut from the New York Jets as backup quarterback to Joe Namath—that directed him to a bigger plan.

"I had committed my life to Jesus Christ when I was 11, but in my pursuit to make a name for myself in football, I left God next to my dust-covered Bible.

"But after getting cut from the Jets, I pulled out my Bible and found comfort in a verse I had memorized in Sunday school: 'Trust in the Lord with all thine heart; and lean not unto thine own understanding. In all thy ways acknowledge him, and He shall direct thy paths' (Proverbs 3:5-6).

"I asked Jesus Christ to take control again.

"My priorities in life are faith, family, and football—in that order."

Personal Challenge:
• *Are you facing difficulty? How can you respond so that you become more committed to Jesus Christ?*
• *Thank God that He rules your life even when heart-break comes.*

Thought to Apply: Faith like Job's cannot be shaken because it is the result of having been shaken.

—ABRAHAM HESCHEL (Jewish author)

Up Close & Personal with Tony Evans

Strangled by Worry?

Q. What's so bad about worry?

A. The word *worry* is from a word that means "to strangle." That's what worry does to us. It chokes us. It cuts off our emotional and spiritual air supply so that we get frustrated and angry.

Worry is like fog. I'm told that a fog that can cover up to seven blocks contains less than one glassful of water. Fog is a lot of smoke and almost no substance. It's the same with worry. It's like a rocking chair, taking you back and forth but never getting you anywhere.

In Matthew 6:25-34, Jesus tells us not to worry about what we are going to eat or drink or wear.

How can I stop worrying? If we get our lives straightened out before God and learn to trust Him and rely on him, he's going to assume responsibility for our tomorrows.

If you want to see how this works, Jesus says, "Look at the birds of the air" (6:26). God is the Creator of birds, but He is not their Father. He's your Father. So if He takes such magnificent care of birds He's not even related to, what are you worried about?

If you saw me feeding birds in my backyard, would you wonder if I'm feeding my kids? You would probably think that any father who takes the time and trouble to feed birds is going to feed His children. That's what Jesus wants us to think about our heavenly Father.

Tony Evans is senior pastor of Oak Cliff Bible Fellowship in Dallas, Texas, and author of No More Excuses.

Trust in God   Sunday, Week 11

For Personal Study or Group Discussion

Real Life Application

Key Bible Verse: Some trust in chariots and some in horses, but we trust in the name of the Lord our God *(Psalm 20:7). Bonus Reading: Philippians 3:4-14; Psalm 23*

Think and pray about these sentence starters on your own. Or, if you meet with other men, use them to trigger your discussion.

☐ One experience that has made it harder for me to trust in God is ...

☐ I'm tempted to trust in created or human things like ...

☐ One time God showed me He could be trusted was ...

☐ I want to trust more in the Lord because ...

Credits: Monday: *Being a Child of God: Your Guide for the Adventure* (Thomas Nelson, 1996); Tuesday: *If God Is So Good, Why Do I Hurt So Bad?* (Spire, 1995); Wednesday: *Grace Walk* (Harvest House,1995); Thursday:Testimony used with permission; Friday: Greg Asimakoupoulos with Mike Holmgren, *Decision* (10/97); Saturday: *No More Excuses* (Crossway, 1996).

It Takes More Than Sperm

Key Bible Verse: He will turn the hearts of the fathers to their children, and the hearts of the children to their fathers *(Malachi 4:6). Bonus Reading: Proverbs 10:1*

Some fathers come to the conclusion that there is something more important than their wives and children. It's not unusual for a man to walk out on his family and think that he can still be a father. But kids who are abandoned by their fathers know the truth. Their lives have been altered. The family has died. And things will never be the same. It takes more than sperm to be a father. It takes commitment.

But commitment can be hard. And a lot of fathers simply aren't wiling to pay the price.

There can be no fathering without commitment. To be a father you must first be committed to your marriage. Committed to your kids. Committed to staying instead of leaving.

A real dad does more than simply produce children. A real dad keeps his promises. He chooses to work through the tough times, for the sake of his family. He provides for them and protects them, both emotionally and physically. These things he cannot do once he walks out the door.

—Steve Farrar, founder Men's Leadership Ministries

Personal Challenge:
• *Do you ever think about leaving your family? Determine today that this is not an option.*

Thought to Apply: Fathering makes a man, whatever his standing in the eyes of the world, feel strong and good and important, just as he makes his child feel loved and valued. —FRANK S. PITTMAN III (author)

Soaking Up Dad

Key Bible Verse: I have chosen Abraham, so that he will direct his children and his household after him to keep the way of the Lord by doing what is right and just *(Genesis 18:18). Bonus Reading: Deuteronomy 11:18-21*

We teach our children even when we don't think school is in session. Too often, we think our lessons are the sit-down kind, the planned-out kind. But our lessons are also how we react as a Little League coach when the ump blows a call, and how we treat our wives after we've both had rugged days at work, and what we say when we see a homeless man on the street.

Sometimes our lessons are good ones. I hope my sons—without me saying a word—have become more color-blind by our attending a church with a black pastor and linking arms with a black ministry in rural Mississippi.

Sometimes my lessons are the wrong kinds. As a boy, what hurt so deeply was to hear my mother and father fight; though it wasn't a common scene, the most perfect day could turn blustery cold when their relationship iced up. Without intending to, I've taught a few similarly chilly lessons to my own sons.

Our sons are sponges, quietly soaking up all we say and do.

—*Bob Welch, author*

Personal Challenge:
• *What is one thing you do that you're glad your children have "soaked up"?*

Thought to Apply: By profession I am a soldier and take pride in that fact. But I am prouder—infinitely prouder—to be a father.

—DOUGLAS MACARTHUR (American five-star general, World War II)

He Had a Hold on Me

Key Bible Verse: He must manage his own family well and see that his children obey him with proper respect. If anyone does not know how to manage his own family, how can he take care of God's church? *(1 Timothy 3:4). Bonus Reading: Proverbs 14:26*

My father would tell me, "I want you home at 10:00 P.M. That's not 10:01. You be in here at 10:00, or it's fire!"

I would get upset and say, "Why do I have to be in here at 10:00? My friends are making fun of me. They can stay out until 2:00 and 3:00 in the morning."

And Dad would say, "Well, maybe their parents don't care. But I care. Be in here at 10:00."

When I go back to Baltimore where I grew up, guess where many of those guys are? Still hanging out on the corner until 2:00 and 3:00 in the morning.

I can trace where I am today back to a father who had a hold on me, who disciplined me, and who would not let me have my way all the time.

What is missing in so much of our well-intentioned parenting is enforcement, which represents the strength of our convictions.

—*Tony Evans*
pastor and author
Dallas, Texas

Personal Challenge:
• *What is one limit your parents put on you that you're grateful for now?*
• *If you have children, ask God for wisdom to know where to put limits on them.*

Thought to Apply: It's easier to build a boy than to mend a man. —Anonymous

Mr. Consistency

Key Bible Verse: Train a child in the way he should go, and when he is old he will not turn from it *(Proverbs 22:6). Bonus Reading: Proverbs 22:13-26; Ephesians 6:4*

When a child of a consistent father interacts with his dad, the child knows what to expect. There are few surprises and no scares.

A consistent father governs his moods. He is not affectionate one minute and angry the next, with no reason for the sudden mood swing. Inconsistent fathers are emotionally erratic. Years later, their children will stand up and confess, often through tears, "Whenever I approached my dad, I had no idea whether he was going to hug me or belt me."

A consistent father also governs his behavior. His children can count on his always being their father, always coming back home. Children of an inconsistent dad live with the threatening sense that their father's bags are packed and waiting by the door.

He also governs his behavior by practicing what he preaches. When he makes a promise, his children can count on his keeping it.

He also practices what he preaches by being consistent in his moral behavior. He avoids hypocrisy at all costs.
—*Ken Canfield
executive director, National
Center for Fathering*

Personal Challenge:
• *What excuses have you made for your unpredictable behavior?*

Thought to Apply: Where a man belongs is up early and alone with God seeking vision and direction for his family.   —JOHN PIPER (pastor and author)

The Last Thing He Wrote

Key Bible Verse: Honor your father and your mother, so that you may live long in the land the Lord your God is giving you *(Exodus 20:12). Bonus Reading: John 17; Romans 12:10*

In an age of parent-bashing, it honors our father and mother to remember their positive qualities. My dad taught me powerful lessons about giving.

When I was a teenager, Dad would come in my room and say, "C'mon, kid, let's go."

"Where to?"

"Lucy's." Once a month he would visit Lucy Butchko, a woman whose body was twisted and pinned into a wheelchair by arthritis. He would reach his big arms around her frail body and lift her out of the wheelchair and place her in the front seat of our brown station wagon. Then he would fold the wheelchair, throw it in back, and drive Lucy to the monthly Communion service for shut-ins.

Here was a vice-president of a publishing company, shuttling shut-ins.

Later, while in the hospital, trying to recover from a massive heart attack, Dad found out that a family down the street didn't have enough money to buy groceries. So he wrote them a check.

It was the last thing he ever wrote, and a lasting lesson in giving.

—Kevin A. Miller
an editor near Chicago

Personal Challenge:
• *What positive lessons did your parents give you?*
• *If your father and mother are still alive, how could you honor them?*

Thought to Apply: Children not only need a father, they long for one, irrationally, with all the undiluted strength of a child's hopeful heart. —MAGGIE GALLAGHER (writer)

Up Close & Personal with Gary D. Chapman

How to Really Love a Child

Q. ▪ Why do you say it is not enough just to love your child?

A. Most fathers love their children, but thousands of children do not *feel* loved by their fathers.

How does a father get his love message across?
After 20-plus years of counseling, I am convinced that there are only five basic languages of love. All of them can be used to communicate love to a child, but one of them will be more important than the other four. Each child has a primary love language. If you discover this language and speak it often, your child will genuinely feel loved.

What are the five basic love languages?
Physical touch, words of affirmation, quality time, giving gifts, and acts of service.

The importance of discovering your child's primary love language is illustrated by the 12-year-old who runs away from home and in due time is sitting in the pastor's or counselor's office saying: "My parents don't love me. They love my brother, but they don't love me."

The parents are shocked to hear these words because the fact is they have always loved their son. However, the painful reality is that the child does not *feel* loved.

Perhaps they have given ball gloves and bicycles to show their love and perhaps the 12-year old is feeling, *I wish Dad would play ball with me. I wish Dad would go riding with me. We never do anything together.*

The child is crying for ▶

quality time, but the parents are expressing their love with gifts. The parents are sincere, but they are not connecting with their child emotion- ally.

Gary D. Chapman leads marriage seminars and is co-author of The Five Love Languages of Children *(Moody, 1997).*

Sunday, Week 12

Fathering

For Personal Study or Group Discussion

Real Life Application

Key Bible Verse: Choose for yourselves this day whom you will serve. ... But as for me and my household, we will serve the Lord *(Joshua 24:15). Bonus Reading: Proverbs 20:7*

Think and pray about these sentence starters on your own. Or, if you meet with other men, use them to trigger your discussion.

☐ What I like best about being a father is ...

☐ When it comes to disciplining my children, I ...

☐ Something good I learned from my father ...

☐ The greatest challenge of being a father is ...

☐ To be a more godly father, I need ...

Credits: Monday: *Anchor Man* (Thomas Nelson, 1998); Tuesday: *A Father for All Seasons* (Harvest House, 1998); Wednesday: *No More Excuses* (Crossway, 1996); Thursday: *The 7 Secrets of Effective Fathers* (Tyndale, 1992); Friday: *Leadership* (Winter, 1996); Saturday: *The Five Love Languages of Children* (Moody, 1997).

The Boxer Comes Back

Key Bible Verse: With man this is impossible, but not with God; all things are possible with God *(Mark 10:27). Bonus Reading: Philippians 4:12-13*

Heavyweight boxer Evander Holyfield remembers: "After I lost the fight against Mike Moorer, I felt that my boxing career was over. I was not upset by it. I was thankful for all that I had done, including being two-time heavyweight champion of the world. But God wasn't finished with me yet in the boxing game.

"He healed me, and when He did, He changed everything: my boxing, my health, everything. He brought my family together. After the doctors said that I had a bad heart, God touched me. I went back to the hospital, and they gave me a clean bill of health. I got my boxing license back, winning numerous fights and falling short again but not giving up.

"I knew He brought me back for a reason, which led to the fight with Mike Tyson. Then the world got an opportunity to see that God still lives. God could take a person like Evander Holyfield, when the people were saying he's out—he's too old, it's impossible for him to win—and do what seemed impossible. They saw that I could do all things through Christ, and the Lord got the glory. I'm still in this boxing game because of the Lord."

Personal Challenge:
• *What do you believe makes it "impossible for you to win" in life? Ask God to help you do all things through Christ.*

Thought to Apply: Failure doesn't mean God has abandoned you ... it does mean God has a better idea!

—ROBERT SCHULLER (pastor and author)

What You Can Control

Key Bible Verse: Perseverance must finish its work so that you may be mature and complete, not lacking anything *(James 1:4)*. *Bonus Reading: Psalm 119:65-80*

In dealing with losses in my own life, I have learned one major lesson. I cannot control my circumstance; but I can control my response.

Coming to this realization puts a major building block in place to rebuild the wounds of loss. The key to living victoriously with loss is *how I respond over time*. Most of us cannot control our immediate response to losses. It simply takes time to reflect on them, to understand our feelings about them and to reorder our thinking.

The most fundamental biblical truth is that God is sovereign in all the circumstances of my life. He never places us in circumstances without purpose and design. Therefore this can be the time of greatest personal and spiritual growth in my life. It is through difficult circumstances that we grow. In many sports, the saying "No pain, no gain" is often posted in full view of the athletes. Similarly, in the Christian life little growth occurs without discipline and pain.

God's purpose is the "harvest of righteousness"— right living that pleases Him.
—Jerry White, president
The Navigators

Personal Challenge:
• *How did you respond immediately to a recent loss? How would you like to respond over time? Ask God to help you do that.*

Thought to Apply: It's always too soon to quit.
—V. RAYMOND EDMAN (4th president of Wheaton College)

"I Was Angry at God"

Key Bible Verses: We are hard pressed on every side, but not crushed; perplexed, but not in despair; persecuted, but not abandoned; struck down, but not destroyed *(2 Corinthians 4:8-9). Bonus Reading: Psalm 34*

One particularly dark time for us as a family happened while I was in high school. My dad always worked to improve our lifestyle and provide for us. But through a bad business venture, we lost everything.

I remember how angry I was at God. I went through a period of doubting and questioning Him. Mom and my two brothers also struggled with anger toward God, and we seemed to all retreat to deal with our hurt differently. All except Dad.

I remember seeing him faithfully, every morning, beside his chair on his knees praying for us. Even though I was mad at God, just knowing my dad was consistently praying gave me the assurance we would pull through—and it gave me the courage to hope. Even when we didn't have a kind word for my dad, he was still the one encouraging us.

Seeing his response to this trial affected me more than any other experience in my Christian walk. I'm thankful I have a father who shows me the holiness that comes through simply struggling. I'm proud to be the daughter of Adolph Diaz—an overcomer.

—Tracey D. Lawrence
research writer, All Men's
Outreach, Promise Keepers

Personal Challenge:
• *Get on your knees today and pray for your family.*

Thought to Apply: It is better to fail in a cause that will ultimately succeed than to succeed in a cause that will ultimately fail. —PETER MARSHALL (late Senate chaplain)

Storm Warning

Key Bible Verse: Whoever exalts himself will be humbled, and whoever humbles himself will be exalted *(Matthew 23:12). Bonus Reading: Hebrews 12:4-13*

Perhaps no other storm signal is meant to give a more urgent warning that something is wrong and needs to be addressed than what we call the power of guilt. It is a message that comes deep from the soul saying that something is terribly wrong.

More than a feeling or an emotion, guilt is the pain message of the spiritual system. It speaks to the person on a divergent path from God. It calls attention to choices and values that are likely to be destructive and harmful. It warns when someone is on the verge of breaking or has already broken covenants and trusts.

The pain message of guilt as a storm signal does not last indefinitely. It appears that men can outlive guilt by ignoring it or rationalizing that its message is untrue or unreliable. Many men live beyond guilt, and they generally pay a strong price for it.

The message behind guilt is one of repentance, an ancient word that basically means "to turn around and choose another direction." That's a hard thing for a man to do, especially if it challenges his pride and self-image. But I know of nothing more powerful when it's done.

—Gordon MacDonald
pastor, Grace Chapel
Lexington, Massachusetts

Personal Challenge:
• *Have you been feeling guilt for a sin? Call out to God for forgiveness.*

Thought to Apply: The healthy and strong individual is the one who asks for help when he needs it—whether he's got an abscess on his knee or in his soul. —ANONYMOUS

No More Party Animal

Key Bible Verses: If by the Spirit you put to death the misdeeds of the body, you will live, because those who are led by the Spirit of God are sons of God *(Romans 8:13-14). Bonus Reading: Romans 8*

I went to Promise Keepers knowing I needed a great spiritual uplifting. I had already accepted Jesus Christ as Savior and Lord of my life, but I was living a lie.

I was traveling both sides of the fence, praising the Lord one day, then falling into the same old sins the next.

My intentions were admirable, but I kept feeling the guilt of my sins. I wanted to do right but oftentimes found myself following the crowd, doing what I knew was wrong.

I was at the end of my rope with the way I was living—drinking and partying. I really love the Lord and wanted to please him, but I kept wanting to please my friends as well.

When I went up to the stage Friday night at the Hoosier Dome, I lost all desire to sin against God. I wept uncontrollably, leaving my pain there and giving it to God.

I am now confident that with God's help, I can be the Christian man He intends me to be.

—A promise keeper
from Ohio

Personal Challenge:
• *Are you more likely to follow God or the guys?*
• *Are there men who will help you stay close to God? Talk to one of them this week.*

Thought to Apply: Hell is the place where one has ceased to hope.   —A.J. CRONIN (British physician and novelist)

Up Close & Personal with Phillip H. Porter, Jr.

Coming Back from Moral Failure

Q. ▪ When have you had to "come back" in your Christian life?

A. I wish I could say that I have never wandered off that path, but I have.

As a freshman in college, I was dating Lee. We met in the church and both of us loved God.

Several months before our wedding, we made a big mistake and conceived our first child, Phillip. There was no question of our love for each other and our intention for marriage, so we were married in July 1957. Phillip was born in November.

How were you restored?
We had to confess our sin to God, accept His forgiveness, and return to the path of following Jesus.

That is the Good News about our faith: God's grace is always greater than our sin.

What would you say to the man who has suffered a moral failure?
No matter what sins you have committed in your life or what sort of holy relationship you once had with God, the important thing is to decide where you are today.

God doesn't accept or reject us on the basis of holy living.

I learned afresh that by His grace, God accepts me just as I am. It is a daily process to learn to lean on Jesus and gradually leave our sinful ways behind. Philippians 1:6 says, "He who began a good work in you will carry it on to completion until the day of Christ Jesus."

Phillip H. Porter, Jr., is chairman of the board of directors of Promise Keepers and senior pastor of All Nations Pentecostal Center in Aurora, Colorado.

Coming Back   Sunday, Week 13

For Personal Study or Group Discussion

Real Life Application

Key Bible Verse: Let us then approach the throne of grace with confidence, so that we may receive mercy and find grace to help us in our time of need *(Hebrews 4:16). Bonus Reading: Proverbs 24:16*

Think and pray about these sentence starters on your own. Or, if you meet with other men, use them to trigger your discussion.

☐ One time I had to "come back" to God was ...

☐ A person who has modeled coming back is ...

☐ The difference Jesus makes for those who are trying to bounce back is ...

Credits: Monday: *New Man* (March/April, 1998), interview by Stephen Strang; Tuesday: *Dangers Men Face* (NavPress, 1997); Wednesday: *The Promise Keeper* (May/June, 1998); Thursday: *When Men Think Private Thoughts* (Thomas Nelson, 1996); Friday: Testimony used by permission; Saturday: *Better Men* (Zondervan, 1998).

Skillfully Disguised Disciple

Key Bible Verse: If you hold to my teaching, you are really my disciples *(John 8:31). Bonus Reading: Matthew 28:18-20; 1 Thessalonians 4:11-12*

At one small group meeting, I turned to one person obviously anxious to participate and asked, "Would you mind telling us your name, please?"

"Sure. Nancy," she replied.

"And tell us what you do."

"I'm a disciple of Jesus Christ very skillfully disguised as a machine operator," she responded.

Even as the others laughed at the way she responded, they realized Nancy had not only made a personal statement but had presented a challenge to everyone in the room.

The laughter soon subsided, and in its place a sense of introspection settled on the group. We all began to think how we would have answered the question, "And what do you do?" Of course, the most common way to answer is to state an occupation. "Oh, I sell insurance." But to see oneself as first and foremost a disciple of Jesus Christ is refreshingly different. Our discipleship is something lived out on a factory floor amid the noise and clamor of machines and the hustle and bustle of labor-management relations.

—Stuart Briscoe, pastor and author

Personal Challenge:
• *Is there a Christian man who understands your type of work? Talk to him about how serving Jesus affects your work.*

Thought to Apply: It's important that I have good numbers and I'm well-respected as a player. But I think it's more important that I'm respected as a man.

—DAVID ROBINSON (San Antonio Spurs basketball star)

How to Do Noble Things

Key Bible Verse: The noble man makes noble plans, and by noble deeds he stands *(Isaiah 32:8). Bonus Reading: 2 Corinthians 4:18; Philippians 4:8-9*

Mike Kami is a strategic planning consultant. I went to Mike because I wanted him to do for my life what he does so well for business: Draw up a strategic plan. I needed him to show me how to live so I was not plagued by a growing sense that I was missing out.

I went to Mike with tons of questions: What should I do with my life? How could I be most useful? Where should I invest my time, talents and treasures?

Mike asked me a simple, penetrating question: "What's in the box?"

I didn't have a clue as to what he was getting at.

"I can't put together an honest plan for your life until I identify the mainspring. I've been listening to you for a couple of hours, trying to figure out what's in your box. It's either money or Jesus Christ. If you can tell me which one it is, I can tell you the strategic planning implications of that choice. If you can't tell me, you're going to bounce between those two values and be confused."

After a few minutes (which seemed like hours), I answered, "Well, if it has to be one or the other, I'll put Jesus Christ in the box."

—Bob Buford, Buford Television, Dallas, Texas

Personal Challenge:
• *Set a work goal for the year ahead that is spiritual in nature.*

Thought to Apply: Work as if you were to live a hundred years; pray as if you were to die tomorrow.
—BENJAMIN FRANKLIN (1706-1790)

Getting a New Boss

Key Bible Verse: Whatever you do, work at it with all your heart, as working for the Lord, not for men *(Colossians 3:23). Bonus Reading: Colossians 3:22-4:1*

If you don't go to work tomorrow thinking, *I'm going to work for the Lord,* then you've missed the meaning of work. The quickest way to transform a bad job is with a new attitude.

And the quickest way to get a new attitude is to change bosses.

Paul says if you work for the Lord, you get your reward from Him. If you're just working for "the man," the man can give you whatever reward he wants. But if you're working for the Lord, the man has to give you what the Lord tells him to give you.

This is a subtle yet significant reorientation to work.

God wants you to find meaning in your work, but the thing that makes it meaningful is not the task itself, but your relationship with God in the task.

Tasks can change. But even if you get a project you're not excited about, if your attitude is that you are participating with God in the project, He can change the meaninglessness of work into the meaningfulness of work.

—*Tony Evans*
pastor and author
Dallas, Texas

Personal Challenge:
• *Is God your real boss?*
• *This week remind yourself that you are working for Jesus.*

Thought to Apply: The highest reward for a man's toil is not what he gets for it, but what he becomes by it.

—JOHN RUSKIN (19th century writer)

From Workaholism to Worship

Key Bible Verse: [The Lord] has filled them with skill to do all kinds of work ... all of them master craftsmen and designers *(Exodus 35:35). Bonus Reading: Exodus 35:30—36:8; 1 Peter 4:10-11*

After five years at Hallmark, artist Thomas Blackshear left to open his own studio. He quickly earned clients like Disney Pictures, Coca-Cola, The Hamilton Group, Jim Henson Studios and Lee Jeans. "I was running like a maniac, and it was intensely exciting. I was doing exactly what I wanted to do in life," Blackshear says.

His canvas was full—but what was wrong with this picture? "I turned into an obsessed workaholic. I'd made a name for myself, but inside I felt empty." That didn't change with his 1986 marriage to Ami, a popular figurine artist. The couple struggled with his workaholism. Blackshear's dark days led to a three-year depression.

The artist credits his survival to Jesus Christ. Blackshear had made a faith commitment while growing up. One day he had his inspiration for "Forgiven," a picture that has inspired believers all over the world. Thereafter his art was informed by his faith.

Blackshear never forgets who really holds the brush.

—W. Terry Whalin, writer
Colorado Springs, Colorado

Personal Challenge:
• *Dedicate your talents to the purposes of God.*

Thought to Apply: It is our best work that God wants, not the dregs of our exhaustion.

—GEORGE MACDONALD (19th century Scottish author)

Bank on Me

Key Bible Verse: All hard work brings a profit, but mere talk leads only to poverty *(Proverbs 14:23). Bonus Reading: Ephesians 4:28*

One common sentiment says, "If a man thinks his work is important, then obviously he's depriving his kids." Our culture for the past few decades has perhaps overemphasized the role of father as financial provider, but the effective father says, "While financial provision is not my only role, it is a role and one I consider important."

Providing financially for your family is related to protecting them. When you provide a roof over their heads, you protect them against snow and hail and lightning storm. When you provide grocery money, you protect them against starvation. We could even say that when you pay taxes, you protect your children against crime, since a portion of those taxes goes to support a police force.

What effective fathers tell us is that we should not feel guilty about going to work. If we never come home from work, then we should feel guilty, but while doing our jobs and drawing our paychecks we should feel proud that we are faithfully meeting the needs of our children and dutifully fulfilling our roles as fathers.

—*Ken R. Canfield, executive director, National Center for Fathering*

Personal Challenge:
• *Ask God for wisdom on how to juggle the demands of work and family.*

Thought to Apply: I can see the work I do as either a problem or a privilege. —Anonymous

Up Close & Personal with Phil Downer

Q. ¤ **What is success?**

A. ¤ Success is nothing more than the feeling of reaching our goals. The Lord is more interested in our significance.

How can we have greater significance?

God wants us to make a difference in the lives of other people. I have two business friends—both Christians—who passed away recently. Chuck built a huge factory. He also discipled many believers.

I also visited Randy, a man with a healthy business but an unhealthy heart. He realized no one would weep when he died. I want to go out like Chuck.

Phil Downer is president of the Christian Businessmen's Committee. (Written by Chip MacGregor).

For Personal Study or Group Discussion

Key Bible Verse: Diligent hands will rule, but laziness ends in slave labor *(Proverbs 12:24). Bonus Reading: 2 Thessalonians 3:6-13*

Think and pray about these sentence starters.

☐ God has given me the ability to ...

☐ God could work through me more on the job if I ...

Credits: Monday: *Discipleship for Ordinary People* (Shaw, 1995); Tuesday: *Halftime* (Zondervan, 1996); Wednesday: *No More Excuses* (Crossway, 1996); Thursday and Saturday: *Stand Firm* (May, 1998); Friday: *The 7 Secrets of Effective Fathers* (Tyndale, 1992).

Zero Gravity

Key Bible Verses: Suffering produces perseverance; perseverance, character; and character, hope *(Romans 5:3-4). Bonus Reading: 2 Peter 1:5-9*

On December 29, 1987, a Soviet cosmonaut returned to the earth after 326 days in orbit. He was in good health, which hadn't always been the case in those record-breaking voyages.

Five years earlier, touching down after 211 days in space, two cosmonauts suffered from dizziness, high pulse rates and heart palpitations. They couldn't walk for a week.

After 30 days, they were still undergoing therapy for atrophied muscles and weakened hearts.

At zero gravity, the muscles of the body begin to waste away because there is no resistance.

To counteract this, the Soviets prescribed a vigorous exercise program for the cosmonauts. They invented the "penguin suit," a running suit laced with elastic bands. It resists every move the cosmonauts make, forcing them to exert their strength. Apparently the regimen is helping.

We often long dreamily for days without difficulty, but God knows better. The easier our lives, the weaker our spiritual fiber, for strength of any kind grows only by exertion.

Personal Challenge:
• In the difficulties you face this week, tackle them with a sense of God's purpose. Thank God for the good He wants to accomplish in you.

Thought to Apply: Storms make oaks take deeper root.
—GEORGE HERBERT (17th century English writer)

I Needed Cash

Key Bible Verse: My God will meet all your needs according to his glorious riches in Christ Jesus *(Philippians 4:19)*. *Bonus Reading: Matthew 6:25-34*

F our years ago, I was sitting in my cab in front of a Philadelphia hotel thinking and praying.

This particular Sunday, business had been extremely slow. I was wondering where I was going to get $60 to pay for the daily rent of my cab. I could lose the cab—and my livelihood—if I didn't come up with the money immediately.

Just then, a young woman got into my cab and said, "I know it will cost $25 for this ride, but I can only afford to pay you $15. I work for a charity, and that's all they gave me for cab fare."

I thought about it for a minute. *I am probably going to lose my cab anyway. Why not* *help someone else have a good day?*

I agreed to do it.

At her destination, the woman paid her $15 fare, then reached into her purse and laid a $100 bill next to me on the seat!

"The $15 fare was the charity's money," she explained. "This is my own money. God told me you needed it." With that, she was gone.

Through tears of joy, I thanked God for supplying my daily needs.

—Bruce Watson

Personal Challenge:
• *Thank God for the many ways He has provided for your daily needs.*
• *Can you be God's means of providing for someone else?*

Thought to Apply: The lowest ebb is the turn of the tide.
—HENRY WADSWORTH LONGFELLOW (19th century American poet)

Thrown from a Speedboat

Key Bible Verse: I will exalt you, O Lord, for you lifted me out of the depths *(Psalm 30:1).*
Bonus Reading: Psalm 107

Some years ago a speedboat driver who had survived a racing accident described what had happened. He said he had been at near top speeds when his boat veered slightly and hit a wave at a dangerous angle. The combined force of his speed and the size and angle of the wave sent the boat spinning crazily into the air. He was thrown from his seat and propelled deeply into the water—so deep, in fact, that he had no idea which direction the surface was.

He had to remain calm and wait for the buoyancy of his life vest to begin pulling him up. Once he discovered which way was up, he could swim for the surface.

Sometimes we find ourselves surrounded by confusing options, too deeply immersed in our problems to know which way is up. When this happens, we too can remain calm, waiting for God's gentle tug to pull us in the proper direction.

Our "life vest" may be other Christians, Scripture, or some other leading from the Holy Spirit, but the key is recognizing our dependency upon God and trusting Him.

Personal Challenge:
• *Are you needing to make an important decision? What do you believe is God's gentle tug? Talk about that with a trusted Christian brother.*

Thought to Apply: Many men owe the grandeur of their lives to their tremendous difficulties.
—CHARLES H. SPURGEON (19th century English pastor)

Beneath the Bluster

Key Bible Verse: We cannot do anything against the truth, but only for the truth *(2 Corinthians 13:8).*
Bonus Reading: John 1:43-47; Philippians 2:14-16

I was (at one time) a very young pastor, and each Monday I met with the chairman of the church's board. In the middle of one such meeting, the chairman, a wise and rather tough man, suddenly waved his arm as if to call time-out to our conversation.

He said, "Pastor, I need to tell you something. I've met with you week after week and noticed that you have a difficult time ever listening to difficult news. You want to give one excuse after another. You spend more time trying to explain yourself than you do listening and asking where the point of truth might be. You better beat this one, or you're never going to be an effective leader."

My defensiveness was an indicator of just how unsure of myself I really was. On the surface, I tended to act as if I had everything under control, as if I knew exactly what was happening and should happen. But the truth was that I didn't know half as much as I tried to pretend.

Some men need to listen to their prevailing tendency to whine or complain about everything that appears to go against them.

—Gordon MacDonald
pastor and author

Personal Challenge:
• *What are you tempted to complain about right now? Or make excuses about? Ask God for courage to face the truth and do His will.*

Thought to Apply: The Christian ideal has not been tried and found wanting. It has been found difficult and left untried.　　—G. K. CHESTERTON (20th century English journalist)

Fighting through Darkness

Key Bible Verse: God is our refuge and strength, an ever present help in trouble *(Psalm 46:1). Bonus Reading: Psalm 62*

I came to Promise Keepers in 1992, and it challenged me at a time when my spiritual life, my work, and my marriage were about to fall apart. One week after the 1992 conference, my wife told me she wanted to leave me. She said she had lost all respect for me and wanted her freedom.

I went from a mountain peak to the lowest valley in my life. I thought of suicide because of the rejection I felt. There was no one to turn to except my pastor. He loved me and encouraged me.

The year was painful, and it seemed as though I could not break out of the darkness around me. Then I came to Promise Keepers in 1993, and God gave me new insight into the battle raging in my life. I had once prayed that God would make me a soldier of the Cross, but until I heard and saw the clear message of the Cross through the Promise Keepers speakers, I had no idea which direction to go to battle.

Things are better in my family. Without Promise Keepers, my family would be in ruins today.

—A promise keeper from Indiana

Personal Challenge:
• *What spiritual battle are you facing? Ask God to give you strength for it and to build your character through it.*

Thought to Apply: What we do in the crisis always depends on whether we see the difficulties in the light of God, or God in the shadow of the difficulties.

—G. CAMPBELL MORGAN (English pastor and author)

Up Close & Personal with Dr. Ben Carson

How to Pray When Handling Dynamite

Q. ▪ As one of the world's leading neurosurgeons, what sort of challenges do you face in your work?

A. Most of my patients are children. They have tumors. They have spinal deformities. They suffer from debilitating seizures. Or, on rare occasions, they are connected to a sibling, each sharing parts of their skull, blood vessels and tissue with the other.

To perform one recent surgery on a 7-year-old's spinal column was like unwrapping a bunch of rubber bands from a stick of dynamite while knowing that moving the wrong band at the wrong time would cause an explosion—in this case, paralysis.

I perform as many as 500 surgeries each year.

How does your relationship with God help you face such awesome challenges?

I say a prayer before every operation. I pray for wisdom. I pray for guidance. And I pray for God's direct intervention should it become necessary.

I have a motto: "Do your best and let God do the rest." But you have to do your part. You can't sit and wait and say, "Oh Lord, take care of this ▶

problem." Man's extremity is unreasonable to expect God's opportunity. But unless you do your part, it's Him to intervene.

Dr. Benjamin Carson is director of pediatric neurosurgery at Johns Hopkins Medical Institutions. (Written by Stephen Caldwell.)

Sunday, Week 15   **Meeting Challenges**

For Personal Study or Group Discussion
Real Life Application

Key Bible Verse: The battle is not yours, but God's *(2 Chronicles 20:15). Bonus Reading: 2 Chronicles 20:1-30*

Think and pray about these sentence starters on your own. Or, if you meet with other men, use them to trigger your discussion.

☐ One of the biggest challenges I have faced was ...

☐ Through that the Lord taught me ...

☐ When I pray about the problems I'm trying to solve ...

☐ For me, perseverance is ...

Credits: Monday and Wednesday: *Illustrations for Preaching and Teaching: From Leadership Journal* (Baker, 1993); Tuesday: *Christian Reader* (Jul/Aug, 1998); Thursday: *When Men Think Private Thoughts* (Thomas Nelson, 1996); Friday: Testimony used by permission; Saturday: *Life@Work* (Vol. 1, No. 1)

Who Owns Your Money?

Key Bible Verses: You are not your own; you were bought at a price *(1 Corinthians 6:19-20). Bonus Reading: Matthew 25:14-30*

We must recognize who owns us. If we are Christians, the Lord owns us—all of us. We were bought by the blood of Jesus and his substitutional death on the cross. The symbolism is that we were purchased as slaves on the auction block. God, as our new master, purchased us with the precious blood of His Son, who was executed in our place.

The first step, then, in making godly financial decisions is to realize that God doesn't own just 10 percent but everything—100 percent of our paychecks, our homes, our household goods, our cars, our jobs, our retirement plans, our mates and even our kids. And since He owns everything and we are His property, our job is to be caretakers or stewards over His property.

Funk & Wagnalls dictionary defines a steward as one "entrusted with the management of property, finances or other affairs not his own." The key phrase is "not his own." Once we allow this concept fully to penetrate our hearts and minds, it will revolutionize our financial behavior.

—Jerry and Ramona Tuma and Tim LaHaye

Personal Challenge:

• *Do you really believe everything you have belongs to God? What difference would that make in the way you handle money?*

Thought to Apply: Our faith becomes practical when it is expressed in two books: the date book and the check book.   —ELTON TRUEBLOOD (late Christian author)

Money

You Love Money If...

Key Bible Verses: People who want to get rich fall into temptation and a trap and into many foolish and harmful desires that plunge men into ruin and destruction. For the love of money is a root of all kinds of evil *(1 Timothy 6:9-10). Bonus Reading: 1 Timothy 6:6-19*

That's how money works: You think you have it, but it has you. God is not trying to keep us from something good. An inordinate desire for money leads to "many foolish and harmful desires that plunge men into ruin and destruction." Does that sound like a route you want to take?

The problem is that the love of money doesn't make you more generous and loving. It doesn't make you a better husband or father or promise keeper.

You know you love money if your passion for it outweighs your passion for God. You know you love money when you have to choose between money and God, and money wins. You know you love money when your career keeps you off your knees, out of the Word, and out of fellowship with the saints.

Satan is going to try and change your priorities. He's going to try to get you to fix your hope on the uncertainty of riches rather than on God, "who richly provides us with everything for our enjoyment" (1 Timothy 6:17).

—Tony Evans, pastor and author

Personal Challenge:
• *If someone were to measure your love for God by looking at your check book, what would he conclude?*

Thought to Apply: For every verse in the Bible that tells us the benefits of wealth, there are ten that tell us the danger of wealth. —HADDON ROBINSON (author and professor)

When Money Isn't Just Money

Key Bible Verse: Watch out! Be on your guard against all kinds of greed; a man's life does not consist in the abundance of his possessions *(Luke 12:15). Bonus Reading: Luke 12:13-21*

My personal struggle with money issues is on the emotional side.

I do not feel driven to have things. It is fairly easy for me to keep a car for years and be satisfied with it, running the mileage up to over 150,000. But it is harder for me to stand by and watch certain members of my family get a lot of attention just because they have money.

Just as sex is never just sex, money is never just money. It is almost always something else.

Something deeper is going on in us than the pure motivation to make money.

One powerful motivating factor is that having money feeds feelings of self-worth. You always hear people say things like "He's worth two million."

This is how who we are gets mixed up with how much money we have.

If you have made a lot of money, it becomes easier to think of yourself as a hard worker, bright, diligent, clever and even superior to all those who have tried and failed. Having money can make us feel good about ourselves.

We need to pursue God and God's work, not money.
—Tom L. Eisenman, pastor in California

Personal Challenge:
• *Ask God to show you what money means to you beyond just money.*

Thought to Apply: Money is a terrible master but an excellent servant. —P. T. BARNUM (20th century showman)

The Nerves in Your Wallet

Key Bible Verse: Each man should give what he has decided in his heart to give, not reluctantly or under compulsion, for God loves a cheerful giver *(2 Corinthians 9:7). Bonus Reading: 2 Corinthians 8:1-9*

When you go to a doctor for your annual check-up, he or she will often begin to poke, prod and press various places, all the while asking, "Does this hurt? How about this?"

If you cry out in pain, one or two things has happened. Either the doctor has pushed too hard, without the right sensitivity. Or, more likely, there's something wrong, and the doctor will say, "We'd better do some more tests. It's not supposed to hurt there!"

So it is when pastors preach on financial responsibility, and certain members cry out in discomfort, criticizing the message and the messenger.

Either the pastor has pushed too hard, or perhaps there's something wrong. In that case, one could say, "My friend, we're in need of the Great Physician because it's not supposed to hurt there."

Personal Challenge:
• *As you consider God's principles for your finances, what are the tender places in your life?*

Thought to Apply: Money will buy a bed but not sleep; books but not brains; food but not appetite; finery but not beauty; a house but not a home; medicine but not health; luxuries but not culture; amusements but not happiness; religion but not salvation—a passport to everywhere but heaven. —UNKNOWN

Paying with Your Time

Key Bible Verses: Honor the Lord with your wealth, with the firstfruits of all your crops; then your barns will be filled to overflowing, and your vats will brim over with new wine *(Proverbs 3:9-10). Bonus Reading: Numbers 18:29*

There is always a trade-off between time and effort and money and rewards. You've heard the phrases, "There's no such thing as a free lunch," and "You can't get something for nothing." Those are very important understandings. Money should always be thought of as linked to work and the sweat of our brow.

Here's how this principle has meaning for us. Think for a moment of the most worthless, unnecessary purchase you have made in recent years. Perhaps it was an electric shaver that now sits in the garage, or an article of clothing that will never be worn. It is important to realize that this item was not purchased with your money; it was bought with your time, which you traded for money. In effect, you swapped a certain proportion of your allotted days on earth for that piece of junk that now clutters your home.

When you understand that everything you buy is purchased with a portion of your life, it should make you more careful with the use of money.
—*Dr. James Dobson president, Focus on the Family*

Personal Challenge:
• *Make a sacrificial offering to your church as a way of saying to God that you are giving him your life.*

Thought to Apply: There is no dignity quite so impressive, and no independence quite so important, as living within your means.   —Calvin Coolidge (U.S. President)

Up Close & Personal with Steve Farrar

Q. Sometimes it seems God isn't providing as much as we need. Why?

A. If we always have money in the bank, if we always have everything we need, then, quite frankly, we miss out on some great blessings.

In recent years, corporations have gone to "just-in-time" inventory. Instead of keeping big inventories in their warehouses, the shipments from their suppliers show up just a day or so before they actually need them.

Most businessmen don't know it, but God is the originator of "just-in-time" inventory. God will meet your need. But He won't meet it until exactly the right time.

Steve Farrar is founder of Men's Leadership Ministries in Dallas, Texas.

For Personal Study or Group Discussion

Key Bible Verses: Do not store up for yourselves treasures on earth ... store up for yourselves treasures in heaven *(Matthew 6:19-21). Bonus Reading: Luke 19:1-10*

Think and pray about these sentence starters.

☐ One time I saw God provide for me was ...

☐ The biggest growth point for me when it comes to finances is ...

Credits: Monday: *Smart Money* (Multnomah, 1994); Tuesday: *No More Excuses* (Crossway, 1996); Wednesday: *Temptations Men Face* (InterVarsity, 1990); Thursday: *Illustrations for Preaching and Teaching: From Leadership Journal* (Baker, 1993); Friday: *Life on the Edge* (Word, 1995); Saturday: *Anchor Man* (Thomas Nelson, 1998).

The Seven Promises of a Promise Keeper

1. A Promise Keeper is committed to honoring Jesus Christ through worship, prayer and obedience to God's Word in the power of the Holy Spirit.
Core Issue: Intimacy with God.
Key Passage: Psalm 73:25

2. A Promise Keeper is committed to pursuing vital relationships with a few other men, understanding that he needs brothers to help him keep his promises.
Core Issue: Brotherhood.
Key Passage: Hebrews 3:12-13

3. A Promise Keeper is committed to practicing spiritual, moral, ethical and sexual purity.
Core Issue: Faithfulness.
Key Passage: 1 Corinthians 4:2

4. A Promise Keeper is committed to building a strong marriage and family through love, protection and biblical values.
Core Issue: Servanthood.
Key Passage: Matthew 20:27-27

5. A Promise Keeper is committed to supporting the mission of his church by honoring and praying for his pastor, and by actively giving his time and resources.
Core Issue: Honor.
Key Passage: 1 Thessalonians 5:12-13

6. A Promise Keeper is committed to reaching beyond racial and denominational barriers to demonstrate the power of biblical unity.
Core Issue: Unity.
Key Passage: John 17:20-23

7. A Promise Keeper is committed to influencing the world, being obedient to the Great Commandment and the Great Commission.
Core Issue: Mission.
Key Passage: Mark 12:30-31, Matthew 28:19-20.

Living Two Lives

Key Bible Verse: Teach me your way, O Lord, and I will walk in your truth; give me an undivided heart, that I may fear your name *(Psalm 86:11).*
Bonus Reading: Psalm 119:5-16

No one ever kidded himself by thinking that attending a conference, wearing a shirt, or drinking from a Men of Integrity coffee mug made one a bona fide promise keeper. The Word says, "Man looks at the outward appearance, but the Lord looks at the heart" (1 Samuel 16:7).

In much the same way, being founder of a fast-growing Christian men's movement didn't automatically make me a true man of integrity. A man of integrity is someone whose public persona is squarely reconciled to, and in full agreement with, his private reality. Therein lay the problem. Therein had always been the problem—the undeniable contradictions between who I wanted to be and who I was.

The tightrope I was walking in the spring of 1993, juggling a frantic coaching load while serving as Promise Keepers' vocal, visible front man, drove a wedge further still between my private and public selves.

After wrestling with this maddening tension for years, I made a silent decision to myself: Loving God would be my top priority. And I *would* be a promise keeper to my family.

—Bill McCartney, founder
Promise Keepers

Personal Challenge:
• *Talk to a trusted Christian man about any divisions between your private and public lives.*

Thought to Apply: People already know we make mistakes. They want to know if we have the integrity to admit them.   —BILL HYBELS (pastor and author)

Contagious Character

Key Bible Verse: Let your light shine before men, that they may see your good deeds and praise your Father in heaven *(Matthew 5:16). Bonus Reading: Matthew 5:1-15*

In a profile of U.S. Congressional representative Tony Hall, Frederica Mathewes-Green writes:

The event that began to awaken him spiritually was a prayer breakfast in 1980. Chuck Colson would be the featured speaker. What he heard that day, he says, "stunned" him.

What brought Hall up short was not so much the content of Colson's speech as the witness of his life; it was, Hall recalls, "his sincerity. Here was a guy who'd had wonderful success, been a counselor to the President, and he was saying it wasn't enough.

"I knew that was true. I had success and was doing well, but I began to think, 'Is that all there is?'"

The experience at the prayer breakfast kicked off a year-long spiritual search for Hall. Eventually he attended a small gathering where he heard Campus Crusade's Bill Bright speak, and all the pieces fell into place. "It was exactly what I was looking for and, boom! I went for it."

When Tony Hall's wife, Janet, came to faith a year after her husband, it was not due to his badgering but due to the witness of his life. "I was changing toward her, toward the children, and toward life overall."

Personal Challenge:
• *Ask God to make you a man who draws others to Christ by your life.*

Thought to Apply: When a Christian jealously guards his secret life with God, his public life will take care of itself. —OSWALD CHAMBERS (minister and author, 1874-1917)

Church Mechanics

Key Bible Verse: Encourage one another daily ... so that none of you may be hardened by sin's deceitfulness *(Hebrews 3:13). Bonus Reading: Hebrews 10:24-25; Matthew 9:9-13*

From the sound of Alex's voice, I knew it was important. "Could you come by the dealership tomorrow? We need to talk," the new car salesman asked.

Alex and I go to the same church. The next day, in his office, he got straight to the point. "Jim, I feel like a hypocrite every time I go to church because I fail to live for Christ so often."

"Alex, what do you call this part of the dealership?" I asked, nodding to the area outside his cubicle.

"You mean the showroom?"

"Yes. And what's behind the showroom, past the parts counter?"

"The service department,"

Alex said.

"What if I told you I didn't want to bring my car to the service department because it was running rough?"

"That would be crazy! That's the whole point of service departments—to fix cars that aren't running right."

"You're absolutely right," I replied. "Now, instead of thinking of church as a showroom where image is everything, start thinking of it as God's service department. Helping people get back in running order with God is what the church is all about."

—*Jim Corley, Tucson, Arizona*

Personal Challenge:
• *Have you been skipping church? Attend this week.*

Thought to Apply: Labor to keep alive in your breast that little spark of celestial fire called conscience.

—GEORGE WASHINGTON (U.S. President)

They Thought I Was Crazy

Key Bible Verse: Blessed are they who maintain justice, who constantly do what is right *(Psalm 106:3)*.
Bonus Reading: Psalm 15

I t's the toughest decision I ever made," says Ed Allen, a West Virginia native and former golf pro. "All my friends thought I was crazy. They said eliminating beer sales at Sugarwood Golf Club would hurt us."

Instead, a year after his beer license expired, Allen's business in southwestern West Virginia rose 19 percent (in one month compared to the same month the previous year).

Now behind the evergreens and spruce trees lining the fairways, no inebriated golfers wander off to relieve themselves. Nor do tipsy drivers wreck carts. It's just as pleasant inside the clubhouse, where Allen has also halted the poker games that used to run until midnight.

Where did Allen get the courage to say no? It wasn't overnight. Over three years Allen eliminated smoking, gambling, and beer. Interestingly, dropping poker elicited the biggest outcry.

The alcohol ban also brought passionate protest, but nine out of ten customers approved.

"I don't have any fear now of people leaving the golf club drunk and causing an accident," Allen says.

—*Ken Walker, writer*

Personal Challenge:
• *Does something about your work not honor the Lord? Pray for wisdom about what to do.*

Thought to Apply: Courage faces fear and thereby masters it. Cowardice represses fear and is thereby mastered by it.   —MARTIN LUTHER KING, JR. (civil rights leader)

Inspecting Lady Liberty

Key Bible Verse: Whatever your hand finds to do, do it with all your might *(Ecclesiastes 9:10).*
Bonus Reading: Daniel 6:1-5

Integrity is more than not being deceitful or slipshod. It means working "with all your heart, as working for the Lord" (Colossians 3:23). In his book *Lyrics* Oscar Hammerstein II points out why:

On the cover of the *New York Herald Tribune* Sunday magazine, I saw a picture of the Statue of Liberty taken from a helicopter, and it showed the top of the statue's head. I was amazed to see the detail there. The sculptor had done a painstaking job with the lady's coiffure, and yet he must have been pretty sure that the only eyes that would see this detail would be the uncritical eyes of sea gulls.

He could not have dreamt that any man would ever fly over this head. He was artist enough, however, to finish off this part of the statue with as much care as he had devoted to her face and her arms and the torch and everything that people can see as they sail up the bay.

When you are creating a work of art, or any other kind of work, finish the job off perfectly. You never know when a helicopter, or some other instrument not at the moment invented, may come along and find you out.

Personal Challenge:
• *Where are you tempted to let something go rather than do it well to God's glory?*

Thought to Apply: A time like this demands strong minds, great hearts, true faith, and ready hands.
—JOSIAH GILBERT HOLLAND (19th century author and editor)

Up Close & Personal with Gordon MacDonald

Q. What shows you have godly character?

A. Character is seen in a thousand small bit parts. How I react to the guy behind me in the jetway at the airport who thinks I'm moving too slowly and says, "Why don't you get out of the way and let the rest of us get by?" What I do when the clerk gives me change that is $5 over what I had coming. What I say when a man shows up who wrote me off ten years ago but now wants support for his beleaguered organization.

People of notable character do something that may be to their disadvantage to come to the aid of another person.

Gordon MacDonald is an author and pastor of Grace Chapel in Lexington, Massachusetts.

For Personal Study or Group Discussion

Key Bible Verse: May integrity and uprightness protect me, because my hope is in You *(Psalm 25:21). Bonus Reading: 1 Thessalonians 2:1-6*

Think and pray about these sentence starters.

☐ I feel good about my integrity when ...

☐ I want greater integrity in the area of ...

Credits: Monday: *Sold Out* (Word, 1997); Tuesday: *Christianity Today* (1997); Wednesday: *Christian Reader* (Jan/Feb, 1998); Thursday: *Christian Reader* (Jan/Feb, 1995); Friday: *Illustrations for Preaching and Teaching: From Leadership Journal* (Baker, 1993); Saturday: *When Men Think Private Thoughts* (Thomas Nelson, 1996).

Battleground: Your Mind

Key Bible Verse: God is faithful; he will not let you be tempted beyond what you can bear. But when you are tempted, he will also provide a way out so that you can stand up under it *(1 Corinthians 10:13).*
Bonus Reading: James 1:13-15

For men, the area of sexual purity is an enormous challenge. Most Christian men tend to deny this and pretend they are above sexual temptation. Those are usually the ones who fall.

I'm the first to admit that I find women beautiful and that the way they are presented in the media makes them even more alluring. Let's not kid ourselves and think that only the other guy is vulnerable. The first step in keeping yourself sexually pure is to be honest with yourself and admit that it's a struggle. Here are strategies that have helped me deal with sexual temptation:

1. When sexual thoughts come to mind, immediately short-circuit those thoughts with something else, for if you dwell on the thought, it opens the door to possibly following through with the fantasy.

2. When you near a sexual temptation, run away from it.

3. Replace those sexual temptations with positive acts.

4. As you attempt to live a sexually pure life, a key principle is to have at least one spiritual brother with whom you have accountability.

—Phillip Porter, Jr., chairman of the board, Promise Keepers

Personal Challenge:
•*Which of the four steps above do you need to do?.*

Thought to Apply: Each temptation leaves us better or worse; neutrality is impossible.

—ERWIN W. LUTZER (pastor and author)

Lethal Low Voltage

Key Bible Verse: The one who sows to please his sinful nature, from that nature will reap destruction; the one who sows to please the Spirit, from the Spirit will reap eternal life *(Galatians 6:8). Bonus Reading: John 10:10*

In *All Thumbs Guide to VCRs*, a repair guide for amateurs, Gene Williams begins with a warning:

"Getting a jolt from the incoming 120 volts AC is more than just unpleasant; it can be fatal. Studies have shown that it takes very little current to kill. Even a small amount of current can paralyze your muscles, and you won't be able to let go. Just a fraction more and your heart muscle can become paralyzed."

Williams knows that the amateur repairman does not have sufficient respect for the lethal power of electricity.

The amateur knows that a shock hurts, but he thinks he can always let go of the wire. It is the paralyzing power of even a small amount of electricity that makes it so dangerous.

So it is with sin. People dabble with sin because they don't fear its power to paralyze the soul. Then it's too late: people know a sinful behavior is hurting them and they want to quit, but they can't let go.

—Craig Brian Larson
pastor and author
Chicago, Illinois

Personal Challenge:
• *Is there some ongoing sin in your life that you think won't hurt anything? If so, do whatever it takes to save yourself!*

Thought to Apply: He who feeds a wolf strengthens his enemy.   —DANISH PROVERB

Power to Change

Key Bible Verse: Live by the Spirit, and you will not gratify the desires of the sinful nature *(Galatians 5:16).*
Bonus Reading: Galatians 5:17-25; Romans 8:1-16

I began my new life in Christ about 19 years ago, with the last 17 in a backslidden condition much of the time. When I went to Promise Keepers in Minneapolis, I hoped and prayed that God would use the speakers to tell me something that would help me get out of my backslidden condition. I was skeptical, though, because I felt so powerless as a Christian.

However, in the first session on Saturday morning, God used the speaker to convict me as never before. As I stood to sing after he spoke, I found myself spontaneously raising my arms. With tears streaming down my face I knew I was at the foot of the Cross, closer than I had ever been in my life.

Since those moments, I have a new power and courage through the Holy Spirit.

The most important action point for me has been to read the Word of God and pray daily for discipline, strength and courage in order to live for Christ.

I know that without doing this I will be as powerless as I was before.
—A promise keeper from Minnesota

Personal Challenge:
• *Ask God each day to fill you again with His Holy Spirit.*
• *Memorize today's Key Bible Verse.*

Thought to Apply: Temptation rarely comes in working hours. It is in their leisure time that men are made or marred.
—W.T. TAYLOR (writer)

Checklist: Are You in Danger?

Key Bible Verses: It is God's will that you should be sanctified: that you should avoid sexual immorality; that each of you should learn to control his own body in a way that is holy and honorable, not in passionate lust like the heathen, who do not know God *(1 Thessalonians 4:3-5). Bonus Reading: 1 Peter 4:1-8*

Sexual purity is a direct command of Scripture. There are no excuses. Repentance, yes. Forgiveness, yes. Excuses, no. Here are some principles and observations:

1. Sexual sin is always generated in the mind before it is acted out in the body. Thus, to guard one's thoughts is absolutely indispensable.

2. A struggling marriage is never an excuse for sexual sin.

3. A widowed, divorced, or sexually-experienced man will likely have more temptation, mainly due to knowledge.

4. Some common threads seem characteristic of men who have fallen into sexual impurity:

• The macho image and a sense of dominance.

• A perceived failure in one's job or a blow to one's pride.

• A feeling of being above the rules.

• Going easy on one's self in many areas like diet or exercise.

• Carelessly allowing one's self to be in places or situations that boost temptation.

• A roving and undisciplined eye.

—Jerry White, president
The Navigators

Personal Challenge:
• *If any points in the above list are a weakness for you, talk to God and your pastor about it.*

Thought to Apply: It is easier to stay out than to get out.
—MARK TWAIN (19th century author)

Chasing Coyotes

Key Bible Verses: Be self-controlled and alert. Your enemy the devil prowls around like a roaring lion looking for someone to devour. Resist him *(1 Peter 5:8-9)*. *Bonus Reading: Matthew 4:1-11*

The *Denver Post* reports: "Like many sheep ranchers in the West, Lexy Lowler has tried just about everything to stop crafty coyotes from killing her sheep. She has used odor sprays, electric fences, and 'scare-coyotes.' She has slept with her lambs during the summer and has placed battery-operated radios near them. She has corralled them at night, herded them at day. But the southern Montana rancher has lost scores of lambs—fifty last year alone.

"Then she discovered the llama—the aggressive, funny-looking, afraid-of-nothing llama. 'Llamas don't appear to be afraid of anything,' she said. 'When they see something, they put their head up and walk straight toward it. That is aggressive behavior as far as the coyote is concerned, and they won't have anything to do with that. Coyotes are opportunists, and llamas take that opportunity away.'"

James writes: "Resist the devil, and he will flee from you" (4:7). The moment we sense the devil's attack is the moment we should face it and deal with it.

Personal Challenge:
• *Ask God to give you greater discernment to see when the devil is at work to tempt you.*

Thought to Apply: Temptation is not meant to make us fail; it is meant to confront us with a situation out of which we emerge stronger than we were.

—WILLIAM BARCLAY (late pastor and author)

Up Close & Personal with Edgar D. Barron

Breaking the Death Grip of Porn

Q. How did you get into pornography?

A. As a teenager I felt a void because of a poor relationship with my father. When I was in pain, looking at pornography made me feel good—for at least a few minutes. When I got married, I figured I wouldn't need the pornography anymore. But it had a death grip on me. I couldn't understand it. My love for my wife was deep and true.

Then I had the scariest thought of my life: What if Lucia found out who I really was? I chose to continue to hide this side of my life from her. For years I fought the battle alone. I thought if I could just do enough for God, he would take this sin away from me.

How did you get free?

At a men's retreat I surrendered. God was telling me I had to confess to my wife. It was the hardest thing I've ever done. Only by the grace of God did our marriage survive. Throughout months of Christ-centered counseling, I began to see the root causes of my behavior.

Edgar D. Barron (with wife Lucia) is executive editor of The Promise Keeper.

Men of Integrity is published in association with Promise Keepers by Christianity Today, Inc., 465 Gundersen Drive, Carol Stream, IL 60188. Printed in U.S.A. Canada Post International Publications Mail Sales Agreement No. 546526. **Staff:** Editors: Craig Brian Larson, Ashley Nearn; Design Director: Doug Johnson. **Advisory Board:** Edgar D. Barron, Kevin A. Miller. **Subscriptions:** A one-year subscription to *Men of Integrity* is available for a suggested donation of $20 to Promise Keepers, P.O. Box 103001, Denver, CO 80250-3001.

Credits: Monday: *Better Men* (Zondervan, 1998); Tuesday: *Contemporary Illustrations for Preachers, Teachers, and Writers* (Baker, 1996); Wednesday: Testimony used with permission; Thursday: *Dangers Men Face* (NavPress, 1997); Friday: *Illustrations for Preaching and Teaching: From Leadership Journal* (Baker, 1993); Saturday: *The Promise Keeper* (May/June 1998).

For Personal Study or Group Discussion

Real Life Application

Key Bible Verse: Pray so that you will not fall into temptation *(Luke 22:46). Bonus Reading: Genesis 3*

Think and pray about these sentence starters on your own. Or, if you meet with other men, use them to trigger your discussion.

☐ Since I've become a Christian, temptation has become ...

☐ The people I talk to about my challenges with temptation are ...

☐ When I'm tempted, prayer is ...

☐ A difficult temptation for me is ...

☐ I can overcome temptation when ...

☐ I need God to help me ...

Mad Enough to Kill

Key Bible Verses: If you forgive men when they sin against you, your heavenly Father will also forgive you. But if you do not forgive men their sins, your Father will not forgive your sins *(Matthew 6:14-15). Bonus Reading: Acts 7:54-8:1*

One day a man told me that a bitter divorce had cheated him out of his money and kept him from his children. He was angry at the judge, the lawyer, and everybody involved with the case. He had begun making plans to kill those who had hurt him.

"Every time I drove by that lawyer's office, I advanced a plot to kill him. I stalked the courtroom and devised my plan to have the judge murdered. I had every intention of taking out the two men who had separated me from spending time with my kids."

As he described this, his eyes were piercing, his face taut, his lips stretched tight.

But then he told me how he came to know Jesus Christ as his Lord and Savior. He said to me, "I have actually been able to forgive those people, and now I recognize God was wanting to get my attention through all this so I would follow Him and not chase after my old ways of vengeance."

—*Phil Downer*
president, Christian
Businessmen's Committee

Personal Challenge:
• *Is there anyone you would like to get back at for a wrong he did against you? Forgive that person.*

Thought to Apply: Forgiveness is a required course.
—CHARLES R. SWINDOLL (author and seminary president)

Disobedient Kids

Key Bible Verse: God demonstrates His own love for us in this: While we were still sinners, Christ died for us *(Romans 5:8). Bonus Reading: Romans 5:1-11*

I love my kids so much that I'd die for them. When my children fail, I don't love them any less. I look at one of my kids, sitting there in his or her own little world, bound and determined to do something despite what Mom or Dad might say. Do I love them any less because of it? Of course not. Sure, I'll get angry with them; but my love never disappears because of what they might do.

As I look at a disobedient son or daughter, I see myself. I'm no different than Jonathan or Tiffany—I'm just a bigger, older version!

So what does that mean? Could it mean that God continues to love us despite our sins, just as we continue to love our kids despite theirs?

Absolutely! God does not rejoice when I fall, nor does he rub his hands and say, "Aha! I told you so!"

When we sin terribly, that's when most of us want to run away from God. Yet that's the time we most need to go before God.

God hates our sin and regrets the consequences that come to us because of our sin, but he doesn't love us any less. His love remains constant.
—Dave Dravecky, former Major League pitcher

Personal Challenge:
• *Pray to believe that God loves you no matter what you have done.*
• *If you have been avoiding God because you feel guilty, restore your daily fellowship with Him.*

Thought to Apply: Our God has a big eraser.
—BILLY ZEOLI (Christian filmmaker)

Getting Right with God

Key Bible Verse: There is now no condemnation for those who are in Christ Jesus *(Romans 8:1)*.
Bonus Reading: Ephesians 2:8-9

I always thought Christianity was a task, something I did for God. I began to learn that Christianity is a relationship with God, something He does for us.

The issue is not, "What must I do to be good?" The issue is, "What must I do to be saved?"

I learned that I was separated from God because of my sins. Further, no human effort was sufficient to receive forgiveness for these sins and salvation. Instead, Jesus Christ came into the world to save sinners—like me. After living a sinless life, He voluntarily shed His blood and died on a cross as a substitute for me. He took the penalty for my sins. Remarkable.

I also learned that because He rose from the dead, I, too, could become like Him and live forever in heaven. To accomplish this, I needed to agree with God that I was a sinner, express genuine remorse and a desire to change directions (called *repentance*), and by *faith* receive Christ into my life as my Savior and Lord.

—Patrick M. Morley, business executive and author

Personal Challenge:

• *Have you ever asked God to forgive you of your sins and then asked Jesus to come into your life as your Lord? If not, do so today.*

Thought to Apply: The most marvelous ingredient in the forgiveness of God is that He also forgets, the one thing a human being can never do.

—OSWALD CHAMBERS (writer, 1874-1917)

Democrat Meets Republican

Key Bible Verse: For He Himself is our peace, who has made the two one and has destroyed the barrier, the dividing wall of hostility *(Ephesians 2:14).*
Bonus Reading: Matthew 5:38-48

Soon after my commitment to Christ, some friends arranged for me to meet other Christians. Sitting across the room was a great big bear of a man named Harold Hughes, a liberal Democratic senator from Iowa. If you want to talk about being poles apart, take Chuck Colson, Nixon aide and conservative Republican from the East, and place him across the room from a liberal Democratic senator from Iowa. I slowly told the story of my conversion.

About halfway through, this big, burly guy, who used to be a truck driver and an alcoholic, stood up and said, "I've heard enough." And he started across the room toward me. I was a little nervous. He's a big guy.

He reached down, picked me up, and said, "I believe Jesus Christ has come into your life, and therefore we are brothers, and I will stand with you."

And so he did, all through Watergate. Two people who were absolute political poles apart, drawn together by the love of Christ. That's what overcomes this world.

—*Chuck Colson, Watergate conspirator, and founder Prison Fellowship*

Personal Challenge:
• *Who is "poles apart" from you? How can you show love to that person?*

Thought to Apply: Forgiveness is not an occasional act; it is a permanent attitude.

—Martin Luther King, Jr. (civil rights leader, 1929-1968)

He Forgives the Molester

Key Bible Verses: If anybody does sin, we have one who speaks to the Father in our defense—Jesus Christ, the Righteous One. He is the atoning sacrifice for our sins *(1 John 2:1-2). Bonus Reading: Romans 3:10-26*

All around us we see man killing man. Man gunning down his fellowman on the street. All around us we see men killing their "seed." Men making babies and then not having the desire or taking the time to be fathers to them. Men impregnating women and then not marrying them; encouraging women, by their lack of involvement and provision, to get abortions. Men abandoning their children and teenagers, leaving their sons to struggle with finding their identity in a godless world.

We've all hurt some people, betrayed some covenants, made some mistakes, blown some money, missed some opportunities, and sinned against God.

But thank God, He is merciful. The good news—the very best news—is that God forgives. He forgives the molester. He forgives the abuser. He forgives the addict. He forgives the liar and the thief. He forgives the sinner.

The Devil may be out to defeat you, but God is out to defeat the Devil. Stay on God's side. Receive His forgiveness.

—T. D. Jakes, pastor

Personal Challenge:
• *Ask God to help you not dredge up confessed sins.*

Thought to Apply: If God forgives us, we must forgive ourselves. Otherwise it is almost like setting up ourselves as a higher tribunal than Him.

—C. S. LEWIS (Oxford professor and author, 1898-1963)

Up Close & Personal with Mark Mittelberg

What's Unique about Christianity?

Q.▮ What's the difference between Christianity and other religions?

A.▮ Other religions are spelled *d-o* because they teach that people must do a bunch of religious rituals to work their way to God. But Christianity is not spelled *d-o*. It's spelled *d-o-n-e* because it's *done*. Jesus Christ has done what needed to be done on the cross. We just need to receive Him.

Give me an illustration of this. Compare a parable taught by Jesus with a similar story found in Buddhist literature.

Both stories involve sons who became rebellious and left home in a huff, but who later saw the error of their ways and decided to return home to be reconciled with their families.

In the Buddhist story, the errant son is required to work off the penalty for his past misdeeds by spending years in servitude.

But the Christian parable of the Prodigal Son ends with the repentant son being warmly welcomed home by a loving father who showers him with undeserved forgiveness and grace.

Mark Mittelberg is executive vice president of the Willow Creek Association and co-author of Becoming a Contagious Christian *book and training course (Zondervan, 1994-95).*

For Personal Study or Group Discussion

Real Life Application

████████████████████████████████████

Key Bible Verse: Bear with each other and forgive whatever grievances you may have against one another. Forgive as the Lord forgave you *(Colossians 3:13)*.
Bonus Reading: Matthew 18:21-35

████████████████████████████████████

Think and pray about these sentence starters on your own. Or, if you meet with other men, use them to trigger your discussion.

☐ I have trouble shaking free from guilt when ...

☐ I know I am forgiven of my sins because ...

☐ One person I need to contact to make things right is ...

☐ One thing I don't understand about forgiveness is ...

☐ Because God has forgiven me, I am compelled to ...

Credits: Monday: *Eternal Impact* (Harvest House, 1997); Tuesday: *The Worth of a Man* (Zondervan, 1996); Wednesday: *The Seven Seasons of a Man's Life* (Zondervan, 1997); Thursday: *A Life of Integrity* (Multnomah, 1997); Friday: *So You Call Yourself a Man?* (Albury, 1997); Saturday: *Leadership* (Summer 1998).

What Makes People Clam Up

Key Bible Verse: My tongue will tell of your righteous acts all day long *(Psalm 71:24). Bonus Reading: Psalm 9:1-2, 7-14*

Recently I attended a Colorado Rockies game in Denver with my grandson. As we searched for our seats, I bumped into a friend who keeps in contact with some of my former players. He's a Christian.

"Did you see the fight?" "Have you got the coaching itch yet?" "The Rockies could sure use some pitching."

I asked about a former player of mine he knew—I'll call him *Ron*—who I'd heard had recently given his life to the Lord. "How's Ron doing? How's his walk with the Lord?"

"Hmmm," he said. "You know, I should know that." He rubbed his chin and finally shrugged his shoulders. "Mac, I'm embarrassed to say it, but I just don't know."

The question clearly made him uncomfortable. It should have been the most natural thing in the world for two Christians to discuss the Lord in normal conversation. We shook hands and went back to our seats. I continually marvel that so many God-fearing Christians are eager to take random conversation anywhere but to Jesus. Whenever Jesus is mentioned, people clam up.

Oh, if we only knew—God *loves* it when we talk lovingly about Him to one another.
—*Bill McCartney, founder and CEO of Promise Keepers*

Personal Challenge:

• *This week bring Jesus Christ into a conversation with Christian friends.*

Thought to Apply: Tell me whom you love, and I will tell you what you are.   —ARSENE HOUSSAYE (writer, 1815-1896)

No Retreat

Key Bible Verse: Now, Lord, consider their threats and enable your servants to speak your word with great boldness *(Acts 4:29). Bonus Reading: Acts 4:1-31*

Isn't it strange that the group prayed for boldness? We might have expected them to pray, "Lord, help us find a safe shelter now. We need to 'lie low' for a few weeks until the heat goes away. We'll stay out of sight, and if you could just make the Sanhedrin sort of forget about us..."

Not at all. If anything, they prayed against backing down. They asked God to help them press on. Retreat was the furthest thing from their minds.

And how did God react?

"After they prayed, the place where they were meeting was shaken. And they were all filled with the Holy Spirit and spoke the word of God boldly" (v. 31).

When we sincerely turn to God, we will find that his church always moves *forward*, not *backward*. We can never back up and accommodate ourselves to what the world wants or expects.

The apostles realized that without a bold, aggressive attitude in proclaiming God's Word, they would not build the church Jesus intended.

—Jim Cymbala
pastor and author
Brooklyn, New York

Personal Challenge:
• *In what situation are you tempted to back down from saying what God wants? Ask God to fill you with the Holy Spirit so you can speak boldly for Him.*

Thought to Apply: Boldness enables Christians to forsake all rather than Christ, and to prefer to offend all rather than to offend Him.

—JONATHAN EDWARDS (preacher and philosopher, 18th c.)

White-Hot Fastball

Key Bible Verse: I am not ashamed of the gospel, because it is the power of God for the salvation of everyone who believes *(Romans 1:16). Bonus Reading: Philippians 1:19-26*

On July 15, 1986, Roger Clemens, the sizzling right-hander for the Boston Red Sox, started his first All-Star Game. In the second inning he came to bat, something he hadn't done in years because of the American League's designated-hitter rule. He took a few uncertain practice swings and then looked out at his forbidding opponent, Dwight Gooden, who the previous year had won the Cy Young award.

Gooden wound up and threw a white-hot fastball past Clemens. With an embarrassed smile on his face, Clemens stepped out of the box and asked catcher Gary Carter, "Is that what my pitches look like?"

"You bet it is!" replied Carter.

From that day on, Clemens later said, with a fresh reminder of how overpowering a good fastball is, he pitched with far greater boldness.

Sometimes we forget the Holy Spirit within us and how powerful our witness can be.
—*Craig Brian Larson pastor and author*

Personal Challenge:
• *The next time you give someone the good news about Jesus, put your confidence in the message more than in how you present the message.*

Thought to Apply: Having thus chosen our course, let us renew our trust in God and go forward without fear and with manly hearts.

—ABRAHAM LINCOLN (U.S. President during the Civil War)

Keep Spelling It Out

Key Bible Verse: How can they believe in the one of whom they have not heard? And how can they hear without someone preaching to them? *(Romans 10:14).* *Bonus Reading: Matthew 28:18-20*

One popular version of evangelism says, "If I just live as a consistent Christian, people will see it, figure it out, and come to Christ."

But that approach isn't biblical, and it doesn't work.

In Romans 10:14 Paul said we have to go and give people the message. We have to initiate conversations and trust the Holy Spirit will work as we bring the message to them.

Years ago a girl I knew started coming to a Bible study I was leading. She learned the songs and started talking like us and hanging out with us. One day I said to her, "I'm glad you're part of our group."

"I love it," she said.

"I'm just wondering, have you ever committed your life to Christ so you know you're forgiven of your sins?"

"No, I've never done that," she said, "and no one ever told me I needed to."

I learned we have to keep spelling out the basics. When I did that, she made a commitment right away.

—*Mark Mittelberg*
executive vice president
Willow Creek Association

Personal Challenge:
• *Are there any "may be Christians" or "almost Christians" in your life that you have avoided discussing Christ with? Make it your goal to talk to them as soon as possible.*

Thought to Apply: God is not saving the world; it is done. Our business is to get men and women to realize it.

—OSWALD CHAMBERS (minister and author, 1874-1917)

No Secret Agent

Key Bible Verses: You are the light of the world. A city on a hill cannot be hidden. Neither do people light a lamp and put it under a bowl. Instead they put it on its stand, and it gives light to everyone in the house. In the same way, let your light shine before men *(Matthew 5:14-16). Bonus Reading: Mark 8:34-38*

My notion of what it means to be a Christian has changed. I used to be a "secret agent." I wouldn't share my faith with people around me, and I wouldn't act like a Christian (most of the time). But now I'm trying to be Christian in action. Of course it's not easy, but God I know is on my side, which is cool.

My most important action point from the PK conference was to be the light to the world.

I had read this Bible passage about being the light before, but Tony Evans really opened my eyes. I don't know how to explain it, but his message has changed me inside.

I have begun to be more open with my friends, and I feel more comfortable and confident in sharing. And they have noticed.

—*A promise keeper from California*

Personal Challenge:
• *Who in your network of relationships would be surprised to learn that you are a Christian?*
• *Ask God to help you be more "comfortable and confident" in talking about Christ with others.*

Thought to Apply: I don't have to light all the world, but I do have to light my part.   —Anonymous

Up Close & Personal with T. D. Jakes

Becoming a Bold Man

Q. How can we become bold men for Jesus, like Peter and John were when they ministered to the lame man at the temple (in Acts 3:1-10)?

A. There are people around you today who need for you to speak the right name into their lives—the name of Jesus—and they need for you to help them get to their feet spiritually and emotionally, and in some cases, physically and materially. It is your hand reached out in love and compassion, with genuine help that is not born of sympathy but which is born of faith, that will help them stand.

Won't that make others dependent on us?
You don't need to be their crutch. You don't need to spend the rest of your life helping them. But you do need to pull them to their feet so that God can heal and strengthen the lameness in their lives.

What if I'm the one who is "lame"?
If you are the one who is being helped to your feet by a Christian brother, then rise up in faith on the inside even as you are helped to rise. Don't place your confidence in the person who is lifting you or praying for you. Put your trust in the name of Jesus. He is the One who will heal you of your lameness, strengthen you in your weakness, and cause you to walk in boldness. He alone is the One who can make you whole.

What do I need to know to act in boldness?
Believe that God is desiring

to work in you and through you today. Speak boldly and act boldly when he reveals to you the person you are to help.

T.D. Jakes is the founder and senior pastor of The Potter's House church in Dallas, as well as an author and conference speaker.

For Personal Study or Group Discussion

Real Life Application

Key Bible Verse: When I called you, you answered me; you made me bold and stouthearted *(Psalm 138:3). Bonus reading: 2 Timothy 1:7-12*

Think and pray about these sentence starters on your own. Or, if you meet with other men, use them to trigger your discussion.

☐ The main thing that keeps me from sharing Christ more with others is ...

☐ When I have been bold with others about Christ ...

☐ I want to be bold because ...

☐ People whom I want to receive Jesus are ...

Credits: Monday: *Sold Out* (Word, 1997); Tuesday: *Fresh Wind, Fresh Fire* (Zondervan, 1997); Wednesday: *Illustrations for Preaching & Teaching: From Leadership Journal* (Baker, 1993); Thursday: *Leadership* (Summer 1998); Friday: Promise Keepers testimony used by permission; Saturday: *So You Call Yourself a Man?* (Albury, 1997).

Fix Your Antenna

Key Bible Verses: Set your minds on things above, not on earthly things *(Colossians 3:1-2).*
Bonus Reading: Hebrews 12:2

We were having problems with our television reception some months ago. The repairman I had to call told me my antenna had been knocked around by a recent storm. It needed to be turned back toward the signal.

That helped a lot, but it didn't completely fix the trouble because I had a second problem.

Our house is in a gully amid lots of tall trees. The trees were interfering with the signal, so the repairman had to put an extension on our antenna to lift it above the interference so it could receive the signal clearly.

It's easy to fiddle with the buttons in our lives, trying to get a clear picture of this thing called life. But that's starting in the wrong place. Until the antenna of your mind is turned toward the divine signal, messing with the other stuff in your life won't help.

In addition, daily stuff like job, family problems, and cars that need tires can grow up and crowd out God's signal. If you will get your mind turned to the divine signal and lifted up above the "trees" of circumstances and other people, you will get the right picture, the divine viewpoint.
—*Tony Evans*

Personal Challenge:
• *Ask God to teach you how to discern His voice.*

Thought to Apply: One of the highest and noblest functions of man's mind is to listen to God's Word, and so to read His mind and think His thoughts after Him.
—JOHN R. W. STOTT (British Christian leader, 1921-)

Pleasing God or People?

Key Bible Verses: Am I now trying to win the approval of men, or of God? Or am I trying to please men? *(Galatians 1:10). Bonus Reading: 1 Thessalonians 2:4-6*

Both Jan and I struggle with pleasing other people rather than God. When you know that you're walking according to God's leading, you find the strength to stand against human expectations. We've learned to go to God in prayer, hear His voice, find His leading, and then stand in our decision and withstand all the repercussions it may bring.

This year I took a trip where I committed to speak four times in two days. Now, why would I do that?

Well, for one thing, I was tired when I said yes. For another, I didn't want to disappoint the people who asked me to speak. And I ended up paying for it.

The point is, it's one thing to say that we're creating boundaries by listening to God's voice; it's another to admit that those boundaries seem to change all the time. We cannot say, "We've got the answers now, and everything's cool. Here we go on this wonderful ride of life, this fantasy dream of happiness. No more problems!" We're not there. But I can assure you that in these last five years I have learned a lot about where I should be and the journey I should be on.

That's a big, big step in the right direction.

—Dave Dravecky, author and former all-star pitcher for the San Francisco Giants

Personal Challenge:
• *Are you bending to please a person instead of the Lord?*

Thought to Apply: Please all, and you will please none.

—AESOP (Ancient author of fables)

How to Listen to God

Key Bible Verses: The Lord came and stood there, calling as at the other times, "Samuel! Samuel!" Then Samuel said, "Speak, for your servant is listening" *(1 Samuel 3:10). Bonus Reading: 1 Samuel 3:1-19*

I have not met many who know how to listen to God. Busy people find it hard to learn how.

Most Christians learned at an early age how to talk to God, but they did not learn to listen as well.

We listen every time we open the Scriptures and place ourselves at the feet of the inspired writers who unfold the mysteries of God.

We listen when we sensitize ourselves to the proddings of God's indwelling Holy Spirit.

Listening happens when the preacher or teacher of Scripture, empowered by God's Spirit, brings instruction.

When I studied some of the contemplative Christians, I found that one practical way to learn to listen to God speak was to keep a journal.

With a pencil in hand ready to write, I found that there was an expectancy, a readiness to hear anything God might wish to whisper through my reading and reflection.

— *Gordon MacDonald*
pastor and author

Personal Challenge:

• *Try writing what God may be saying to you in a spiral notebook today. Does it help you hear God?*

Thought to Apply: Prayer begins by talking to God, but it ends by listening to Him.

—FULTON J. SHEEN (Radio preacher, early 20th century)

Taking Time Out

Key Bible Verses: Very early in the morning, while it was still dark, Jesus got up, left the house and went off to a solitary place, where He prayed *(Mark 1:35)*.
Bonus Reading: Daniel 6

We have to allow quiet time in the midst of our busy schedules so we can turn to God during the peaks and valleys of life's experiences.

These valleys and peaks are inevitable. If we insist on going at full speed, we rush blindly ahead without God's help and guidance. We reach canyons and dead-ends that would not have concerned us if we had checked out the land ahead of time. We would have better prepared to face the giants that could be lurking there unseen.

Taking time out was important to the Lord Jesus when He walked the earth.

The crowds pursued Him. Yet, as we read in Mark 1:35, after one of His busiest days, Jesus got up early in the morning and went out to pray.

The only means that I have discovered to walk in purity is to have a day-to-day relationship with Jesus Christ through reading God's Word and applying it carefully to my daily life. It is indeed a day-to-day process.

—Phillip H. Porter, Jr., board chairman, Promise Keepers

Personal Challenge:
• *Don't miss time with the Lord this week. If you've never made 7 out of 7 days in the week, go for it.*

Thought to Apply: The voice of God is a friendly voice. No one need fear to listen to it unless he has already made up his mind to resist it.

— A. W. TOZER (author)

No Easy Formula

Key Bible Verse: He who belongs to God hears what God says. The reason you do not hear is that you do not belong to God *(John 8:47). Bonus Reading: Ephesians 2:1-7*

If you have trouble hearing God speak, you are in trouble at the very heart of your Christian experience.

The key to knowing God's voice is not a formula. It is not a method you can follow. Knowing God's voice comes from an intimate love relationship with God. That is why those who do not have the relationship ("do not belong to God") do not hear what God is saying (John 8:47).

You are going to have to watch to see how God uniquely communicates with you. You will not have any other crutch.

An intimate love relationship with God is the key to knowing God's voice, to hear-ing when God speaks. You come to know His voice as you experience Him in a love relationship. As God speaks and you respond, you will come to the point that you recognize His voice more and more clearly.

Some people try to bypass the love relationship. Some look for a miraculous sign or try to depend on a "formula" or a set of steps to discover God's will. No substitute, however, exists for the inti-mate relationship with God.
—*Henry Blackaby, author*

Personal Challenge:
• *How intimate would you say your relationship with God is? Why?*

Thought to Apply: For years the Bible was a dead book to me ... like grits without salt. But after I gave my life to Jesus Christ, it became alive. I saw that the Bible was God's way of talking to me.
—STEVE BARTKOWSKI (Former quarterback, Atlanta Falcons)

Up Close & Personal with Bill McCartney

Finding Time to Pray

Q. You're a busy leader. When do you pray?

A. Years ago I began to discipline myself to rise each morning before dawn. When others were catching a final hour or two of sleep before a demanding day, I was keeping the most pressing appointment of my day.

I was meeting with God when I was fully alert, unhurried, and totally engaged. There was no push to rush off to a coaches' meeting or a business function. I had more important business to attend to. I needed uninterrupted time to complete it without having to check the clock every five minutes.

What difference does early morning prayer make?
For the first time, I wasn't concerned with distracting details; I wasn't trying to rush through my devotions. It was God and me *alone*. It immediately became the best time of my day.

How do you function during the day?
Believe me, I know how tiring life can be. I'm not proposing that we deny ourselves adequate rest. But spending time alone with God is the most revitalizing thing we can do for ourselves.

I tapped into the awesome privilege of starting each day in God's presence. "In the morning, O Lord, you hear my voice; in the morning I lay my requests before you and wait in expectation" (Psalm 5:3).

When He shows up in the morning, I am filled with an inexpressible joy—the kind that tells me I'm exactly where I'm supposed to be, exactly where I was created to be. I'm talking to God and basking in His resplendent love. Nothing my mind can conjure approaches the sheer delight of calling His name and hear-ing His soft reply.

Bill McCartney is the founder and CEO of Promise Keepers, and author of Sold Out *(Word, 1997).*

Hearing God

For Personal Study or Group Discussion

Real Life Application

Key Bible Verse: Today, if you hear His voice, do not harden your hearts *(Hebrews 3:7-8). Bonus Reading: 1 Corinthians 2:9-16*

Think and pray about these sentence starters on your own. Or, if you meet with other men, use them to trigger your discussion.

☐ One time I knew God was leading me was ...

☐ One confusing experience I've had when trying to follow God's direction is ...

☐ On a scale of 0 to 10, my ability to hear from God is ...

☐ I would probably do better at hearing from God if ...

Credits: Monday: *What a Way to Live!* (Word, 1997); Tuesday: *The Worth of a Man* (Zondervan, 1996); Wednesday: *Ordering Your Private World* (Oliver-Nelson, 1984, 1985); Thursday: *Better Men* (Zondervan, 1998); Friday: *Experiencing God* (Broadman & Holman, 1994); Saturday: *Sold Out* (Word, 1997)

Rock-Throwing Rage

Key Bible Verse: Get rid of all bitterness, rage and anger, brawling and slander, along with every form of malice *(Ephesians 4:31). Bonus Reading: Ephesians 4:25-5:2*

The Academy Award-winning movie *Forrest Gump* has been viewed by millions of Americans. Most people remember its line, "Life is like a box of choklits," but there is another line worth noting.

One of the central characters, Jenny, returns to her old home after her father has died. The farmhouse is dilapidated and abandoned.

As she reflects on the sexual abuse that she endured as a child, she is overcome by rage and begins throwing rocks at the house. She violently throws them at the house until she falls to the ground in exhaustion.

The scene closes with Forrest Gump sympathizing, "Sometimes there just aren't enough rocks."

Many of us struggle with anger, and some anger seems justifiable. Yet unresolved anger leaves us reaching and crying out for more rocks. The rage is never satisfied, and contentment is never found.

Only through the power of Christ can we find the strength to lay down rocks of anger rather than needing to reach for more.

—Raymond McHenry, pastor Beaumont, Texas

Personal Challenge:
• *What are you "throwing rocks at"? Ask Jesus to help you get to the root of your anger and find peace.*

Thought to Apply: Anger is a weed; hate is the tree.
—AUGUSTINE (Christian leader, 354-430)

God-Centered Anger

Key Bible Verse: Jesus made a whip out of cords, and drove all from the temple area ... he scattered the coins of the money changers and overturned their tables *(John 2:15). Bonus Reading: John 2:12-22*

A man may get angry at his father for not including him in the business, at his wife for not serving the dinner he expected, at his daughter for telephoning at midnight for a ride home from a party. He may explode with rage at a driver who cuts him off on the freeway or at a long red light that makes him late for an appointment. In short, self-centered anger erupts when you don't get what you want when you want it. This kind of anger is out of bounds.

Self-centered anger is not what Jesus experienced and expressed in the Bible. He wasn't ticked at the money-changers for offending Him, but for desecrating His Father's house and disrupting the worship of the people. Jesus never got angry at the wrongs done to Him—including the ultimate wrong, the crucifixion. Instead He forgave. But He did get angry whenever someone cast a slur on His Father or treated others unjustly.

In order to defuse our anger, we need to examine our motives to see if they are springing from self-centeredness or God-centeredness.

—David Stoop and Stephen Arterburn counselors and authors

Personal Challenge:
• *Have you ever felt God-centered anger? What did you learn from the experience?*

Thought to Apply: Anybody can become angry—that is easy; but to be angry in the right way—that is not easy.

—ARISTOTLE (Ancient Greek philosopher)

When Kids Light Your Fuse

Key Bible Verse: Fathers, do not exasperate your children ... bring them up in the training and instruction of the Lord *(Ephesians 6:4). Bonus Reading: Proverbs 12:16, 18*

Our children need good models, not perfect models. They need to watch adults handle anger in mature and appropriate ways.

I remember one incident when my son was about 9 years old. He was stirring his iced tea and kept clinking the spoon against the side of the glass.

I had had a pretty rough day, and just the sound of the consistent clinking glass irritated me. So I asked him to stop. He did, for a few seconds. Then he began to clink again.

Once again I asked him to stop, this time with a little more intensity in my voice. Once again he cooperated, for a few seconds.

The third time it hap-pened, I turned to him, asked him to look me straight in the eye and said with more intensity than ever, "Kenton, I've asked you to stop two times already. Now please obey me. That noise makes me angry!"

My son looked at me somewhat startled. Then with a calm spirit, he said, "Oh, okay, Dad! I understand."

This time he really understood and stopped. He needed to hear me share my anger in a direct but nonabusive way.

—*Gene A. Getz,*
pastor and author

Personal Challenge:

• *What has your example been teaching your children about how to handle anger? Apologize to your children if that is in order.*

Thought to Apply: Speak when you are angry and you will make the best speech you will ever regret.

—AMBROSE BIERCE (American author, 1842-1914)

Fooling Around with Anger

Key Bible Verse: A fool gives full vent to his anger, but a wise man keeps himself under control. An angry man stirs up dissension, and a hot-tempered one commits many sins *(Proverbs 29:11,22). Bonus Reading: Galatians 5:23-25*

In *Currents,* Jim Taylor tells the following story about his friend, Ralph Milton:

One morning Ralph woke at five o'clock to a noise that sounded like someone repairing boilers on his roof.

Still in his pajamas, he went into the back yard to investigate.

He found a woodpecker on the TV antenna, "pounding its little brains out on the metal pole."

Angry at the little creature who ruined his sleep, Ralph picked up a rock and threw it. The rock sailed over the house, and he heard a distant crash as it hit his car.

In utter disgust, Ralph took a vicious kick at a clod of dirt, only to remember—too late—that he was still in his bare feet.

Uncontrolled anger, as Ralph learned, can sometimes be its own reward.

—Brian Weatherdon
pastor
Nova Scotia

Personal Challenge:
• *What is the dumbest thing you've done because you were angry?*
• *What is the dumbest thing you've seen someone else do?*
• *Ask God for self-control, a fruit of His Holy Spirit.*

Thought to Apply: When anger enters the mind, wisdom departs. —THOMAS A KEMPIS (Christian writer, 1380-1471)

Afraid to Tell What They Feel

Key Bible Verses: Confess your sins to each other and pray for each other so that you may be healed *(James 5:16). Bonus Reading: James 5:12-16*

Many of God's men are silent today. They come home and say to their wives and children: "Why haven't you cleaned the house?" "Why aren't you making better grades in school?"

They are scared that they are about to lose their jobs, but they'll never say a word about it. Instead, they'll march around with a chip on their shoulders. They are afraid that if they tell what they feel, others will lose respect for them or will take advantage of them.

Our fears can erupt in anger and in criticism. But most of the time, they lie just under the surface of our stone-cold silence. As long as they remain there, they will foment and brew —unhealed, unchanged, unresolved. We will remain weak on the inside even though we may seem strong on the outside.

David said, "O Lord my God, I cried unto thee, and thou hast healed me" (Psalm 30:2).

Hasn't the time come for you to break your silence so God can heal you? Tell God what you are feeling. Tell your wife and children today how you feel about them. Express to them what you need emotionally—first, that you have emotional needs, and second, what they are.

—T. D. Jakes, pastor
and author

Personal Challenge:
• *This weekend, tell a loved one how you feel.*

Thought to Apply: Hot heads and cold hearts never solved anything.   —BILLY GRAHAM (Evangelist)

Up Close & Personal with Dave Dravecky

The Anger Curve

Q. How have you learned to handle your anger?

A. Professional counselor Gary Oliver introduced me to what he calls "The Anger Curve." He draws a curved arch and along the ascending line writes, "hurt, frustration, fear." At the height of the arch goes the word "anger."

Gary explains how many people (including me) don't register much, if any, emotional connection with their hurt, frustration, and fear. They don't feel anything until they get to the point of anger. Once many guys become angry, they may be unable to stop their heated outbursts.

How did this help you?
This tool showed me how to track the origins of my rising anger back to hurt, frustration, or fear. I've learned to ask myself, *Why am I angry?*

Give us an example.
Since losing one arm to cancer, I have a hard time putting on my pants with one arm. I don't like it, nor the feeling of helplessness it causes. One day I was struggling to get my pants on and Jan was sitting right there. I kept trying and could feel the anger rising.

By understanding and using the anger curve, I was able to realize, *I am getting really frustrated right now, and if somebody doesn't step in and help me, I'm going to blow!*

In that situation I didn't blow up. I could deal with my frustration by saying, "Hey, Honey, I'm getting really frustrated here. Do you think you could help me?"

Believe me, Jan appreci-

ates that far more than an angry tirade.

Dave Dravecky (with Jan, left) is an author and former all-star pitcher for the San Francisco Giants.

Sunday, Week 22   **Handling Anger**

For Personal Study or Group Discussion

Real Life Application

Key Bible Verses: "In your anger do not sin": Do not let the sun go down while you are still angry, and do not give the devil a foothold *(Ephesians 4:26-27).*
Bonus Reading: Proverbs 15:1, 16-18

Think and pray about these sentence starters on your own. Or, if you meet with other men, use them to trigger your discussion.

☐ Some things I lose my temper about are . . .

☐ When I get really angry I . . .

☐ The way I rationalize losing my temper is . . .

☐ I would like God to help me with anger by . . .

Credits: Monday: *Something to Think About* (Hendrickson, 1998); Tuesday: *The Angry Man* (Word, 1991); Wednesday: *The Measure of a Man* (Regal, 1995); Thursday: *Leadership* (Winter 1988); Friday: *So You Call Yourself A Man?* (Albury, 1997); Saturday: *The Worth of a Man* (Zondervan, 1996)

Priority One

Key Bible Verse: Love the Lord your God with all your heart and with all your soul and with all your strength *(Deuteronomy 6:5). Bonus Reading: Revelation 2:3-5*

One of our church members always was having difficulty in his personal life, his family, at work, and in the church. One day I went to him and asked, "Can you describe your relationship with God by sincerely saying, 'I love You with all of my heart'?"

The strangest look came over his face. He said, "Nobody has ever asked me that. No, I could not describe my relationship with God that way. I could say I obey him, I serve him, I worship him, and I fear him. But I cannot say that I love him."

I realized that everything in his life was out of order because God's basic purpose for his life was out of order.

God created us for a love relationship with Him. If you cannot describe your relationship with God by saying that you love Him with all your being, then you need to ask the Holy Spirit to bring you into that kind of a relationship.

If I were to try to summarize the entire Old Testament, it would be expressed in this verse: "You shall love the Lord your God with all your heart, with all your soul, and with all your strength" (Deuteronomy 6:5).

—*Henry Blackaby, author*

Personal Challenge:
• *Do you love the Lord with all your heart? Pray about that today.*

Thought to Apply: A man's spiritual health is exactly proportional to his love for God.

—C. S. LEWIS (Oxford professor and author, 1898-1963)

Why I Go to Rotten Holes

Key Bible Verses: We love because He first loved us. If anyone says, "I love God," yet hates his brother, he is a liar *(1 John 4:19-20). Bonus Reading: 1 John 3:16-20; Matthew 25:31-46*

When I reflect on what God has done for me, you know what I appreciate the most?

I think most about the fact that Jesus Christ, the Son of God, went to a cross, was nailed to it, and died there in payment of my sins so that the stuff in my heart is removed, and I can live free. The Son of God, sinless, died that I might be free. It has to fill you with awe and gratitude to God. God loved me. How can I repay Him?

I've been in 700 prisons in 49 countries. I was in prison this morning, and it was great to see men coming to know Christ. Of course, the prisons are rotten holes. I've been in places in South America where you slip on the sewage coming out of the cells. I've been in prisons in Zambia where the men haven't anything to wear or eat, and your heart breaks.

People say to me, "Why do you keep doing this? Why do you keep going back and back and back to these prisons?"

I do it because it is my duty, out of gratitude to God, for what he has done in my life. I can do nothing else.

—Chuck Colson, founder
Prison Fellowship

Personal Challenge:
• *One way to express your love for Jesus is to help needy people in your world. Who comes to mind?*

Thought to Apply: The poor come to all of us in many forms. Let us be sure that we never turn our backs on them.   —MOTHER TERESA (1910-1997)

He Wants Us

Key Bible Verses: The Lord answered, "You are worried and upset about many things, but only one thing is needed" *(Luke 10:41-42). Bonus Reading: Luke 10:38-42*

A man married the love of his life. He worshiped the very ground she walked on. From sunup to sunset, thoughts of how to make her happy consumed him.

Because he diligently worked so hard to provide for her, he spent most of his time away from her. The harder he worked to serve her, the happier he was, but the less time he actually spent with her. She, on the other hand, missed the time they once spent together when they first met.

Perhaps the single greatest risk of walking with Jesus is that we would lose our first love. What starts out as a wonderful love relationship is reduced to an endless repetition of religious tasks and activities—all of which are intended to please Him.

Yet what He wants most is not what we can do for Him. He wants us. He wants a relationship. He wants us to talk with Him and spend time with Him.

If we love Him with all our hearts, then we will serve Him with all our might. Yet, we don't love God because we serve Him; we serve God because we love Him.

—*Patrick M. Morley, author*

Personal Challenge:
• *Take an extra chunk of time this week to enjoy being in God's presence without any agenda.*

Thought to Apply: We can get so caught up in the work of the Lord that we forget the Lord of the work.

—Anonymous

"You Love Yourself Too Much"

Key Bible Verses: I have been crucified with Christ and I no longer live, but Christ lives in me. The life I live in the body, I live by faith in the Son of God, who loved me and gave Himself for me (*Galatians 2:20*).
Bonus Reading: Colossians 3:1-14

The Lord revealed to me that I love myself too much.

My whole life I have been overweight, up and down, up and down. Currently I weigh 335 pounds. My love life with my wife is stale, and I needed an answer from the Lord as to what to do.

He told me at the L.A. Promise Keepers conference, "Son, you love yourself too much, more than you love Me."

I realized from Tony Evans's speech that my weight represented the "cracks in my spiritual house."

My spiritual house would get in order only when I surrendered; my foundational re-lationship with the Lord Jesus Christ needs to be fixed, modified, patched, and restored.

Lord Jesus, here I come. Thanks for loving me!
—*A promise keeper from California*

Personal Challenge:
• *Is there anything in your life that signals selfishness? The way you spend money or time?*
• *Pray about those things: "Lord, I die to myself so that I can live for You. I say no to selfishness and yes to You. I want to know You, love You, and center my life on You. Jesus, your love means most to me."*

Thought to Apply: If we build to please ourselves, we are building on the sand; if we build for the love of God, we are building on the rock.
—OSWALD CHAMBERS (preacher, 1874-1917)

No Locked Closets

Key Bible Verse: [God] testified concerning [David]: "I have found David son of Jesse a man after my own heart; he will do everything I want him to do" *(Acts 13:22). Bonus Reading: Psalm 19:14*

What does it mean to be a person after God's own heart? Seems to me, it means that you are a person whose life is in harmony with the Lord. What is important to Him is important to you. What burdens Him burdens you. When He says, "This is wrong, and I want you to change," you come to terms with it, because you have a heart for God.

When you are deeply spiritual, you have a heart that is sensitive to the things of God. "For the eyes of the Lord move to and fro throughout the earth that He may strongly support those whose heart is completely His" (2 Chronicles 16:9).

What is God looking for? He is looking for men and women whose hearts are completely his—*completely.* That means there are no locked closets. Nothing's been swept under the rugs. That means that when you do wrong, you admit it and immediately come to terms with it. You're grieved over wrong. You're concerned about those things that displease Him. You long to please Him in your actions.

—Charles R. Swindoll, president, Dallas Seminary

Personal Challenge:
• *What areas of your life are locked to God?*

Thought to Apply: I have found that the most extravagant dreams of boyhood have not surpassed the great experience of being in the will of God, and I believe that nothing could be better. —JIM ELLIOT (martyred missionary, 20th c.)

Up Close & Personal with David Robinson

The Admiral and The Lord

Q. When did you start taking "loving God" seriously?

A. On June 8, 1991, I was talking with a minister from Champions for Christ. The first question he asked was, "David, do you love God?"

I was a little surprised and said, "Of course, I love God."

Then he asked, "How much time do you spend praying?"

I said, "I eat three times a day, and I pray then."

"How much time do you spend reading your Bible?"

"There's one around here somewhere ..."

"Then he said, 'When you love someone, don't you usually take time to get to know that person? Don't you want to get to know that person better?' "

What happened next?
That day, Christ became a real person to me.... I felt like a spoiled brat. Everything was about me, me, me. How much money can I make? It was all about David's praise and David's glory. I had never stopped to honor God for all He had done for me.

That really hit me. I cried all afternoon. That very day, I was saved.

David Robinson is an NBA all-star center for the San Antonio Spurs.

Tom DiPace

For Personal Study or Group Discussion

Real Life Application

Key Bible Verse: Love the Lord your God and keep His requirements, His decrees, His laws and His commands always *(Deuteronomy 11:1).*
Bonus Reading: Deuteronomy 11:1-32

Think and pray about these sentence starters on your own. Or, if you meet with other men, use them to trigger your discussion.

☐ Some things I admire most about Jesus Christ are ...

☐ I love Jesus because ...

☐ For me, expressing my love for God means ...

☐ Compared to where I was a year ago, my love for God is ...

☐ One thing that I really love that sometimes competes with my love for God is ...

Credits: Monday: *Experiencing God* (Broadman & Holman, 1994); Tuesday: *A Life of Integrity* (Multnomah, 1997); Wednesday: *The Seven Seasons of a Man's Life* (Zondervan, 1997); Friday: *David: A Man of Passion & Destiny* (Word, 1997); Saturday: *Christian Reader* (Mar/Apr, 1998)

Decisions When You're Not Happy

Key Bible Verse: The man who looks intently into the perfect law that gives freedom, and continues to do this, not forgetting what he has heard, but doing it —he will be blessed in what he does *(James 1:25)*. *Bonus Reading: James 1:22-27*

Ron, sitting in his office, pored over the latest episodes in his marriage. "I know God wants me to be happy. He loves me more than anything. But I'm not happy; I really think I need to make a change. Maybe it's all right if I divorce Janie—if it will make me happy."

I told him his happiness was not God's first concern. Ron's *holiness* was what the Lord was most concerned about.

Then I showed him Malachi 2:16, where God gives the very clear message, "I hate divorce." I told Ron I didn't think he had any biblical grounds for divorcing his wife; instead, he had a commitment to remain married, and within his marriage God could provide the fulfillment and happiness he sought. God is more concerned about the condition of our hearts and our obedience than He is about our feeling good.

The real problem of determining God's will is most people aren't in close contact with the Father; they rely on their selfish desires.

*—Phil Downer, president
Christian Business
Men's Committee*

Personal Challenge:
• *In any decision, are you unsure whether you're deciding based on selfishness? Ask a pastor or other wise Christian for counsel.*

Thought to Apply: Our scientific power has outrun our spiritual power. We have guided missiles and misguided men. —MARTIN LUTHER KING, JR. (Civil rights leader, 1929-1968)

Avoiding Shipwreck

Key Bible Verse: Direct me in the path of your commands, for there I find delight *(Psalm 119:35).*
Bonus Reading: Psalm 119:1-40

A certain harbor in Italy can be reached only by sailing up a narrow channel between dangerous rocks and shoals. Over the years, many ships have been wrecked, and navigation is hazardous.

To guide the ships safely into port, three lights have been mounted on three huge poles in the harbor. When the three lights are perfectly lined up and seen as one, the ship can safely proceed up the narrow channel. If the pilot sees two or three lights, he knows he's off course and in danger.

God has also provided three beacons to guide us. The same rules of navigation apply—the three lights must be lined up before it is safe for us to proceed. The three harbor lights of guidance are:

1. The Word of God (objective standard)
2. The Holy Spirit (subjective witness)
3. Circumstances (divine providence).

Together they assure us that the directions we've received are from God and will lead us safely along His way.
    —Bob Mumford
    author and speaker

Personal Challenge:
• *What does the Word of God say about a decision you face? Talk with a Christian brother about how you feel led.*

Thought to Apply: However far you go, it is not much use if it is not in the right direction.
    —WILLIAM BARCLAY (Bible scholar, 1907-1978)

Flight 007

Key Bible Verses: Just as He who called you is holy, so be holy in all you do; for it is written: "Be holy, because I am holy" *(1 Peter 1:15-16).*
Bonus Reading: 1 Peter 1:13-16; Proverbs 4:25-27

On October 31, 1983, Korean Airlines flight 007 departed from Anchorage, Alaska, for a direct flight to Seoul, Korea.

Unknown to the crew, however, the computer engaging the flight navigation system contained a 1-$\frac{1}{2}$ degree routing error. At the point of departure, the mistake was unnoticeable.

One hundred miles out, the deviation was still so small as to be undetectable. But as the giant 747 continued through the Aleutians and out over the Pacific, the plane strayed increasingly from its proper course. Eventually it was flying over Soviet air space.

Soviet radar picked up the error, and fighter jets scrambled into the air to intercept. Over mainland Russia the jets shot flight 007 out of the sky, and all aboard lost their lives.

Choose your direction well. Although poor choices may hurt you in only minor ways for a while, the longer you go, the more harm they bring.

—George O. Wood
author and minister

Personal Challenge:
• *In what "small ways" are you straying from God's will for your life? Don't excuse them any longer. Get things right.*

Thought to Apply: Most of us follow our conscience as we follow a wheelbarrow. We push it in front of us in the direction we want to go.   —BILLY GRAHAM (Evangelist)

How to Find God's Will

Key Bible Verse: Teach me to do your will, for you are my God; may your good Spirit lead me on level ground *(Psalm 143:10). Bonus Reading: Isaiah 30:21*

Here is how George Mueller [a 19th century orphanage founder famous for prayer] summed up the way he learned to discern God's voice:

• I seek at the beginning to get my heart into such a state that it has no will of its own in regard to a given matter. Nine-tenths of the difficulties are overcome when our hearts are ready to do what His will is.

• I do not leave the result to feeling or simple impression. If so, I make myself liable to great delusions.

• I seek the will of the Spirit of God through, or in connection with, the Word of God. If the Holy Ghost guides us at all, He will do it according to the Scriptures and never contrary to them.

• I take into account providential circumstances.

• I ask God in prayer to reveal His will to me.

• Thus, (1) through prayer to God, (2) the study of the Word, and (3) reflection, I come to a deliberate judgment according to the best of my ability and knowledge, and if my mind is thus at peace, and continues so after two or three more petitions, I proceed accordingly.

—*Henry Blackaby*

Personal Challenge:
• *Is there a matter where your heart is not "ready to do what His will is"?*

Thought to Apply: [God's] voice will always be in harmony with itself, no matter in how many different ways he may speak.   —HANNAH WHITALL SMITH (19th c. teacher)

Swimming in the Fog

Key Bible Verses: The Lord gave and the Lord has taken away; may the name of the Lord be praised *(Job 1:21). Bonus Reading: Job 1:1-22*

Once a friend of mine went swimming in a large lake at dusk. As he was paddling about 100 yards offshore, a freak evening fog rolled in across the water. Suddenly he could see nothing: no horizon, no landmarks, no objects or lights on shore. Because the fog diffused all light, he could not even discern which direction the sun was setting.

For thirty minutes my friend splashed around in panic. He would start off in one direction, lose confidence, and turn ninety degrees to the right. Or left—it made no difference which way he turned. He was utterly lost until, finally, he heard voices calling from shore and was able to guide himself by the sounds.

Something like that feeling of utter lostness must have settled in on poor Job. He too had lost all landmarks, all points of orientation. Where should he turn? God, the one Person who could guide him through the fog, kept silent.

Although Job questioned everything about God, he stubbornly refused to give up on God. "Though He slay me, yet will I hope in Him," Job defiantly maintained. He believed when there was no reason to believe, when nothing at all made sense. He believed in the midst of the Fog.

—*Philip Yancey*
Christian writer

Personal Challenge:
• *Unsure what direction to turn? Turn to God.*

Thought to Apply: Where there is no longer any opportunity for doubt, there is no longer any opportunity for faith either.   —PAUL TOURNIER (Swiss psychologist)

Up Close & Personal with Haddon Robinson

Q. Why don't wise decisions always lead to positive results?

A. Someone has said that life is what happens to you after you've made your decisions. There are times when we make our decisions as best we can, and suddenly life crumbles in on us.

Where do we find hope? God is not limited to what we decide to do. In God's sovereignty, He can work *in* our choices, *through* our choices, and *in spite* of our choices to accomplish His will. We may not choose to help, we may not be able to see; but, God is at work.

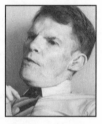

Haddon Robinson is professor of preaching at Gordon-Conwell Theological Seminary in South Hamilton, Massachusetts.

For Personal Study or Group Discussion

Key Bible Verse: If any of you lacks wisdom, he should ask God, who gives generously to all without finding fault, and it will be given to him *(James 1:5).*
Bonus Reading: Colossians 1:9-14

Think and pray about these sentence starters.

☐ One thing that still puzzles me about Christian decision making is ...

☐ I make my wisest decisions when ...

Credits: Monday: *Eternal Impact* (Harvest House, 1997); Tuesday: *Take Another Look at Guidance* (Lifechangers, 1993); Wednesday: *Pentecostal Evangel* (3-26-95); Thursday: *Experiencing God* (Broadman & Holman, 1994); Friday: *Disappointment with God* (Zondervan, 1988); Saturday: *Decision-Making by the Book* (Victor, 1991)

Raising the Bar Too High

Key Bible Verses: Each one should test his own actions. Then he can take pride in himself, without comparing himself to somebody else, for each one should carry his own load *(Galatians 6:4-5). Bonus Reading: Matthew 17:20*

We all tend to set unrealistic goals. There's something masculine about doing the impossible.

The summer Olympics in 1992 provided a great example of this myth. In anticipation of the Games, Reebok invested over $15 million in ads asking whether Dan O'Brien or Dave Johnson was the world's greatest decathlete. They were considered a slam dunk to make the U. S. Olympic team and compete in Barcelona.

Everything went great until it came to the pole vault event at the U. S. Olympic Trials. The bar started at 14'5-1/4". O'Brien had jumped this height and more hundreds of times. So rather than play it safe, he decided to pass at several lower heights before opening at 15'9".

The athletic world was shocked when he failed on all three attempts to clear the bar. If he had cleared the lowest of the lower vaults, even 14'5-1/4", he would have earned enough points to finish second and make the Olympic team. He spent the 1992 Olympics in the broadcasting booth rather than on the field.

God wants us to dream great dreams and attempt great things. But He knows we need to do them one step at a time.   —*John Trent*
author and counselor

Personal Challenge:
• *What is a reasonable and achievable goal for your spiritual life?*

Thought to Apply: The journey of a thousand miles begins with one step.   —CHINESE PROVERB

Investor or Trader?

Key Bible Verse: The king ... renewed the covenant in the presence of the Lord—to follow the Lord and keep His commands, regulations and decrees with all his heart *(2 Chronicles 34:31, 33). Bonus Reading: Mark 4:1-20*

In his newspaper column "Market Report," Bill Barnhart explained the difference between investors and traders.

"A trader in a stock," writes Barnhart, "is making decisions minute-by-minute in the hope of shaving off profits measured in fractions of a dollar. An investor, on the other hand, typically buys or sells a stock based on views about the company and the economy at large."

In other words, traders pursue short-term profits. By contrast, investors are in it for the long haul. They commit their money to a stock, believing that over years the stock will grow in value. Investors aren't flustered by the ups and downs of the market because they believe in the quality of the company.

In the kingdom of God there are also investors and traders. They come to Christ with very different goals. Traders in the kingdom want God to improve their lot in this world. If following Christ means pain or hardship, they sell out.

But investors in the kingdom stay true to Christ no matter what happens in this world, knowing eternal dividends await them.

—*Craig Brian Larson*

Personal Challenge:
• *Settle that you are going to follow Christ no matter what the repercussions are.*

Thought to Apply: It doesn't take much to say, "I quit." It takes a lot more to say, "I'll try."

—THELMA WRIGHT (Wife of Wilbur, a stroke victim)

Lost in Space

Key Bible Verses: I will show you what he is like who comes to me and hears My words and puts them into practice. He is like a man building a house, who dug down deep and laid the foundation on rock *(Luke 6:47-48). Bonus Reading: Luke 6:46-49*

In space astronauts have to be strapped in someplace, or they float. They wear suction cups on their feet to enable them to stand. These suction cups release with a twist of the foot, then hold firm again with the proper placement. Astronauts need to be attached somewhere in order to work. If they aren't, they can't even push a switch on a computer, for in trying they push themselves backward. That's a problem with weightlessness.

And when they sleep, it doesn't matter whether they sleep on the "top" of the bunk or even sleep standing up. There is no "top" or "bottom," no "up" or "down" in space.

In today's society, it seems, there are no fixed reference points, no "up" or "down," no right way or wrong way. In a society without fixed points we have to make our own or we will be adrift, and every action will have a counter thrust to it.

Men have to be committed. Only those who determine that they will be, who have a reference point, will ever touch the world in a meaningful way.

—*Roger Palms, author*

Personal Challenge:
• *What values are you most committed to?*

Thought to Apply: The foundation of all human excellence must be laid deep in the blood of the Redeemer's cross and in the power of His resurrection.

—FREDERICK WILLIAM ROBERTSON (1816-1853)

"That's My Boy"

Key Bible Verse: A voice from heaven said, "This is my Son, whom I love; with Him I am well pleased" *(Matthew 3:17). Bonus Reading: Colossians 3:21*

In Kansas, when you go pheasant hunting, you have to stop at the farmer's house first to ask permission to walk his fields. The farmer will likely be in the shed working on some piece of rusty equipment. As you pull up into the driveway, he'll look up. Eventually he'll walk out to meet you. He'll rub his greasy hands off on an equally greasy rag and then shake your hand and introduce himself. Then invariably he'll nod his head over his left shoulder and say, "This's my boy, Jim."

In some ways, it's not even an introduction—it's a claim, a fact of the universe. This "boy" may actually be a strapping 22-year-old hunk of farm stock who looks like he could throw a hay bale over the barn, but that's the term of endearment: "My boy."

Telling children "you are mine" and telling the world "they are mine" is the first stage of a father's commitment. Such an expression of commitment gives a child a sense of belonging and connectedness. Fathers who tell their kids "you are my children" give them an invaluable point of reference. Children then feel secure in exploring the world because they always know where they belong.

—Ken R. Canfield, author and executive director, National Center for Fathering

Personal Challenge:
• *Tell your child, "You are mine."*

Thought to Apply: Children must be valued as our most priceless possession. —JAMES C. DOBSON (Psychologist and author)

Commitment

The Devil's Nail

Key Bible Verses: Do not give the devil a foothold ... Be strong in the Lord and in His mighty power. Put on the full armor of God so that you can take your stand against the devil's schemes *(Ephesians 4:27; 6:10-11).* *Bonus reading: Matthew 12:43-45*

One Haitian pastor illustrates the need for total commitment to Christ with this parable:

A certain man wanted to sell his house for $2,000. Another man wanted very badly to buy it, but because he was poor, he couldn't afford the full price.

After much bargaining, the owner agreed to sell the house for half the original price with just one stipulation: he would retain ownership of one small nail protruding from just over the door.

After several years, the original owner wanted the house back, but the new owner was unwilling to sell.

So the first owner went out, found the carcass of a dead dog, and hung it from the nail he still owned. Soon the house became unlivable, and the family was forced to sell the house to the owner of the nail.

The Haitian pastor's conclusion:

"If we leave the Devil with even one small peg in our life, he will return to hang his rotting garbage on it, making it unfit for Christ's habitation."

Personal Challenge:
• *Commit every area of your life to Jesus Christ, your Lord.*
• *Renounce any claim the Devil has on you.*

Thought to Apply: What does God require? Everything!

—ERWIN W. LUTZER (Pastor and author)

Up Close & Personal with Steve Farrar

Q. What if your marriage seems tougher than you can handle?

A. The Genesis 2:24 prescription is this: *Never, ever, ever, leave your wife.* Did you get that? That's your job. You stay married. You don't walk.

So your wife has lost her health? Maybe she's lost a breast to cancer. Or maybe she has plummeted into a deep depression. Then it's time to step up to the plate and be a man.

You and your wife don't see eye to eye on anything? Well, that's exactly why you made the commitment. And there's no rational, biblical reason to walk. But let me warn you. If you ever do it, you'll just start another crisis.

Steve Farrar is an author and founder of Men's Leadership Ministries, Dallas, Texas

---

For Personal Study or Group Discussion

Key Bible Verses: Commit your way to the Lord; trust in Him and He will do this: He will make your righteousness shine like the dawn *(Psalm 37:5-6). Bonus Reading: 2 Timothy 2:1-13*

Think and pray about these sentence starters.

☐ The toughest commitment I've ever kept has been to ...

☐ One man whom I respect for his deep commitment is ...

Credits: Monday: *Go the Distance* (Focus on the Family, 1996); Tuesday: *Contemporary Illustrations for Preachers, Teachers, and Writers* (Baker, 1996); Wednesday: *What Makes a Man* (NavPress, 1992); Thursday: *The 7 Secrets of Effective Fathers* (Tyndale, 1992); Friday: *Illustrations for Preaching and Teaching* (Baker, 1993); Saturday: *Anchor Man* (Nelson, 1998)

Lying to the Boss

Key Bible Verse: Each of you must put off falsehood and speak truthfully to his neighbor *(Ephesians 4:25).*
Bonus Reading: John 1:47-49

I was asked by a manager of another division to interview several candidates for a job opening. I said I would, but a week went by, and I let it sit.

Then I received a call from my boss's boss, asking me specifically about the two candidates, and what my progress was in interviewing them. I was stunned to receive a call from someone this high up about these candidates, but someone was obviously using some favors to land a job.

I told the executive I was going to interview them next week, when in fact I had nothing set up. Needless to say, as soon as the phone was down, I called the candidates and set up the interviews. But I had let my integrity lapse.

With the Lord's help, I have not repeated that folly. I realize when I am about to lie to get out of a jam, I need to fear the Lord before the world. If I love the world more than God, I will eventually disappoint Him by breaking His commands. If I claim to love God more than the world, then obedience to His commands demonstrates my love.

—*Dave Endrody, account executive, Wheaton, Illinois*

Personal Challenge:
• *Have you lied to someone at work recently? Confess that to God.*

Thought to Apply: A half-truth is a dangerous thing, especially if you have got hold of the wrong half.
—MYRON F. BOYD (Writer)

Smash-up in Dad's Car

Key Bible Verse: An honest answer is like a kiss on the lips *(Proverbs 24:26). Bonus Reading: Acts 5:1-11*

My buddies and I were 17 or 18 years old, and my dad let us take his Ford station wagon. We were driving on a muddy path to get to our campsite and I stepped on the gas. "Boom!" —the car fishtailed into a tree.

That night I decided, along with the other guys, to drink. Well, I got drunk. I climbed in my dad's car and started doing fishtails in the field, where I ran over a tree trunk and stripped the muffler completely off the car.

The next day I pulled up to the front curb of my house. When my dad looked at his beat-up car, he pulled my brother and me into the house and asked, "Dave, did you guys get drunk?"

I replied, "Yes, we did."

I figured it was better to be honest since the punishment was going to be a lot worse if I wasn't.

Because I was honest, my dad responded in a gentle way. Oh, we did get punished. But we deserved it. That day I saw a loving father in my dad, who responded to us out of both mercy and justice.

Somehow I can't help but think that is how God responds to us when we come home in less than mint condition.

—Dave Dravecky
former all-star pitcher
for the San Francisco Giants

Personal Challenge:
• *In prayer today, be totally straight with God about your sins. Trust Him to show a Father's mercy.*

Thought to Apply: Better the ugly truth than a beautiful lie.   —UNKNOWN

Breach of Contract

Key Bible Verses: Do not lie to each other, since you have taken off your old self with its practices and have put on the new self *(Colossians 3:9-10). Bonus Reading: Psalm 15*

A man I was discipling was involved in a difficult suit with his partners; they had committed acts that breached their contracts and given them substantial liability.

His business partners wouldn't admit the problem. So he arranged a luncheon where he introduced me as his personal lawyer, familiar with the case. His partners were surprised and even irritated as we began talking about the case, but after about thirty minutes they seemed relieved to finally be directly confronting issues.

After about two hours, it was agreed they would try to settle the case. My friend—who was mostly to blame for the problem—agreed to bear a disproportionately larger part of the financial settlement.

The case was settled within thirty days, the impact on their reputation and customer base was minimal, and the partners saw their junior partner in a new light. He was someone who had courage, conviction, and conscience. He was a man of character.
—Phil Downer, president
Christian Business
Men's Committee

Personal Challenge:
• *This week face any problems or failures you've been running from and begin working to make things right.*

Thought to Apply: I am not bound to win, but I am bound to be true. I am not bound to succeed, but I am bound to live by the light that I have.
—ABRAHAM LINCOLN (U. S. President)

What to Give Your Kids

Key Bible Verse: You shall not give false testimony against your neighbor *(Exodus 20:16).*
Bonus Reading: Daniel 5

Someone once asked me on a program, "If you had only one thing to give your four children, what would you give them?"

I had thought a great deal about that, so I answered immediately, "Honesty." You show me a person who is honest with God, who is honest with other people, and, most of all, who is honest with himself, and I will show you a man of integrity.

There are two lines to every man's life: a purpose line and a life line. The moment the purpose line begins to fall off, it's just a question of time before the life line goes too. But here was a man [the prophet Daniel] at the latter end of his life who had not lost his sense of purpose. He was an honest man, a man of integrity—not because it was convenient, not because it had a cheap price tag, but because that was his conviction.

Can your family trust you? Can your company have total confidence in you? Whether you're an employee or an employer, you ought to be the very best employee or the most trusted employer it's possible to be in the sphere of influence where God has placed you.

—Howard Hendricks
seminary professor

Personal Challenge:
• *Ask God to help you be the most trustworthy man where you work.*

Thought to Apply: If you tell the truth, you have infinite power supporting you; but if not, you have infinite power against you.   —CHARLES GEORGE GORDON (1833-1885)

Prison Visit

Key Bible Verse: The Lord detests lying lips, but he delights in men who are truthful *(Proverbs 12:22).* *Bonus Reading: Luke 2:1-20*

I first learned about the value of honesty in prison.

Not when I was in prison, but when in high school I visited a prison with my sociology class. Every one, especially the guys, were acting totally cool, as if we'd been to lots of prisons, and prisoners didn't scare us, and we could handle ourselves. You know, smart remarks, jokes, all the guy baloney.

We were finally escorted into a room with three prisoners whom we were going to talk with. We all took our chairs in a circle and sat and stared at each other, everyone looking as cool as ever.

After introducing the men, the teacher asked if we had any questions. There was a long silence.

Margie, a tall, thin girl who appeared as in control as the rest of us, said, "I don't know about anyone else, but I'm kind of scared."

Everyone laughed—not at her, but with her: we were all feeling the same thing. And all of us, like Margie, had been putting on an act. Now because of her honesty, we didn't have to.

With that, a genuine conversation with our hosts began.
—*Mark Galli*
author and editor
Chicago, Illinois

Personal Challenge:
• *Ask the Lord to help you be more open with others.*

Thought to Apply: An honest man's the noblest work of God.   —ALEXANDER POPE (English poet, 1688-1744)

Up Close & Personal with Tony Evans

Q. How should we respond when others encourage us to lie?

A. I used to work at the bus station in downtown Dallas on the graveyard shift. The workers had a system going whereby they would punch each other's time cards in and out and grab an extra hour or two for lunch.

When I started working there, the other employees began educating me to the system.

I said, "I can't do that."

"No, you don't understand. Everybody does it."

"Well, I'm a Christian," I said. "The Bible tells me this is dishonest."

Tony Evans is senior pastor of Oak Cliff Bible Fellowship in Dallas, Texas, and author of No More Excuses *(Crossway, 1996).*

For Personal Study or Group Discussion

Key Bible Verse: Love does not delight in evil but rejoices with the truth *(1 Corinthians 13:6).*
Bonus Reading: 1 Peter 2:12

Think and pray about these sentence starters.

☐ I am tempted to lie when ...

☐ If God were to describe my level of honesty over the last year, he would probably say ...

Credits: Tuesday: *The Worth of a Man* (Zondervan, 1996); Wednesday: *Eternal Impact* (Harvest House, 1997); Thursday: *A Life of Integrity* (Multnomah, 1997); Saturday: *No More Excuses* (Crossway, 1996)

55 Years of Love

Key Bible Verse: Husbands, love your wives, just as Christ loved the church and gave himself up for her *(Ephesians 5:25). Bonus Reading: Ephesians 5:26-27*

You and I are called to be lovers of our wives. This begins by telling our wives very simply, "I love you."

I recently had the privilege of going to an executive's birthday party in Miami, Florida. The man was 80 years old, and he and his wife were celebrating fifty-five years together as a couple.

His words marked him as a covenant keeper, as one who recognizes the need to love and care for his wife. He had written the following: "We've been married fifty-five years, and we still tell each other 'I love you' all the time. We say it the first thing every morning, and it's the last thing we say to each other before we go to sleep."

He went on to write, "My only regret is that my wife is most likely to outlive me. I won't always be around to take care of her. I know the Lord will do it, but in the meantime I am glad he uses me."

As I publicly repeated the words of this octogenarian at his party, he began to weep. But I wish you could have seen the look in his wife's eyes—she began to beam. He had told his wife he loved her in a simple, yet profound way.

—*Dennis Rainey, author and executive director of Family Life Today*

Personal Challenge:
• *If you're married, tell your wife "I love you."*

Thought to Apply: Love is that condition in which the happiness of another person is essential to your own.

—ROBERT A. HEINLEIN (Author)

Alone on the Couch

Key Bible Verse: Husbands, in the same way be considerate as you live with your wives, and treat them with respect *(1 Peter 3:7). Bonus Reading: Hebrews 13:4*

Excerpt from a letter received by pastor and author Weldon Hardenbrook:

The kids are in bed. There's nothing on TV tonight. I ask my husband if he minds if I turn the tube off. He grunts.

As I walk to the set my mind is racing. *Maybe, just maybe, tonight we'll talk.* I mean, we'll have a conversation that consists of more than my usual question with his mumbled one-word answer or, more accurately, no answer at all.

Silence—I live in a world with continuous noise but, between him and myself, silence. *Please—God, let him open up.* I initiate (once again; for the thousandth time). My heart pounds—oh how can I word it this time? What can I say that will open the door to just talk? I don't have to have a deep meaningful conversation. Just something!

As I open my mouth—he gets up and goes to the bedroom. The door closes behind him. The light showing under the door gives way to darkness. So does my hope.

I sit alone on the couch. My heart begins to ache. I'm tired of being alone. Hey, I'm married. I have been for years. Why do I sit alone?

—*Patrick M. Morley, author*

Personal Challenge:
• *Sit down tonight or tomorrow and talk to your wife for longer than you normally would.*

Thought to Apply: He is a creature of vision and she is a lover of touch. By a little unselfish forethought, each can learn to excite the other.

—JAMES C. DOBSON (President, Focus on the Family)

A Thoroughbred Wife

Key Bible Verses: Husbands ought to love their wives as their own bodies.... After all, no one ever hated his own body, but he feeds and cares for it *(Ephesians 5:28-29).*
Bonus Reading: Proverbs 31:10-31

I remember an important moment when a mentor-friend said to me regarding my wife, "Gordon, she's a thoroughbred of a woman. Don't squelch her gifts. Encourage them."

Gail said to me one day with a smirk, "Think of it. What woman wouldn't give everything to be known as a thoroughbred." But she and I both knew the intent of the observation.

I discovered that my wife had great growth potential, and that her growth could be accelerated as I got behind her and helped. Today, people often ask my wife to speak at their conferences, consult with their organizations, and counsel them in their difficult moments. I take immense pride in her efforts because at a critical time in her life and mine, I began to see her potential and decided to do everything I could to get behind her development.

There are many areas of life where I feel that she is far ahead of me in maturity and insight and capacity. Devotion means that I not only got behind her and pushed, but that I delighted when she jumped way ahead in some things.

—*Gordon MacDonald*

Personal Challenge:
• *What are your wife's two strongest gifts? Ask God to help you nurture these gifts.*

Thought to Apply: It's the man's role to nurture and affirm his wife, so she can blossom and flourish in all of her rich womanhood and God-given gifting

—BILL MCCARTNEY (Founder of Promise Keepers)

Repeating the Vows

Key Bible Verse: Each one of you also must love his wife as he loves himself *(Ephesians 5:33).*
Bonus Reading: 1 Corinthians 13:4-8

When we made our vows at the wedding ceremony, our wives heard us pledge our faithfulness: "for richer, for poorer, in sickness and in health, from this day forward, till death do us part." Marriage lets us separate those vows into more demonstrable pieces.

During periods of richness and health, we get to say, "Honey, things are really going well, and I want you to know that I can't think of another woman I would choose to enjoy all of this with."

During periods of poverty and sickness, we repeat our vows: "Sweetheart, we may be struggling right now, but I want you to know that I'm going to stick it out with you."

Our wives need to hear us repeat our vows over the years and in as many different situations as possible.

—Ken R. Canfield, author
and executive director
National Center for Fathering

Personal Challenge:
• *What part of your wedding vows is most needed in your marriage now?*

Thought to Apply: He who does not honor his wife dishonors himself.   —SPANISH PROVERB

Men of Integrity is published in association with Promise Keepers by Christianity Today, Inc., 465 Gundersen Drive, Carol Stream, IL 60188. Printed in U.S.A. Canada Post International Publications Mail Sales Agreement No. 546526. **Staff:** Editors: Craig Brian Larson, Ashley Nearn; Design Director: Doug Johnson. **Advisory Board:** Edgar D. Barron, Todd McMullen, Kevin A. Miller, Keith Stonehocker. **Subscriptions:** A one-year subscription to *Men of Integrity* is available for a suggested donation of $20 to Promise Keepers, P.O. Box 103001, Denver, CO 80250-3001. **Credits:** Monday: *A Life of Integrity* (Multnomah, 1997); Tuesday: *The Seven Seasons of a Man's Life* (Zondervan, 1997); Wednesday: *When Men Think Private Thoughts* (Nelson, 1996, 1997); Thursday: *The 7 Secrets of Effective Fathers* (Tyndale House, 1992). www.promisekeepers.org

Confrontation at the Reunion

Key Bible Verse: Confess your sins to each other and pray for each other so that you may be healed *(James 5:16). Bonus Reading: 1 Peter 3:1-9*

Popular singer Steve Green was at a family reunion when, according to Joan Brasher in *Marriage Partnership*: "An older brother, Randy, noticed Steve's hesitancy to answer direct questions about his faith. Randy was eager to talk about his own recent spiritual renewal, and he asked Steve if he was merely going through the motions.

In an emotional confrontation, Randy said he thought Steve was covering some hidden sin. Steve responded in anger. Wasn't he part of a well-known Christian music group? Wasn't God using him? Yet even as he defended himself, he knew his brother was right.

"His direct confrontation made me admit I was deceiving myself," Steve says. "I wanted to define Christianity in my own terms. God could have a certain part of me, but the rest of my life was my own."

That night he fell to his knees, asking God for forgiveness. Then Steve poured out his heart to his wife, Marijean. He confessed his hypocrisy and spiritual hollowness. "I told Marijean things I had never told anyone," he recalls.

The result was a spiritual renewal—a "resuscitation," as Steve calls it—for them both.

"When Got got hold of Steve, he began doing a deeper work in me, too," Marijean says.

Personal Challenge:
• *How could you make time in the next month to talk about important things with your wife?*

Thought to Apply: Confession is necessary for fellowship.

—ERWIN LUTZER (pastor and author)

Up Close & Personal with Holly Phillips

How Can Men and Women Connect?

Q. **Many husbands feel frustrated: "I just don't know what my wife wants." What causes that?**

A. I've seen firsthand at Promise Keepers gatherings how frustrated some men are. They're isolated. They're trying to do things without the help of older males and without the help of women who are on their side.

Also, the idea of preferring one another in love, whether you're a husband or a wife, is absent today. We tend to think more in terms of "me," so we're not tuned in to our spouse's needs, fears or troubles.

In your book, you write that small hurts can make a woman feel devalued. What happens then?

I struggled for three years before I finally decided to deal with the anger and frustration that resulted from nearly 11 years of my husband, Randy, not meeting my needs.

When our needs aren't met, women tend to wait until we're so stinking frustrated that we blow up. Instead of taking the time to understand the cause of our frustration or anger, we come at our husbands with both barrels. Until I started getting counseling, I was a woman in a rage—a walking time bomb. And I didn't even know why.

What's the way out of this cycle?

Women and men need to spend more time listening and giving each other permission to vent. Once we get past the venting, we can get down to the real stuff. From there God can move our hearts with compassion; and we can start helping one another instead of being each other's biggest "enemy." The bottom line is the Scripture in Ephesians 5— "Love one another in the fear of Christ."

Holly Phillips is co-author of What Does She Want from Me, Anyway? *(Zondervan, 1997) and wife of Promise Keepers executive vice-president Randy Phillips. Interview by Louise A. Ferrebee.*

Sunday, Week 27 **Enriching Your Wife**

For Personal Study or Group Discussion

Real Life Application

Key Bible Verse: Husbands, love your wives and do not be harsh with them *(Colossians 3:19).*
Bonus Reading: Song of Songs 8:7

Think and pray about these sentence starters on your own. Or, if you meet with other men, use them to trigger your discussion.

☐ One thing about my wife I'm grateful for is ...

☐ Something that keeps me from enriching my wife is ...

☐ I would like God's help to ...

Credits: Adapted from—Friday: *Marriage Partnership* (Summer, 1998); Saturday: *Marriage Partnership* (Summer 1997)

Given a Job by God

Key Bible Verse: The Lord God took the man and put him in the Garden of Eden to work it and take care of it *(Genesis 2:15). Bonus Reading: Genesis 2:2*

In the beginning God is presented to us as a worker. In Genesis 2, man and woman are placed in the garden as workers, employed at tasks assigned by their Maker. When Jesus stood up in the Nazareth synagogue to announce that he was going to work, and how he was going to go about it, he said, "The Spirit of the Lord is upon me because he has *anointed* me ..." (Luke 4:18).

Being anointed means being given a job by God. We're told that there's a job to be done and that we're assigned to do it—and that we *can* do it.

Anointing connects our work with God's work.

The first thing David does after he's anointed is go to work. He enters Saul's court and becomes his righthand man. Saul is anointed but is no longer acting like it—not letting the anointing shape his work.

When we're working well, we are tempted to think we don't need God, or at least not very much. Saul was ruined as a God-anointed king while doing his God-appointed work.

Work is a more common source of temptation than sex.

—Eugene H. Peterson
author, Bible translator

Personal Challenge:
• *Are you aware of being given a job by God? What is it?*
• *Thank God for enabling you to accomplish what He has assigned.*

Thought to Apply: Oh, how sweet to work all day for God, and then lie down at night beneath His smile!

—ROBERT MURRAY MCCHEYNE (Scottish preacher, 19th century)

Addicted to Work?

Key Bible Verses: May the favor of the Lord our God rest upon us; establish the work of our hands for us— yes, establish the work of our hands *(Psalm 90:17).* *Bonus Reading: 1 Timothy 3:4, 12*

Dave is a very successful entrepreneur who loves Jesus Christ, his wife and his kids. About a year ago he got conned into making some bad decisions about his time and commitments on the job. He's putting in 80-hour weeks. He's just too busy to hear his wife and his kids crying out for his attention. And he keeps digging himself deeper.

The Enemy loves to take Christian fathers and get their careers out of balance. He ususally does this with highly motivated self-starters—guys who want to do a job and do it right. Those great traits can distract men from their central responsibilities as fathers. Dave's workload, although re-warding, is simply too much. He's paying a very high price for self-fulfillment.

Let's be gut-level honest about this. The temptation for fathers who love what they're doing is to spend too much time at it. Success came Dave's way as a result of the quality of work that he puts out. But another result is that he has become as addicted to his work as the guy smoking crack in some back alley. It's a different kind of addiction but just as devastating to his family.

—*Steve Farrar, founder of Men's Leadership Ministries*

Personal Challenge:

• *If your loved ones cried out for your attention, what would it sound like?*

Thought to Apply: I believe the family was established long before the church, and my duty is to my family first; I am not to neglect my family. —D. L. MOODY (Evangelist, 19th century)

The Man Behind the Mask

Key Bible Verses: After this, Jesus went out and saw a tax collector by the name of Levi sitting at his tax booth. "Follow me," Jesus said to him, and Levi got up, left everything and followed him *(Luke 5:27-28)*.
Bonus Reading: Mark 8:34-37

At a party, as guests poured in, our host led them to me: "Meet the chief operating officer of ... "

I heard someone introduce my wife: "This is Teri. Her husband is the C.O.O. of ... "

I overheard a guest: "He looks familiar to me. Oh, I know, he's the chief operating officer of ... "

I left sadly knowing who I had become. While I was proud of my job, I had allowed my identity to evolve into that position. I was living behind the mask of my job.

Is your identity being erased by your work?

• Listen the next time you refer to yourself. Do you automatically tell people your position and where you work?

• Look at your friendships. If your wife asked you to arrange dinner with a couple you know best, would that be a work relationship? Could you avoid excessive "work-talk"?

• Consider life without your job. Would your friends be the same? Would you be more stressed from giving up the *image* of your job or the *security* of a trade you know well?
—*Bill Nix, president, Faith@Work and WorkLife*

Personal Challenge:
• *Which of the questions above hit you hardest? Why?*

Thought to Apply: You may get to the very top of the ladder and find it has not been leaning against the right wall.
—A. RAINE

Removing the Mask

Key Bible Verses: Nobody should seek his own good, but the good of others. *(1 Corinthians 10:24).*
Bonus Reading: Philippians 2:3-4

If you have discovered a high dependence on your job, what can you do to take off this mask and stop living the masquerade?

• *Pray.* Ask God for courage, wisdom, discernment and humility as you seek to remove the mask.

• *Become more interested in others.* When asked who you are, respond first by describing your roles as husband, father, son, Little League coach, etc.

• *Develop interests other than your work.* Pick up a good book or a new sport. Pick up your Bible. Spend more time with your family.

• *Develop nonwork relationships.* Find friends who appreciate your position and level of skill but are not impressed by them. Agree to keep your conversations from becoming dominated by work-talk.

Our identity can be found in the unchanging, all sufficient person of Jesus Christ.

• *Begin every day with Galatians 2:20:* "I have been crucified with Christ and I no longer live, but Christ lives in me. The life I live in the body, I live by faith in the Son of God, who loved me and gave himself for me."

Remove the mask and allow the radiance of Christ to mark your life.

—*Bill Nix, president,
Faith@Work and WorkLife*

Personal Challenge:
• *Bill lists 5 steps; which one can you start to work on?*

Thought to Apply: The Lord frustrates our plans, shatters our purposes, lets us see the wreck of all our hopes, and whispers to us, "It's not your work I wanted, but you."
—ANONYMOUS

Power of the "Bag Lady"

Key Bible Verse: Whatever you do, work at it with all your heart, as working for the Lord, not for men *(Colossians 3:23). Bonus Reading: Exodus 31:1-5*

To Richard Bolles, author of *What Color Is Your Parachute?*, figuring out your calling is figuring out what you are good at (God-given talents), combining it with what you enjoy (God-given interests), and putting it to use in the right job and right company.

Years ago, he read about a woman at Safeway. For him, she illustrates what calling "looks like."

"She worked in the days when there were cash registers rather than bar code readers, and she would get a rhythm going on the keys of the cash register when she was ringing stuff up," Bolles said. "Then she would challenge herself on how she packed the paper bag with groceries." She gave recipes to shoppers who weren't sure how to cook what they were buying. She kept candy for kids.

"That's a basic way calling should get traced out," observes Bolles: "Taking mundane tasks and figuring out how to transfigure them. The story in the Gospels of Jesus going up on the mount and being transfigured before the disciples is to me a picture of what calling is all about. Taking the mundane, offering it to God, and asking Him to help us transfigure it."

—*Stephen Caldwell*
Life@Work Journal

Personal Challenge:
• *Who do you know who can take a mundane task and transfigure it? Ask God to help you develop that art.*

Thought to Apply: If I cannot do great things, I can do small things in a great way.

—JAMES FREEMAN CLARKE (Boston minister, 19th century)

Up Close & Personal with John Beckett

How to Be a Christian at Work

Q. **You chose to serve God in a business rather than a church. Why?**

A. I had to ask myself, *Is my involvement in business truly my calling, or is it personal preference?*

After putting forth my best arguments to the Lord for staying in business, I finally concluded this wasn't a negotiating session. He was probing deep into my heart, examining my motives. After a good deal of soul-searching, I made perhaps the most difficult decision I'd ever made—a decision to release to God my future and all that I owned, including the company.

What happened?
God seemed to be saying, "You are where I want you to be. I have called you to business."

How does your faith influence your work?
Beckett Corporation's core values are integrity, excellence and a profound respect for the individual.

Everyone talks about integrity; what does that mean in business?
The person described in Psalm 15 "swears to his own hurt and does not change." I picture someone who agrees on a handshake to sell a piece of property for a certain sum. The next day another person offers more money. The person of integrity honors the prior commitment, even though backing out would bring greater profit."

Your company allows mothers with newborns to stay home with them for an extended period, and provides subsidies to families who adopt children. Why?
In Genesis we read that God formed men and women in his own image and likeness. When I really saw this, it

changed the way I viewed other people. I concluded I must place a high value on each person, regardless of his or her station in life. If employ- ees are of infinite worth in God's eyes, they certainly deserve no less from us than our profound respect.

John Beckett is CEO *of R. W. Beckett Corporation, an Ohio firm that makes components for heating systems. He is author of* Loving Monday *(InterVarsity, 1998). Interview by Dick Leggatt*

For Personal Study or Group Discussion

Real Life Application

Key Bible Verse: Do you see a man skilled in his work? He will serve before kings; he will not serve before obscure men *(Proverbs 22:29). Bonus Reading: Psalm 15*

Think and pray about these sentence starters on your own. Or, if you meet with other men, use them to trigger your discussion.

☐ One example I saw of integrity at work was ...

☐ I can bring glory to God in my work by ...

☐ I would like to develop my God-given skills by ...

Credits: Monday: *Leap Over a Wall* (HarperCollins, 1997); Tuesday: *Anchor Man* (Thomas Nelson, 1998); Wednesday & Thursday: *The Promise Keeper* (Sept./Oct. 1998); Friday: *Life@Work* (Vol. 1, No. 3) ; Saturday: *The Christian Businessman* (July/Aug. 1998)

God Whispered in Her Ear

Key Bible Verse: Cast all your anxiety on him because he cares for you *(1 Peter 5:7)*. *Bonus Reading: Psalm 127:1-2*

I heard the "voice of God" recently. I almost didn't recognize it. I was taking our four-year-old, Annie, to the day-care center on my way to work. Usually the drive time is filled with sing-along tapes. But this day my mind was elsewhere. Downsizing threatened my day job as a musician. My wife's recent hospital stay [was over], but now the bills were on the way.

Then Annie brought me out of my thoughts. "Dad," she asked, "did God make all these trees?"

"Uh . . . yes, he did."

"He did a pretty nice job." She then pointed out other creations of God: the birds and flowers. Seeing the world through her eyes, the day seemed brighter.

Annie didn't stop there. She reminded me that Jesus had taken care of Mommy in the hospital and that He answers our bedtime prayers. "He's there for us, ya know." It was as if God were whispering into her ear what to say to me.

Following Annie's lead, I allowed the Lord to "be there" for me [and] released my worries to Jesus. The burden was lifted. [Soon] came a contract for unexpected, extra work with the local orchestra. And many issues at my day job were resolved.

—Tom Macklin in Decision

Personal Challenge:
• *What heavy weight are you carrying that Jesus is asking you to give to Him? Pray for His tender release and strength to uphold you.*

Thought to Apply: Relying on God has to begin all over again every day as if nothing has yet been done.

—C. S. Lewis (British scholar and writer)

Learning from a German Shepherd

Key Bible Verse: Though He slay me, yet will I hope in Him *(Job 13:15). Bonus Reading: Matthew 11:28-30*

Our German shepherd has serious congenital problems: both hips malformed and internal problems. Quincy has gone through the first hip operation. He was with the vet for four days in incredible pain.

When we went to pick up Quincy, I was afraid his attitude might have changed toward me. If I had been Quincy, I probably would have been angry at the one who made me go through that. Remember, as a dog, Quincy doesn't know that the pain is necessary for his healing.

Quincy looked horrible. But when he saw us, he started wagging his tail. He pulled at the leash so he could get next to us. And when we got home, he came over and put his head in my lap!

As I was scratching Quincy behind the ears, I prayed, "Lord, make me like Quincy. I know you never hurt me without cause. I know you can't always explain why You do the things You do, but you repeatedly demonstrate Your love for me. Teach me to come to You the way this dog has come to me. Teach me to trust You and love You when it hurts, even when I don't know why I hurt."

—*Steve Brown, teacher and broadcaster*

Personal Challenge:
• *Are you upset with God because something is going wrong?*
• *Make a conscious choice to believe God is working for your good.*

Thought to Apply: I would rather walk with God in the dark than go alone in the light.

—Mary Gardiner Brainard (writer, 17th century)

Give Away My Guitar?

Key Bible Verse: [Jesus] replied, "Blessed rather are those who hear the word of God and obey it" *(Luke 11:28). Bonus Reading: Mark 10:29-30*

In 1989 I took part in the first Soviet-sanctioned Christian music festival, sponsored by Youth for Christ, in Estonia. Enroute, the jet engine couldn't drown out the still, small voice: "Bruce, I want you to give away your guitar in the Soviet Union." At $600, my acoustic, six stringed Takamine guitar was the nicest I had ever owned.

"Lord," I responded, "You know I need my guitar for the ministry You called me to." But the voice persisted.

Seventeen thousand attended the concerts; thousands gave their lives to Christ. After our last concert, we were saying our goodbyes with YFC staff backstage. An Estonian approached me. In broken English, he said, "Your interpreter, Peter, leads praise and worship for his church; he has been praying for five years for an acoustic guitar."

My heart pounded. I went straight over to Peter. I handed him the instrument. "God wants you to have it!"

Not long after I returned, the phone rang. A voice said, "I'm calling from the Gibson Guitar Company. To make inroads into gospel music by way of an endorsement, we'd like to give you a guitar." Within the week, the company sent me a black J200 guitar valued at $3,000!

—Bruce Carroll, gospel singer

Personal Challenge:

• *If God had an errand to be done, would you be available?*

Thought to Apply: Trust involves letting go and knowing God will catch you.

—JAMES DOBSON (psychologist and broadcaster)

"Why Does God Wait?"

Key Bible Verse: Therefore do not worry about tomorrow, for tomorrow will worry about itself. Each day has enough trouble of its own *(Matthew 6:34).*
Bonus Reading: John 11:1-15

You may be going through tough times. You're asking, "Why does God wait? Why won't He help?"

God is waiting simply because His timing is better than yours. Don't push it. When His time has come, it will be done. God is sovereign over not just what we do but the time in which we do it.

My father became a Christian three months before he died of cancer. I had prayed for my father for years and years; so had my mother. Time and time again, I had cried to God, "Why so long? Are You going to let him die in his sins? Aren't You going to draw him to Yourself?"

Then, a short time before my father died, in the most beautiful conversion experience I've ever seen, he received Christ. Do you know what happened as a result? My father almost converted a whole hospital!

I wanted to go out, grab the nurses and doctors, and say, "Come, I want you to watch a Christian man die. I want you to see how this thing really works." It dawned on me then how perfect and right God's timing really is. You can trust God.

—*Steve Brown, teacher and broadcaster*

Personal Challenge:
• *Can you look back and see how God's timing was right for you in the past?*

Thought to Apply: The more we depend on God, the more dependable we find he is.

—CLIFF RICHARDS (British pop singer)

"Who's Your Husband?"

Key Bible Verse: Let him who walks in the dark, who has no light, trust in the name of the Lord and rely on his God *(Isaiah 50:10b). Bonus Reading: Psalm 9:9-10*

Kim Carpenter and his wife, Krickitt, married almost ten weeks, were driving to Phoenix when they were hit by a pick-up truck and rolled one-and-a-half times.

Weeks later, when Krickitt came out of the coma, her nurse asked a routine question: "Who's your husband?"

"I'm not married."

Eighteen months of her life prior to the accident—all the time Krickitt had known Kim—were erased from her memory. And her once bubbly personality had disappeared. She would laugh, cry, be angry without warning.

Five months after the accident, Krickitt went home, to this man everyone said was her husband. Even staring at her wedding photos elicited no response.

"God needed to break me," Kim says. "I had to give everything to Him."

As Kim redated his wife, she began to enjoy his companionship. Then they got married again, giving Krickitt her own memory.

Krickitt continues to improve. "I forget things, yes, but I can walk, I can talk, and I have a wonderful husband!"

"We don't have a story without God," says Kim. "That story really is about commitment—commitment to Him and commitment in marriage."

—*Bonne Steffen, editor*

Personal Challenge:
• *Has a personal crisis helped you surrender more to God?*
• *Can you thank Him for His intervention?*

Thought to Apply: Trust God, even when the pieces don't seem to fit.
—JOHN HERCUS (writer)

Up Close & Personal with Chuck Swindoll

Trusting God When You Hit Bottom

Q. Tell us about a time when your trust in God was tested.

A. My older daughter, Charissa, had an operation on her eye because the muscles caused her eye to turn outward. When her eye was not improving, a pediatric opthalmologist said: "I'll do my best, but now scar tissue has set up. It will be difficult. So I want to tell you ahead of time that it could turn all the way in or out."

What happened?
She came out of surgery bloody, swollen and bruised. I remember standing by the bedside and saying, "Honey, can you open your eye for Daddy?"

Finally, the eye lid came open. The eye was turned all the way in—right against her nose! All one could see was the white part of her eye.

I hit bottom! I did not know how to cope with it. I said to Cynthia, "I'm going."

"Where are you going?" she asked.

"I don't know," I answered. "I'm just leaving."

I got into the car and drove to my office. I went inside the study, put my "Do Not Disturb" sign on the knob, and locked the doors.

How was your trust in God restored?
A very close friend came by and said, "Come on, let's get out of here." He put his arm around me, and we got into his car. He didn't say a lot; we just drove. Just quietness.

About two or three hours later we went back to the hospital. "I'm really going to commit this thing to the Lord," he told me. "But we have to wait on Him. We've got to trust Him, Chuck."

What was the outcome? The next morning we looked again at her eye. It was straightening up! When the opthalmologist checked her later, he said, "Her fusion is perfect. We'll take her out of glasses." Unto this day her eyesight is perfect.

Have you ever had to learn a lesson twice? Would you believe seven or eight times? I had to exchange my weakness for God's strength, even though I didn't deserve the exchange. I simply said, "It is impossible, Lord; you do it." And He did.

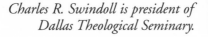

Charles R. Swindoll is president of Dallas Theological Seminary.

Sunday, Week 29   **Trusting God**

For Personal Study or Group Discussion

Real Life Application

Key Bible Verse: "Because he loves Me," says the Lord, "I will rescue him; I will protect him, for he acknowledges My name" *(Psalm 91:14). Bonus Reading: Psalm 91*

Think and pray about these sentence starters on your own. Or, if you meet with other men, use them to trigger your discussion.

☐ The area of my life I find hardest to leave in God's hands is ...

☐ I am asking God for patience to wait for His answer about ...

Credits: Adapted from—Monday: *Decision* (12/98); Tuesday & Thursday: *Jumping Hurdles*; Wednesday: *Christian Reader* (Sept.-Oct./98, as told to Jan Northington); Friday: *Christian Reader* (Nov.-Dec./97); Saturday: *Three Steps Forward, Two Steps Back* (World Wide, 1980)

"Prepare for Impact!"

Key Bible Verse: He who finds a wife finds what is good and receives favor from the Lord *(Proverbs 18:22)*.
Bonus Reading: Psalm 127:3-5

J. Allen Petersen, a Christian counselor and writer, relates:

"The 747 took off at night. I started to doze when I heard a voice announcing, 'We have a serious emergency.'

Three engines had gone out because of fuel contamination; the other would go any second. The plane veered and banked as the crew tried to get it back to the airport.

The steward said, 'Tighten the seat belts tight, pull up your legs, and bury your head in your lap.' Then his voice barked out, 'Prepare for impact.'

Convinced it was over, I said, 'Oh, God, thank you for the incredible privilege of knowing You.' As the plane was going down, my last thought was, 'Oh, God, my wife! my children!'"

Petersen's plane did make it back to the airport:

"As I wandered about in the airport, I ached all over. I thought, 'What were my thoughts? What was the bottom line?'

"Here's the bottom line: relationships."

—*Steve Farrar, Men's Leadership Ministries, Dallas*

Personal Challenge:
• *Make a list of what you value about your family members, then thank God for them.*
• *Go one step further, and tell them what it is about them for which you thanked God.*

Thought to Apply: The security and elevation of the family and of family life are the prime objects of civilization, and the ultimate ends of all industry.

—CHARLES W. ELIOT (President of Harvard University, 19th century)

There When You're Needed

Key Bible Verses: Oh, that my ways were steadfast in obeying your decrees! *(Proverbs 119:5). Bonus Reading: Mark 10:2-12*

I had scheduled a series of meetings in Chicago that were vital to the direction of our ministry. The temperature was in the forties, and the forecast was not too promising. The rain was supposed to turn to freezing rain and then to snow. As I grabbed my bags and got ready to walk out the door, I turned around and said to Karen and the children, "I love you. If you need me, I'll be there."

I made it to Chicago. I conducted that evening's series of meetings. Early the next morning the phone rang. It was Karen. "How are you, honey? How's the weather?" I began.

"There are several inches of snow on the ground. Driving is really treacherous around here . . ."

We went back and forth discussing whether or not I should go home. And although she said she wanted me to stay, I heard her heart. She wanted me to be there.

I went to the airport and secured a flight back to Atlanta. When I arrived home and opened the door, our older son, Bryan, said to me, "Dad, you said if we really needed you that you would be here."

—*Crawford W. Loritts, Jr., national director of Legacy Ministries*

Personal Challenge:
• *What commitments have you made that you need to keep?*

Thought to Apply: The root of all steadfastness is the consecration to God.

—ALEXANDER MACLAREN (British preacher, 19th century)

She Tried to Kiss Me

Key Bible Verse: Flee from sexual immorality. All other sins a man commits are outside his body, but he who sins sexually sins against his own body *(1 Corinthians 6:18).* *Bonus Reading: Proverbs 5:15-20; Genesis 39:6b-12.*

A few weeks ago my wife and I made a decision that strained our marriage: I would serve notice at work; she would support the family while I went back to school.

On my next-to-last work day, a woman with whom I had a friendship asked me to look at something for her in another office. When I went in, she immediately closed the door and tried to embrace and kiss me. She told me she had wanted me for some time and would do anything to have me.

This was the moment for which Promise Keepers had entered my life. I thought of my wife, mother and mother-in-law. Each has been hurt by infidelity. My father had affair after affair when I was growing up. I realized that kind of behavior had to stop here!

I told the woman that I didn't care for the way she was acting, that I had promised my wife and God that I would forsake all others as long as I live, and that I was not about to break that promise.

God has provided magnificently for us as we make this move.

—A promise keeper in Kansas

Personal Challenge:

• *Have you already resolved to flee when and if temptation is placed in your path?*
• *If not, make that resolution now, asking God to protect you.*

Thought to Apply: O heaven! Were men but constant, he were perfect!

—WILLIAM SHAKESPEARE (English playright, 16th century)

Commitment to Family

Revived Vows

Key Bible Verse: This is love: not that we loved God, but that He loved us and sent His Son as an atoning sacrifice for our sins. ... We love because He first loved us *(1 John 4:10, 19). Bonus Reading: Romans 5:6–8*

During a Promise Keepers conference, Gary Rosberg asked us to bow at our seats, hold our cupped hands out to God, and ask him to show us our sins. I couldn't even bear to look at what God was showing me—my forgotten vows to my wife and God. I suddenly realized how much I had hurt God and my wife of 15 years. Immediately, I began to confess my sins and ask for forgiveness.

We went to church on Sunday morning, and I asked the pastor if I could give my testimony during the service. As I began to share the circumstances and events that had unfolded, I began to feel a release and a peace that comes only from God. I confessed my sins, apologized for my failures, and asked my wife to forgive me. She did.

As I recomposed myself, I took out the marriage vow certificate that PK passed out on Saturday. In front of the whole congregation I read it, signed it, and asked my wife to sign it. She did.

I can't say that I'm making incredible, immediate changes. But with God's leading, I am changing for the better.

—A promise keeper in Leonard, Texas

Personal Challenge:
• *Have you been keeping your vows?*

Thought to Apply: The most important thing a father can do for his children is to love their mother.

—THEODORE M. HESBURGH (former president, Notre Dame University)

Duty-Driven

Key Bible Verse: Husbands, in the same way be considerate as you live with your wives, and treat them with respect as the weaker partner and as heirs with you of the gracious gift of life, so that nothing will hinder your prayers *(1 Peter 3:7). Bonus Reading: Ephesians 5:25-27*

I was in the third year of grad school when my wife, Brenda, announced that I was doing a very poor job of being both a husband and a student. Doing well in school consumed a great deal of my energies. But I thought, *Hey, I'm pursuing my life's goal; my wife and family could certainly indulge me a little.*

I didn't see how she could say that I wasn't committed to her. I was doing everything I knew to juggle both family and school. I really didn't believe I'd been that neglectful. I had to eventually admit that my commitment to marriage hadn't really been a commitment to her. I was a duty-driven husband, but I hadn't

invested the same energy in trying to establish an emotional closeness with my wife. I rationalized that since my family was clothed and housed I had adequately fulfilled my marital duty. It pained me to admit that I was wrong, and I left the conversation feeling injured and a little resentful.

I have come to think differently about commitment in marriage since this incident.
—*J. Derek McNeil, family counselor*

Personal Challenge:
• *Can you identify with the feelings Derek relates here?*
• *If you're married, would your wife identify with Brenda's feelings?*

Thought to Apply: Marriage is more than finding the right person; it is being the right person.   —ANONYMOUS

Up Close & Personal with Gary Smalley

Why Is Commitment to Family So Hard?

Q. **Does being a marriage counselor mean that yours has always been together?** Hardly! In the first five years of our marriage, my wife, Norma, and I experienced severe trials. I remember sitting at the breakfast table and asking her, "Norma, what's wrong with our marriage?" and "What would it take to move our marriage toward a 'perfect 10'?" That's when we first committed ourselves to work at learning how to stay in love and build a strong, lasting marriage—whatever it took.

How did that resolve work out?
At first I feared not being able to go the distance—that it would take more out of me than I had to give. The more we talked, the more I didn't get it.

What was Norma telling you?
From my actions, she said, she felt as if everything else on earth was more important to me than her. She patiently repeated the message until I realized for the first time in my life, that I was dishonoring her by making her feel less valuable than practically everything (TV, sports, my ministry) and everyone else.

From that day on, I decided to treasure Norma above all those people and things. I made that commitment out of my love for God, who is my first love.

To be honest, that was a terrifying thing to do. I feared

that Norma would take advantage of me and that my life was over, at least all the fun parts. How wrong I was—again. Norma did just the opposite. As I began treasuring her, making her "number one," her anxieties relaxed, and she became more calm. She enthusiastically pushed me into things she knew I loved to do.

Gary Smalley is president of Today's Family in Branson, Missouri.

Commitment to Family   Sunday, Week 30

For Personal Study or Group Discussion

Real Life Application

Key Bible Verse: The Lord is faithful to all His promises and loving toward all He has made *(Psalm 145:13b).*
Bonus Reading: Psalm 15

Think and pray about these sentence starters on your own. Or, if you meet with other men, use them to trigger your discussion.

☐ For me, commitment to family means ...

☐ One sacrifice I could make to keep my family strong is ...

☐ To make my loved ones feel they are important to me, I could ...

Credits: Adapted from—Monday: *Anchor Man* (Thomas Nelson, 1998); Tuesday: *Never Walk Away* (Moody Press, Moody Bible Institute, 1997); Wednesday: PK Net Testimony of the week (9/4/97); Thursday: PK Net Testimony of the Week (8/28/98); Friday: *Men to Men,* edited by Lee N. June and Matthew Parker (Zondervan, 1996); Saturday: *Go the Distance,* with John Trent (Focus on the Family, 1996)

"I'll Take Care of It"

Key Bible Verse: Dear children, let us not love with words or tongue but with actions and in truth *(1 John 3:18). Bonus Reading: 1 John 3:16-17*

Ted Grigson's neighbor, Hans Hoerler, fell from a tree branch and snapped his neck, leaving him paralyzed, unable to work his farm. Kneeling beside him as the two waited for an ambulance, Grigson, an Arkansas state trooper, made a simple promise: "I'll take care of it."

That day, Grigson and his family were preparing to leave for Disney World on his two-week vacation. Instead, Grigson helped organize a team of volunteers. Over time, the volunteer crew got smaller; but Grigson remained. When he went back to work, he would get home from his police shift at midnight, go to the farm at 5 A.M. and return home in time to dress for his job.

The dairy herd was sold. But the Hoerlers have volunteer help with beef cattle, and they hope to hold onto the land until Jonathan, 14, can begin farming it full-time.

Grigson still helps out about once a week. He feels it's what God calls him to do. "We shouldn't have to tell anybody we're Christians," he said. "They should see it."

The International Association of Chiefs of Police named him National Trooper of the Year in March.

"All I did was milk cows," said Grigson.

—*Laura Kellams,* Arkansas Democrat-Gazette *reporter*

Personal Challenge:
• *Is faith visible?*

Thought to Apply: Do little things as if they were great because of the majesty of the Lord Jesus Christ who dwells in you. —BLAISE PASCAL (French scientist and philosopher, 17th century)

Pulling Rank

Key Bible Verses: Whoever wants to become great among you must be your servant, and whoever wants to be first must be your slave *(Matthew 20:26-27)*. *Bonus Reading: Matthew 20:20-28*

During the American Revolution, a man in civilian clothes rode past a group of soldiers repairing a small defensive barrier. Their leader was shouting instructions at them but making no other attempt to help them. Asked why by the rider, the leader said with great dignity, "Sir, I'm a corporal!"

The stranger apologized, dismounted and proceeded to help the exhausted soldiers. The job done, he turned to the corporal and said, "If you need some more help, son, call me." With that, the Commander-in-Chief, George Washington, remounted his horse and rode on.

Jesus said that the greatest would be the least and the leader would be the servant. We don't buy into that truth much. Perhaps that's why there aren't many true leaders anymore. It wouldn't be a bad idea for our leaders to climb down off their podiums and provide some hands-on help. Once we got over the shock, I think we would listen to them when they returned to their podiums and gave a speech.

—*Steve Brown*
teacher and broadcaster

Personal Challenge:
• *Who is one leader who models servanthood?*

Thought to Apply: If you wish to be a leader you will be frustrated, for very few people wish to be led. If you aim to be a servant, you will never be frustrated.

—FRANK F. WARREN (writer)

Play Like Yankees

Key Bible Verse: Whatever happens, conduct yourselves in a manner worthy of the gospel of Christ *(Philippians 1:27a). Bonus Reading: Philippians 1:27b-30*

Twenty-five years ago, when the New York Yankees were the dominant team in major league baseball, the manager would say to the rookies, "Boys, it's an honor just to put on the New York pinstripes. So when you put them on, play like world champions. Play like Yankees. Play proud."

Paul often urged groups of people to advance the cause of Christ by living for Christ in their particular area of influence. He knows that all kinds of evangelistic actions are generated when believers decide to live like Jesus in the marketplace or in the neighborhood or in schools.

In a way Paul is saying, "Do you really want to make some heads turn? Then you live as ethically, morally, and purely as Jesus lived. You love as deeply as Jesus loved. You serve as humbly as Jesus served. You get elbow deep in people's struggles and problems as Christ did. Get so acquainted with the Jesus of the gospels that it becomes second nature for you to act like he would have acted in each of your daily situations."

You will not lead a comfortable life, but you will also not lead a dull life. Paul tells us there's something to fear that's worse than death—and that's a wasted life, a life that could have advanced the cause of Christ but didn't.

—*Bill Hybels, Illinois pastor*

Personal Challenge:
• *What keeps you from being effective as a servant of the gospel?*

Thought to Apply: A candle loses nothing by lighting another candle. —ANONYMOUS

Consumed with Home Repairs

Key Bible Verse: Remember your leaders, who spoke the word of God to you. Consider the outcome of their way of life and imitate their faith *(Hebrews 13:7).*
Bonus Reading: 2 Corinthians 9:12-13

My husband started a church a little over three years ago. With a rapidly growing church, the pressures on Steve have been extreme. To top things off, we have been getting ready to sell our house, and he has been consumed with home repairs.

I made it a matter of prayer. Two Sundays ago a young woman in our congregation told me she had read an article about the pressures of ministry and wanted to organize something to help our family. I couldn't believe that God had answered my prayers so quickly!

She contacted some of the 150 men in our church who attended Promise Keepers last summer. They organized several work days to work on our projects. The best news of all is they did it to coincide with my husband's trip to attend the Promise Keepers pastors' conference.

Steve knows nothing of their plans, so he will come home not only spiritually renewed but physically relieved because they are planning to repair our bathroom, lay sod in the backyard and, get this, *paint our house!*

I'm so excited I can barely sleep at night.
—*A pastor's wife in California*

Personal Challenge:
• *Think of a way to encourage someone in Christian ministry.*

Thought to Apply: God likes help when helping people.
—IRISH PROVERB

Giving the Best You Can

Key Bible Verses: Greater love has no man than this, that he lay down his life for his friends *(John 15:13)*. *Bonus Reading: 2 Corinthians 11:16-33*

John Payton was finishing seminary and God said, "I want you to go to the New Hebrides Islands."

John Payton said, "God, those are inhabited by cannibals. You want me to go there? Are you sure?"

God said, "Yes."

So he gathered up his young bride and got on a sailing ship, and was let off on the New Hebrides Islands. The ship sailed away and he and his wife were alone.

[Later,] his wife gave birth to their first child, who contracted a tropical disease and died two weeks later. Two days later his wife died. Payton wrote: "I slept on their graves for three days to keep the natives from digging them up and eating them." Then he wrote, "God, how far does love go? How far does obedience and commitment to Christ have to go?"

In God's providence, there was an outcast from one of the tribes who met Payton. He taught John Payton some of the language. John Payton stayed on New Hebrides Islands for thirty-five years. After that, he wrote, "I do not know of a single native in these islands who has not made a profession of faith in Jesus Christ."

—*Roger Barrier,*
Arizona pastor

Personal Challenge:
• *How far does love go? What are you willing to endure for the cause of Christ?*

Thought to Apply: Before the judgment seat of Christ, my service will not be judged by how much I have done but by how much of me there is in it.

—A.W. TOZER (late pastor and author)

Up Close & Personal with Richard J. Foster

Q. **Why is it hard to serve others?**

A. We experience a fear that comes out something like this: "If I do that, people will take advantage of me; they will walk all over me."

How do we overcome that fear? We give up the right to be in charge. There is great free-dom in this. If we voluntarily choose to be taken advantage of, then we cannot be manip-ulated. When we choose to be a servant we surrender the right to decide who and when we will serve. We become available and vul-nerable.

Richard J. Foster is founder of Renovaré, a church renewal effort, and author of Prayer *and other books.*

For Personal Study or Group Discussion

Key Bible Verse: In everything I did, I showed you that by this kind of hard work we must help the weak, remembering the words the Lord Jesus Himself said: "It is more blessed to give than to receive" *(Acts 20:35).*
Bonus Reading: John 13:1-5, 12-17

Think and pray about these sentence starters on your own. Or, if you meet with other men, use them to trigger your discussion.

☐ Helping others is a challenge because . . .

☐ Serving ends up making my day because . . .

Credits: Adapted from—Monday: *Life@Work* (Vol. 1, No. 3); Tuesday: *Jumping Hurdles* (Baker, 1992); Wednesday: *Preaching Today* (#164); Thursday: PK Testimony of the week (9/5/96) Friday: *Preaching Today* (#164); Saturday: *Celebration of Discipline* (Harper & Row, 1978)

A Marine and His Men

Key Bible Verse: I grieve for you, Jonathan my brother; you were very dear to me. Your love for me was wonderful, more wonderful than that of women *(2 Samuel 1:26). Bonus Reading: 1 Samuel 20:16-17, 42*

Some of the best days of my life were in the Marines in 'Nam. I ran with a bunch of guys who went through hell together. We saw men die, get shot to pieces, go crazy. In the midst of it all we got closer as friends than I ever believed possible.

There was nothing we couldn't say to each other, nothing we wouldn't do for one another. You've heard about the guy who throws himself on a grenade to save a friend's life? *Any* of us would have done that.

We talked about everything. We laughed; we cried; we hated; we dreamed; we screamed; even had some fist fights. But one thing we knew: We loved each other—in a way that I have never experienced since.

I don't think I'll ever have friends like that again. I miss that kind of closeness. The guys I know at church, at work? There's nothing like that with them.

—*An Ex-Marine, quoted in* When Men Think Private Thoughts

Personal Challenge:
• *Can you name one guy with whom you can "spill your guts" and who will level with you?*
• *If not, who could become that kind of friend?*

Thought to Apply: There's a kind of emotional exploration you plumb with a friend that you don't really do with your family.   —BETTE MIDLER (actress)

He Kept Looking Beyond Me

Key Bible Verse: I have no one else like him, who takes a genuine interest in your welfare *(Philippians 2:20)*. *Bonus Reading: Philippians 2:4-11*

I'd had an incredibly good day at school and in athletics. I was sure that when my dad heard what had happened to me, he'd be delighted. I think I was always trying to find a way to finally impress him, to get a reaction—any kind—from him.

I remember coming into the room and sitting down and telling him everything that had happened. The television was on, and he was watching the news or sports or something and kept looking beyond me, far more interested in what was on TV than what I was telling him. When I got through, he mumbled a "That's great, Son," and just went on watching television. When the program was over, he just got up and left the room without another word.

I felt like a fool. Everything I'd thought important just didn't count with him.

I don't know what I was looking for. I guess I wanted him to stop everything and share my excitement. It would have been nice to know that what had happened that day was as important to him as it was to me. I don't think I ever bothered to tell him anything important again. I wasn't going to take the risk.

—*Anonymous; quoted in* When Men Think Private Thoughts

Personal Challenge:
• *How can you show someone that you value his words?*

Thought to Apply: It was hard to communicate with you. You were always communicating with yourself. The line was busy.
—JEAN KERR (author)

Brothers-Times-Two

Key Bible Verse: I will sing to the Lord, for He has been good to me *(Psalm 13:6). Bonus Reading: Psalm 142:1-2*

My brother and I grew up in a household that was not necessarily a "touchy-feely" home. My brother and I never communicated any love to each other. I believe that deep down we both knew we loved each other, but to express that love was something totally different.

Unfortunately, due to my brother's job with the State Police, he lives more than 1 ½ hours away from me. Since I was the organizer in our church for the PK conference, I felt a tug on my heart to get my brother involved in Promise Keepers.

Luckily, we were able to sit together for Friday evening's messages. As my brother and I stood and sang together, I began to feel a pull on my heart. Finally, as the evening drew to a close, I grabbed my brother and gave him a hug with so much love and strength that I think his ribs still hurt. Then I told him that I loved him. Immediately he returned my hug and heartfelt sentiment with an "I love you, *too*."

Saturday brought us together again as "brothers-times-two" — brothers in blood and brothers in Christ's blood! Since the event, my brother and I have begun to keep in touch far more than we ever did.

— A promise keeper
from Indiana

Personal Challenge:
•*Whom do you need to tell how you really feel about them? Ask God for courage to share your heart.*

Thought to Apply: The highest sign of friendship is that of giving another the priviledge of sharing your inner thought. —PAUL TOURNIER (late Swiss psychiatrist)

Marriage in the Holy Spirit

Key Bible Verse: Make every effort to keep the unity of the Spirit through the bond of peace. *(Ephesians 4:3)*
Bonus Reading: Ephesians 4:1-6.

Every marriage goes through tests and crises, but these can bring about an increase in love. As Heidi, a cousin of mine who has been married for over forty years, writes, expressions of love do not require much fanfare. Often the simplest gesture says the most.

"My husband, Klaus, and I have gone through many struggles in our relationship with each other, and with our children. Yet through it all our love has grown stronger. Again and again we marvel at the gift God gave us in each other. I do not believe that our relationship could ever exist without romance—the little joys or surprises we make for each other are what confirm and renew our love time and again. I am always happily surprised when Klaus writes me a new poem or makes a little drawing on a stone he has found.

"It is true that marriage is a serious commitment for life, yet I think we can also be very childlike about it and trust in God's leading, taking one step at a time. We stumble along; we make our mistakes. But afterwards we love each other all the more."

—*Johann Christoph Arnold in*
A Plea for Purity

Personal Challenge:
• *What role has the Holy Sprit played in knitting your lives together?*

Thought to Apply: Love gains certainty and firmness only when it is ruled by the Spirit.
— JOHANN CHRISTOPH ARNOLD (author and speaker)

Collarbone Massages

Key Bible Verse: Filled with compassion, Jesus reached out His hand and touched the man *(Mark 1:41).*
Bonus Reading: Daniel 10:18-19

Some of my most cherished memories are of sitting on my dad's lap as a young boy. If he was watching a game and I was hanging in the shadow, he would simply grab me and put me up on his lap.

Often, when we would be coming back from a baseball game in New York, I would fall asleep on the train with his arm draped over me. Then there were his famous collarbone massages. He loved to rub our collarbones, and I don't mean just when we were kids. Sometimes he would walk past me in the kitchen and briefly rub my collarbone, or if I sat next to him watching TV, he would give me the old collarbone touch.

I guess it was his way of saying, "I love you. I would rather be with my family than with anyone else. You matter to me. You are a joy to me."

In a word, Pop's touch affirmed me. At an early age, I experienced the power of a father's touch. Pop's hand became the signature over my soul. I never hungered for his love and affection. I guess I always knew I had it. Although as I was growing up he could never bring himself to say "I love you," we all knew how Pop felt about us.

—*Crawford W. Loritts, Jr.*
National Director
Campus Crusade for Christ's
Legacy Ministries

Personal Challenge:
• *Give a loving touch to a family member today.*

Thought to Apply: Love comforteth like sunshine after rain. —WILLIAM SHAKESPEARE (playwright, 16th century)

Up Close & Personal with Tony Evans

Why Bother to "Connect?"

Q. ▪ **Do guys really need all that 'touchy-feely' stuff?**

A. ▪ I still have a way to go in balancing the need for quality relationships with my task- and goal-oriented makeup as a man. One of my favorite TV programs as a kid was *The Lone Ranger*. He *never* revealed his true identity.

Too many of us are content to pass people by as we continue toward our goals. We don't build significant relationships along the way.

It's not unusual for a man to reach midlife and not have much of a relationship with his wife. His children are ready to leave home, but they don't really know him, and he doesn't know them. Maybe the salary has been made, the position in the corporation has been achieved. But there are relational casualties along the way.

Women are much more oriented to relationships. All of us married men have had our wives say, "I just want to talk."

We want to say, "Well, it's OK to talk if I can do this or that too."

But when the wife slips that word *just* in there, we know they want to do some focused, undistracted talking. And that makes us uncomfortable.

What makes you want to push through the uncomfortable feelings?
I have discovered from God's Word that you can never be what He wants you to be apart from relationships. If we let the world's philosophy of male independence dominate us, we are courting spiritual, personal and family disaster.

God's first comment on the state of human beings was that

Adam needed a helper. But we say it is better that we should be alone as far as relationships are concerned.

If God tells me it's not good for me to be alone, but I insist on being a loner, then I deprive others who are in des-

perate need of what I have to offer. And I also hurt myself, because although I may not know it, I'm in desperate need of what they have to offer too.

Tony Evans is a pastor in Dallas and president of The Urban Alternative.

For Personal Study or Group Discussion

Real Life Application

Key Bible Verse: "Do all that you have in mind," his armor-bearer said. "Go ahead; I am with you heart and soul" *(1 Samuel 14:7). Bonus Reading: 1 Samuel 13:23-14:14*

Think and pray about these sentence starters on your own. Or, if you meet with other men, use them to trigger your discussion.

☐ One time I really connected with another person was . . .

☐ One thing that helps me build signficant relationships is . . .

Credits: Adapted from—Monday & Tuesday: *When Men Think Private Thoughts* (Thomas Nelson, 1996); Wednesday: PK Net Testimony of the Week (9/4/97); Thursday: *A Plea for Purity* (Plough, 1998); Friday: *Never Walk Away* (Moody, 1997) ; Saturday: *No More Excuses* (Crossway, 1996)

Jelly Beans for the Team

Key Bible Verse: Encourage one another and build each other up, just as in fact you are doing *(1 Thessalonians 5:11). Bonus Reading: Romans 1:11-12*

I meet weekly with a community Promise Keepers group of about 10 men. We had been thinking about how we could be role models to the teenage guys in our town.

This winter our boys' basketball team went through a difficult season. One guy in our group felt led to do something to encourage the team. After talking to the other members of the group we sent balloons and jelly beans to the team with the message, "We are behind you, win or lose. Remember: We can do all things through Christ who strengthens us."

We started praying for the boys before each game. After one of these prayer times we talked about doing something more to share the gospel with athletes. We talked to the coaches and decided to serve the students supper after practice one night. We included the girls' basketball team, the girls' volleyball team, the cheerleaders, and the stats people.

About 50 students showed up. In our town, that is nearly half the high school.

Many students stayed to talk with us afterward. We are still hearing how much it meant to them to know we cared.

—A pastor in North Dakota

Personal Challenge:
• *How could you encourage a teen in your church or community?*

Thought to Apply: How many people stop because so few say, "Go!"?   —CHARLES R. SWINDOLL (author and seminary president)

Buddies for the Depressed

Key Bible Verse: If one falls down, his friend can help him up. But pity the man who falls and has no one to help him up! *(Ecclesiastes 4:10). Bonus Reading: Romans 12:15*

I was already in a major depression. Then I got nailed with this intestinal stuff I'm predisposed towards, and just sat home staring at the walls. Feeling totally alone. Crying by the hour. Just numb.

I would get up at about 2:00 P.M. every day, eat a little, stay up until about 7:00 P.M., and then go back to bed.

One day, out of the blue, my two friends called, and asked if they could come visit me. I was terrified at that point, couldn't talk, didn't want to see anybody but my wife. Any little thing set me off crying. Old tapes of "failure, no good, shame, abandoned, worthless, going to end up in the gutter just like your dad" kept running through my head, taking me further down.

My buddies showed up. They just sat down and said, "We care. We don't understand why this is happening, it doesn't make any sense to us, but we care."

Then one of them said, "I've gone through something similar. The pain gets intense, doesn't it? No matter what happens, I value our friendship, and will help in any way I can. It's okay to cry! If I could take some of the pain, I would."

—*Name withheld*

Personal Challenge:

• *Whom do you know who is hurting? How can you take time to be with him?*

Thought to Apply: The men who are lifting the world upward and onward are those who encourage more than criticize. —ELISABETH HARRISON (writer)

Bucky Backers

Key Bible Verse: Let us consider how we may spur one another on toward love and good deeds *(Hebrews 10:24). Bonus Reading: 1 Thessalonians 2:17-3:13*

The Bucky Backers are a group of regular folks who are making it their business to spur on one of minor league baseball's hopefuls: Bucky Jacobsen.

They cheer, shout, make signs, e-mail his stats to each other and even have a web site. Their original intent was to have a good time at a ball game and just make his day.

The reach of their encouragement has amazed everyone in the group, even Bucky himself. They've received e-mail from as far away as Spain from people wanting to register their support. Bucky's family has been encouraged. The cheering has even sparked some razzing in the dugout of the Beloit (Wisc.) Snappers, Bucky's team. They kid about his newfound fame by calling him Bucky.com.

All this encouragement and energy from a bunch of ordinary people cheering on a regular guy at a ball game. Makes you wonder what might happen within the church if we all followed the instructions in Hebrews 3:13 to "Encourage one another daily, as long as it is called Today, so that none of you may be hardened by sin's deceitfulness."

—Michelle Hayes
Christianity.Net

Personal Challenge:
• *How could you get behind someone in your church who is serving and leading?*

Thought to Apply: We cannot hold a torch to light another's path without brightening our own.

—BEN SWEETLAND (speaker)

I'd Given God a Deadline

Key Bible Verse: Your love has given me great joy and encouragement, because you, brother, have refreshed the hearts of the saints *(Philemon 7)*. *Bonus Reading: Philemon 1-25*

I remember being one of the oldest people in a class at Emory University. There was another student there who had also served for some time. We didn't relate too well to the younger students because we didn't have much in common. One day I went over to see this man, who was the only black person in the class, and said, "How about having lunch today?"

We went to the cafeteria and began to talk about our churches. Out of that grew a friendship. One weekend he invited me to go home with him to preach in his church. It was a great church. He said something in his introduc-tion of me that choked me up so much I found it difficult to continue.

He said, "I set a deadline on the day I met this man. I told God that morning that if I didn't meet someone that day who said hello to me and wanted to spend some time with me, wanted to be my friend, then I was giving up my education. I was coming back home."

What I had done was such a small gesture, but God used it to encourage him in a time of bleak despair.

—*William Hinson, pastor Houston, Texas*

Personal Challenge:
• *Reach out to the man who is sitting or standing by himself.*

Thought to Apply: Is anyone happier because you passed his way? Does anyone remember that you spoke to him today?

—ANONYMOUS

No One to Talk To

Key Bible Verse: Let us not give up meeting together, as some are in the habit of doing, but let us encourage one another—and all the more as you see the Day approaching *(Hebrews 10:25). Bonus Reading: Ephesians 6:21-22*

Dave Dravecky, on his late friend Eric Show, who died of a drug overdose:
There were so many things I wish I would have said to Eric but never did: that he was precious to me, that his failures didn't wipe out his worth as a man, that he didn't have to hide from me what was going on in his life.

It's too late now to change anything with Eric, but I can put into practice what I've learned from his life. I can tell others how precious they are to me. I can offer acceptance instead of criticism. I can be honest about my struggles with sin and affirm the worth of others, despite their struggles.

Whenever another man dares to open up his struggles and failures with me, I won't criticize. I will encourage him that he has great worth, regardless of what he has done or what kind of shameful behavior has him trapped.

But perhaps most of all, I am determined to develop friendships with a few other men with whom I can openly share my heart. Eric didn't have that, and it cost him his life.

Personal Challenge:
• *Don't wait until it's too late to encourage the people in your life.*

Thought to Apply: Real men need real men.

—DAVE SIMMONS (writer)

Up Close & Personal with John Trent

How to Encourage Loved Ones

Q. Why do many men have difficulty encouraging their families?

A. A distinguished looking ex-soldier, who in World War II splashed ashore in Sicily and later at Utah Beach on D-Day, waited around to talk to me after a family conference about a battle he's fought for years. "I'm one of those guys," he said, "who could go ashore under fire because we knew the target. But we didn't know how to hit the target when it came to raising our families."

He represents many men who don't bless their sons and daughters because they simply don't recognize the target. As boys, they never received words of praise, love, or blessing. Their dads didn't speak the words that attach high value to a child, that picture a child's special future, and that commit a loved one to the Lord's care.

What can we learn from that? We can learn to tell our wives and children about a specific character trait we appreciate about each of them. Tell them those priceless words, 'I love you.' Put our hands on their shoulders and pray God's best for them. Give them our blessing today."

What kinds of things most encourage a loved one? Tell each member of your family: "I'm proud of you. I forgive you. I believe you. I'm praying for you. Until the day I die, I'm here for you."

John Trent, Ph.D., is a marriage and family counselor and president of Encouraging Words. He is the author of Choosing to Live the Blessing *(WaterBrook, 1998).*

Encouragement   Sunday, Week 33

For Personal Study or Group Discussion

Real Life Application

Key Bible Verse: Strengthen your brothers *(Luke 22:32).*
Bonus Reading: Exodus 17:8-13

Think and pray about these sentence starters on your own. Or, if you meet with other men, use them to trigger your discussion.

☐ The most encouraging person I know is . . .

☐ The encouragement of another person is what brought me through . . .

☐ I am most encouraged by others when they . . .

☐ I am learning to encourage others by . . .

Credits: Monday: *PK Net* (Testimony of the Week, 3/5/98); Tuesday: *Locking Arms* (Multnomah, 1995); Wednesday: *Connection Newsletter* (7/17/98); Thursday: *Preaching Today* (#114); Friday: *The Worth of a Man* (Zondervan, 1996); Saturday: *Christian Parenting Today* (Jan.-Feb./99)

No One's Looking

Key Bible Verse: Above all else, guard your heart, for it is the wellspring of life *(Proverbs 4:23). Bonus Reading: Philippians 4:8*

I'm in London on a business trip. I have some free time, and I'm walking through the city when suddenly I see a theater showing a porno movie. I'm alone. I'm lonely. No one's looking, and something inside me says, "Do it!" In a minute I'm standing in line behind these other guys waiting to buy a ticket.

All kinds of rationalizations are running through my mind. I've never seen a movie like this before. It can't hurt anyone when you're this far away from home. Who's going to find out?

And then an old song we used to sing in church begins to play in my mind: "I would be true, for there are those who trust me; I would be true, for there are those who care."

You have to picture this: the line is moving now; one side of my brain is telling me to do it, and the other side is singing this song louder and louder. I buy the ticket and start in the door. But the song is now so loud I can't hear anything else.

Shoot, how do you beat a song? So I finally turn around, walk out the door and rip up the ticket. Wasted money, but a reasonably clean soul. I'm sure glad I didn't go in.

Anonymous; quoted in When Men Think Private Thoughts

Personal Challenge:
• *Does your heart have a functioning security system?*

Thought to Apply: Unless there is within us that which is above us, we shall soon yield to that which is about us.

—P. T. FORSYTH (British pastor and educator, 19th century)

Counting $1,000 Bills

Key Bible Verse: In the same way, count yourselves dead to sin but alive to God in Christ Jesus *(Romans 6:11).*
Bonus Reading: Romans 6:1-14

I have an attorney friend whose work involves numerous trips to the Federal Reserve Bank. He took me there one afternoon. We were on security cameras all the way.

Behind a large section of bulletproof glass are people who do nothing but count money. There were numerous stacks of crisp, new hundred-dollar bills. He told me there were also stacks of thousand-dollar bills.

I asked him, "How can they stand it behind there?"

He said, "Everything is fine if they remember their job is only to count pieces of paper. If they begin to concentrate on what those pieces of paper represent—If they think, 'Hey, this is a spendable hundred-dollar bill I have in my hand!' or 'Man, a thousand dollars!'—then they're in for trouble."

Open doors to sin face us all each day. The person centered on Christ and His righteousness says, "Nothing doing," and willfully walks away. The person intent on satisfying his own desires for sin (whether he is a Christian or not) says, "Oh, I just can't help myself," and walks in.

The good news for the Christian is that by the power of the Holy Spirit, *we can help it!*
—Charles R. Swindoll
president, Dallas Seminary

Personal Challenge:
• *What, for you, is an open door to sin?*

Thought to Apply: No one knows how bad he is until he has tried to be good. There is a silly idea about that good people don't know what temptation means.
—C. S. LEWIS (British scholar and writer, 20th century)

Curing a Chicken Killer

Key Bible Verse: But now that you have been set free from sin and have become slaves to God, the benefit you reap leads to holiness, and the result is eternal life *(Romans 6:22). Bonus Reading: Romans 6:15-23*

Jack London's *White Fang* tells the story of a dog that is half wolf, half dog. As a puppy, White Fang was abused by his cruel master. After several years, he found his way to a new master.

White Fang was fond of chickens and raided a chicken-roost and killed 50 hens. His master, Weeden Scott, whom White Fang saw as man-God and "loved with a single heart," scolded him and then took him into the chicken yard. White Fang obeyed his natural impulse and lunged for a chicken. He was immediately checked by his master's voice. Every time White Fang made a move toward a chicken, his master's voice would stop him.

In this way he learned what his master wanted—he learned to ignore the chickens.

Weeden's father argued that you "couldn't cure a chicken killer," but Weeden challenged him. They agreed to lock White Fang in with the chickens all afternoon.

"Locked in the yard, White Fang lay down and went to sleep. The chickens he calmly ignored. At four o'clock he executed a running jump, gained the roof of the chicken house and leaped to the ground outside. He had learned the law."

—Steve Farrar, Men's Leadership Ministries, Dallas

Personal Challenge:
• *What is your Master's voice "checking you" about?*

Thought to Apply: He ... got the better of himself, and that's the best kind of victory one can wish for.

—MIGUEL DE CERVANTES (Spanish novelist, 16th century)

Get Lost!

Key Bible Verse: Submit yourselves, then, to God. Resist the devil, and he will flee from you *(James 4:7). Bonus Reading: Ephesians 6:12*

Pete GreyEyes was under attack from other medicine men. His sheep and horses were dying. His family's sickness could not be identified. The medicine men were even sending messages through owls. They sat around his hogan at night and called to him in Navajo: "We are going to kill you, you, you." Tormented, he tried to shoot them with his rifle.

Finally, realizing he was powerless against these attacks, he came 30 miles to the church at Navajo Mountain and committed his life to Christ. Herman, the preacher, spent all night counseling him. Pete told him about the owls and asked, "What should I do?"

"If the owls can speak to you, they can listen to you. Tell them to get lost in Jesus' name!"

Pete went home. The owls were waiting. Pete said, "Last night Jesus Christ became my Savior! I gave Him this land, my hogan, my family, my livestock. You are trespassing on God's property. In the name of Jesus Christ, go!"

One by one those owls left and never returned. His family was healed, the spiritual forces arrayed against him defeated.

—Craig Stephen Smith, C&MA director, Native American district

Personal Challenge:
• *Have you acknowledged that resisting evil is not a do-it-yourself project?*

Thought to Apply: There are two great forces at work in the world today: the unlimited power of God and the limited power of Satan.

—CORRIE TEN BOOM (Dutch speaker and concentration camp survivor)

9 Ways to Stay Pure on the Road

Key Bible Verse: Flee the evil desires of youth, and pursue righteousness, faith, love and peace, along with those who call on the Lord out of a pure heart *(2 Timothy 2:22). Bonus Reading: Proverbs 5:1-2*

1. Ask at the hotel desk to turn off the adult movies or disconnect the cable movies.
2. Have friends (other than your wife) you can call if you are lonely and tempted to do something you know is wrong.
3. Go for a walk to the gym, to the mall or to a bookstore. Physically do something instead of sitting in the hotel room.
4. Decide in advance what the rules will be for male and female client dinners. Avoid them if possible.
5. Never give or get a phone number from a woman you meet on the road.
6. Wear your wedding band if you are married. It makes a statement.
7. If you are traveling with a woman from your company, be sure your wife gets to know her.
8. If you are ever tempted to cross boundaries with someone you work with or for, do not travel with them. Some people have quit their jobs rather than risk this.
9. Alcohol always weakens your defenses. Avoid places like bars, designed with low lighting and seductive music, which may cause you to stumble.

—Cindy Crosby with Mark Sanborn, road warrior

Personal Challenge:
• What precautionary steps are you taking to protect your purity?

Thought to Apply: When fleeing temptation, don't leave a forwarding address. —R. E. PHILLIPS (writer)

Up Close & Personal with Bryan Chapell

How to Fight Temptation

Q. Should men be discouraged that they are not immune from temptation?

A. I don't know how you can be a businessman and not be tempted to sacrifice people for profit, or be in government and not be tempted to sacrifice integrity for success.

Satan says, "It's just you. You've been a Christian how long and you *still* struggle with that?"

Against that comes the voice of God [in 1 Corinthians 10:13]: "Listen, you're experiencing what millions of Christians have struggled with. It's not just you."

So how do we respond to temptation?

[We have] the sovereign promise of God: "I will not allow sin and temptation to be greater than you can stand up under." These are the terms of human resistance. It's the idea that we fight.

How do we fight?

I know a group of Christian businessmen who meet once a month and ask each other questions: The last time you traveled on a business trip did you stay pure in your hotel room? When you returned from your business trip, did you stay honest on your expense reports?

Those are tough questions. They are at war for the goodness of their souls, for their relationships with each other and with the Lord.

It's not just a matter of fighting: it's fleeing it. Look at [1 Corinthians 10] verse 14: "flee from idolatry." That's part of the battle. If you struggle with it, flee. Change the channel. Stay away from her.

Where does the power for resisting come from? When I know God has forgiven me, he releases me from the guilt of my sin, and the power to fight it comes. It's in love for God, taking His grace fully, that the things around us don't tempt us as much.

Bryan Chapell is president of Covenant Theological Seminary in St. Louis, Missouri.

Sunday, Week 34   **Resisting Evil**

For Personal Study or Group Discussion

Real Life Application

Key Bible Verse: No temptation has seized you except what is common to man. And God is faithful; he will not let you be tempted beyond what you can bear. But when you are tempted, he will also provide a way out so that you can stand up under it *(1 Corinthians 10:13).* *Bonus Reading: 1 Thessalonians 4:3-8*

Think and pray about these sentence starters on your own. Or, if you meet with other men, use them to trigger your discussion.

☐ What has helped me resist temptation in the past is . . .

☐ The area of my life where I feel most vulnerable is . . .

☐ I would be willing to be held accountable for . . .

Credits: Adapted from—Monday: *When Men Think Private Thoughts* (Thomas Nelson, 1996); Tuesday: *Three Steps Forward, Two Steps Back* (World Wide, 1980); Wednesday: *Anchor Man* (Thomas Nelson, 1998); Thursday: *Whiteman's Gospel* (Indian Life, 1997); Friday: *Life@Work* (Vol. 1, No. 3); Saturday: *Preaching Today* (#181)

"I'm Green"

Key Bible Verse: He answered: "'Love the Lord your God with all your heart and with all your soul and with all your strength and with all your mind'; and, 'Love your neighbor as yourself'" *(Luke 10:27). Bonus Reading: Luke 10:25-37*

Jesus' heart crossed difficult relational barriers to reach out to others. "When a Samaritan woman came to draw water, Jesus said to her, 'Will you give me a drink?' . . . The Samaritan woman said to him, 'You are a Jew . . . How can you ask me for a drink?' (For Jews do not associate with Samaritans)" (John 4:7-9). Racial differences form some of the most daunting barriers in this world.

Australian Anglican Bishop John Reed relates that early in his ministry he was driving a bus carrying a full mix of black aboriginal boys and white boys on an outing. As they filed in, the white boys took one side and the blacks the other. And as the trip went on, they exchanged jibes with increasing intensity.

Finally Reed could take it no longer. He stopped the bus and ordered everyone off. Then he made every boy say "I'm green" before allowing him back on.

At last the bus was full. Bishop Reed was feeling pretty good about his accomplishment until he heard someone in the back of the bus say, "All right, light green on this side, dark green on the other!"
—*R. Kent Hughes*
Illinois pastor

Personal Challenge:
• *Are there people you look down on?*

Thought to Apply: [Prejudice is] our method of transferring our own sickness to others. It is our ruse for disliking others rather than ourselves.   —BEN HECHT (commentator)

Apartheid, American Style

Key Bible Verse: So God created man in His own image, in the image of God He created him; male and female He created them *(Genesis 1:27). Bonus Reading: Malachi 2:10*

It was October 1955 in Clairton, Pennsylvania. I walked out of the high school stadium, my hair still wet from the shower, and headed downtown with my best friend, "Philco" Batten, a fleet-footed halfback who was the star of our football team.

As we passed Walker's Drugstore I said, "Hey Phil, let's go in and get a Coke."

Philco shrugged and feigned a nonchalant reply, "No, man. Let's skip it."

In my naïveté I pressed my friend to enter. We sat on the red-capped swivel stools. I spoke to the soda jerk, "Two Cokes, please."

Moments later the soda jerk returned with one Coke. He placed it in front of me.

"Where's Phil's Coke?" I said.

The soda jerk nodded over his shoulder to the manager, standing with arms folded. He stepped forward. "We don't serve colored."

Then to Philco he said, "You know better than to come in here, boy."

Again he looked at me: "Now finish your Coke and get out of here!"

I left the drugstore enraged. Obviously, the store owner did not understand the character of God, the Creator who made both blacks and whites in His own image.

—*R. C. Sproul, theologian*

Personal Challenge:
• *Do you also recoil at blatant injustice like this?*

Thought to Apply: We must recognize that the notives and forces behind racism are the anti-Christ, denying that man is made in the divine image.

—TREVOR HUDDLESTON (English missionary)

Part of the Solution

Key Bible Verse: You are worthy to take the scroll and to open its seals, because You were slain, and with Your blood You purchased men for God from every tribe and language and people and nation *(Revelation 5:9).*
Bonus Reading: Revelation 7:9-17

Ernie, owner of E. Horn Construction, was involved in planning our Fort Worth crusade when a police friend was shot by a gang member. After his friend's funeral the Lord spoke to his heart: "If I can't send My people to be part of the solution, who am I going to send?"

The Lord first dealt with Ernie's heart. Ernie had just hired iron workers—all white—for a construction project. Every interview with a black man concluded, "We'll get back with you later."

Ernie called a meeting of some 30 black pastors to enlist support for a youth rally.

Sitting face to face with them, Ernie confessed his prejudice, and asked for forgiveness. With only a few day's notice, 4,000 young people—including rival gang members—showed up for a "reconciliation rally."

Then, spearheaded by Ernie, volunteers canvassed inner-city neighborhoods, inviting young people to the crusade. On youth night, the crowd erupted in applause as three gang members professed their newfound faith in Christ.

—Luis Palau, evangelist

Personal Challenge:
• *When it comes to racial relations, are you part of the problem or part of the solution?*

Thought to Apply: Not the extremists but the great, white midstream America—i.e. Christian America—produces and preserves the racial chasm in American society.

—KYLE HASELDEN (writer)

My Racial Education, Part 1

Key Bible Verse: But if you show favoritism, you sin and are convicted by the law as lawbreakers *(James 2:9)*.
Bonus Reading: Acts 10:34-35

My high school friends roared with laughter at another of my racial jokes. Suddenly their smiles dimmed as they looked past me. I whirled to see Jerry, a black friend, standing behind me. Visibly hurt, he left without saying a word.

Actually, I counted Jerry and other black people as friends. Any accusation of prejudice would have elicited incredulous denial from me. But living in a white community in Pennsylvania, I was taught to avoid predominantly black neighborhoods. We referred to black people in a derogatory manner—not out of hatred, but out of fear and suspicion.

I had accepted Jesus as my Savior when I was 14. That's when God called me to the ministry. My youth pastor discipled me, getting me involved in a Bible quiz program. God used that program to reveal my prejudice. Each year, for three years, the Holy Spirit stunned me with Scriptures that exposed my sinful heart. The key to overcoming my racial prejudice was internalizing the Word of God, which never fails to expose sin and to supply the power to overcome sin.

—James Line, Assemblies of God minister

Personal Challenge:
• *Are you internalizing the Word of God by memorizing parts of it?*
• *Have you noticed change in your attidues or actions?*

Thought to Apply: The chief cause of human errors is to be found in the prejudices picked up in childhood.

—RENÉ DESCARTES (French philosopher, 17th century)

My Racial Education, Part 2

Key Bible Verse: You are all sons of God through faith in Christ Jesus. There is neither Jew nor Greek, slave nor free, male nor female, for you are all one in Christ Jesus *(Galatians 3:26, 28). Bonus Reading: 1 Peter 2:9-10*

At college, as part of a three-month internship, I was required to live with a black family in the government housing projects of Washington, D.C. Thinking of drugs and violence, I was so scared that I cried the night before I moved in with Tony Yates, an assistant pastor.

Tony told me I was family. He and his family immediately accepted me and let me live with them rent-free. The members of his church accepted me; many invited me to their homes.

At the same time, Pastor Bob Mathieu, a white man who had started an inner-city evangelistic work, taught me that my fear of crime and vio-lence among black people was exaggerated. He helped me learn about their culture and feel comfortable among them.

Before I finished college, God called me to work with Pastor Mathieu's ministry. I help low-income families buy and renovate their homes. Whenever people mention that I live in the roughest part of Washington, D.C., I explain that they are talking about *my* family, *my* neighborhood.

—James Line, Assemblies of God minister

Personal Challenge:
• *Are your friendships formed more on the basis of common social background or shared faith?*

Thought to Apply: Skin color does not matter to God, for he is looking upon the heart. . . . When men are standing at the foot of the cross there are no racial barriers.

—BILLY GRAHAM (evangelist)

Up Close & Personal with Joseph L. Garlington

How to Deal with Prejudice

Q. What advice do you have for someone raised in a racially intolerant home?
A. Remember Gideon. God ordered Gideon to tear down his father's altar to Baal [Judges 6:25-26]. Gideon's father had taught him evil traditions that were going to separate him from his inheritance in Abraham if they weren't dealt with. Many dads build altars to racial prejudice. Any tradition, idea or value contrary to God's Word and character *must be torn down.*

How do we find unity with people who are so different from us?
Large families who gather for reunions think nothing of different cultures they experience in different states and regions. Uncle Bob from Klamath Falls, Oregon, can talk by the hour with Buford, his second cousin who hitched a ride to the re-union from Houma, Louisiana. Their resident cultures are different, but their family roots and bloodline are the same. They share the same memories and language of a common source. So it is with everyone who has been baptized by one Spirit into one Lord and Savior.

Who is a good example for you in dealing with race?
I have a friend (who happens to be Caucasian), who kept telling me about another friend of his. He said, "Garlington, you need to meet this guy." For two months he kept encouraging me to meet this guy, and he finally arranged for both of us to meet at a party at his house. When he introduced us, I was shocked. I told the man, "I didn't know *you* were black," and he said, "I didn't know you were black either."

Then it dawned on both of us that our mutual friend had

never discussed skin color or race with either of us. All he had talked about was his friendship with both of us.

I wish we would all see one another as that mutual friend saw us—as people of worth and value.

Joseph L. Garlington is pastor of Covenant Church in Pittsburgh.

For Personal Study or Group Discussion

Real Life Application

Key Bible Verse: I charge you, in the sight of God and Christ Jesus and the elect angels, to keep these instructions without partiality, and to do nothing out of favoritism *(1 Timothy 5:21). Bonus Reading: Romans 2:6-11*

Think and pray about these sentence starters on your own. Or, if you meet with other men, use them to trigger your discussion.

☐ Things that could be "false altars" in my family's traditions are . . .

☐ One way I have seen the Spirit of God bring unity in the Body of Christ is . . .

Men of Integrity is published in association with Promise Keepers by Christianity Today, Inc., 465 Gundersen Drive, Carol Stream, IL 60188. Printed in U.S.A. Canada Post International Publications Mail Sales Agreement No. 546526. **Staff:** Editors: Harry Genet, Craig Brian Larson, Ashley Nearn; Design Director: Doug Johnson. **Advisory Board:** Edgar D. Barron, Todd McMullen, Kevin A. Miller, Keith Stonehocker. **Subscriptions:** A one-year subscription to *Men of Integrity* is available for a suggested donation of $20 to Promise Keepers, P.O. Box 103001, Denver, CO 80250-3001. www.promisekeepers.org

Credits: Adapted from—Monday: *Disciplines of a Godly Man* (Crossway, 1991); Tuesday: *The Character of God* (Servant, 1995); Wednesday: *The Peter Promise* (Discovery House, 1996); Thursday & Friday: *Decision* (10/98, with Chuck Goldberg); Saturday: *Right or Reconciled?* (Destiny Image, 1998)

Sharing the Paddle

Key Bible Verse: For waging war you need guidance, and for victory many advisers *(Proverbs 24:6).*
Bonus Reading: Proverbs 27:5-9

One thing that keeps me turning from sin is an accountability relationship with three other men. Friends for a number of years, in 1988 we decided to formalize our accountability. Our purpose is to help one another keep faithful in our walk with God.

One of the men, Doug Hignell, said, "Humble myself enough to be accountable to another person? Not me, a man who likes to be in control and paddle his own canoe!" That would have been my response 15 years ago.

Doug went on to say, "But as I began to grow in my spiritual walk, and as God brought men with spiritual depth into my life, being a lone ranger became less attractive.
I began to realize that to remain teachable as I got older and to end well in my Christian walk, I needed to develop one or more relationships that would require me to keep open and vulnerable."

Doug, Stan, Chris and I have given one another full permission to invade each other's lives, to ask any questions.

The best accountability is with very close friends who know each other so well that they "sense" when something is going astray, and will say so.
—Jerry White, president of The Navigators and a major general, Air Force Reserve

Personal Challenge:
• *Do you have friends whom you could approach about developing mutual accountability? If not, think how you could cultivate some.*

Thought to Apply: You can never establish a personal relationship without opening up your own heart.
—PAUL TOURNIER (Swiss psychologist)

Building Your Circle of Safety

Key Bible Verse: Brothers, if someone is caught in a sin, you who are spiritual should restore him gently *(Galatians 6:1a). Bonus Reading: Hebrews 3:12-14*

Moral failure is not a team sport, but it requires a team solution. People isolate themselves and remain imprisoned. Often those prisons are addictions—workaholism, alcoholism, sexual addictions, eating addictions.

Pulling out of that spiral requires help. Step one in the recovery process is admitting the failure. Finding and accepting help is step two.

When people come to us in crisis, I ask permission to help them develop a circle of safety around them. How do you do this? Ask yourself two questions:

1. Who are the men and women you trust? Start with three to five. Make sure to pick people who live nearby, not halfway across the country.

2. Why should you trust this person? No "yes people" allowed; no one who will be awed by your achievements, position or power.

You need a circle of safety that will say, "Hey, we are committed over the long haul to you," and you need to trust those people. Learning to trust them with your heart, life and work is really parallel to trusting God.

—Wes Roberts, president of Life Enrichment

Personal Challenge:
• *Answer the two questions in today's reading.*

Thought to Apply: Each one should confidently make known his needs to the other, so that he might find what he needs and minister to him.

—FRANCIS OF ASSISI (Founder of the Franciscans, 13th century)

I Was Depressed Until ...

Key Bible Verse: Carry each other's burdens, and in this way you will fulfill the law of Christ *(Galatians 6:2)*. *Bonus Reading: James 2:8*

Before coming to Korea I prayed that I would be able to attend *Stand in the Gap* because I was due to report here the same month as that event. God worked it so that I could. I made promises in front of my brothers and confessed my sins. It was very difficult leaving my wife and three children behind. I was afraid I would fall into sin and go back to [being] the person I used to be.

When I arrived, I was depressed until I met other soldiers who are part of Promise Keepers at our chapel. We formed an accountability group and confided in each other our deepest concerns. If one of us saw the other slipping, we quickly held each other accountable. We've studied *Tender Warrior* by Stu Weber.

God helped me focus on Him, be a prayer warrior, and have a passion for His ministry. I no longer worry about my family or my career because they are in His hands.

Our group has dedicated itself to witness to soldiers [and] Koreans alike. We are no longer "ashamed of the gospel," and our worship services have intensified because God has given us a vision.

—*a soldier in South Korea*

Personal Challenge:
• *Do you have friends who know the commitments you have made and will help you keep them?*

Thought to Apply: We are born helpless. . . . We need others physically, emotionally, intellectually; we need them if we are to know anything, even ourselves.

— C.S. LEWIS (British scholar and writer)

5 Good Questions

Key Bible Verse: As iron sharpens iron, so one man sharpens another *(Proverbs 27:17). Bonus Reading: Philippians 2:20-21*

Maybe you haven't been able to find a group of men. An alternative is to meet with one person on a regular basis. Find someone with whom you can let down your guard and share your struggles with the confidence that he will care and pray for you.

John Maxwell has spoken at the Promise Keepers gatherings. He says that one of the Devil's best weapons is to keep Christians from being accountable. John has an older friend named Bill with whom he meets regularly. Every time they meet, Bill asks five questions that John must answer:

1. Are you reading your Bible and praying every day?
2. Consider what's running through your mind. Are your thoughts pure?
3. Are you misusing or violating any trust that someone else has given you?
4. Are you living every day in total obedience to God?
5. Have you lied about any of the previous questions?

You may smile at the fifth question, but consider how easy it is to stretch the truth and weasel out of being accountable. John has admitted before thousands of men at the rallies that many times he has had to stop and say, "Yeah, Bill, let's go back . . . "

—Phillip H. Porter, Jr.
Colorado pastor

Personal Challenge:
• *Are you asking or answering questions like these?*

Thought to Apply: Opposition is true friendship.
—WILLIAM BLAKE (English poet and painter, 19th century)

Another Jerk ...

Key Bible Verse: So I strive always to keep my conscience clear before God and man *(Acts 24:16).*
Bonus Reading: Galatians 2:11-14

Tuesday, after I put my kids to bed, I drove over to the church because there was a rehearsal and I wanted to encourage the cast and musicians. I intended to be here just a few minutes, so I drove my car up and parked it between the auditorium and the parking lot. I was in a short time, ran out and drove home.

The next morning I got a note from a staff member: "Bill, a small thing, but Tuesday night you parked in the no-parking area. A reaction from one of my crew, who did not recognize you until after you got out of the car was, 'There's another jerk parking in the no-parking area.' We try hard not to allow people, even workers, to park anywhere other than the parking lots. I would appreciate your cooperation, too. [signed] . . ."

He had the courage to write me about a little slippage in my character. As I drove up, I thought, *I shouldn't park illegally there, but I mean, I am the pastor.*

If people allow me to say I'm an exception to the rules, I am in big trouble. Somebody loved me enough to say, "Don't do it, Bill."

—*Bill Hybels, pastor, Willow Creek Community Church, South Barrington, Illinois*

Personal Challenge:
• *Is there another guy who cares enough about you to confront you if you are getting off track?*

Thought to Apply: An open word spoken directly to another person deepens friendship and is not resented.
—EBERHARD ARNOLD (Founder of the Bruderhof community, 18th century)

Up Close & Personal with Phillip Porter

What It Takes to Be Accountable

Q. How did you get started in an accountability group?

A. A group of men invited me to join their small group. Initially I was suspicious. At my first meeting, I said, "Guys, I'm not sure if I want to be a part of your small group. I'm not sure I want to be vulnerable and transparent with you."

They said, "That's okay. We know it takes time." I have been with this group now for three years. We meet every Tuesday morning, drink coffee, and share what's going on in our lives.

Gradually, I learned to trust these men. These men have been challenging me about my weight and about the intensity of my schedule of activities. Their honest encouragement has helped me.

How can someone get hooked up to an accountability group? First, ask your pastor. Chances are, your church already has groups that would welcome you. If not, take the initiative. Ask a guy to meet you for coffee some morning. Share your desire and see what happens.

Promise Keepers publishes a resource called *The Next Step* (to order, 1-800-456-7594.)

What should the group's ground rules be?
Four things are essential:

First, we're not here to talk about the weather or sports. The purpose is to talk about parts of our lives in which we are struggling.

Second, confidentiality is vital. What is said here stays here.

Third, every person should have the opportunity to speak. No one person is allowed to dominate.

Last, be committed to praying for each other. Prayer allows each man to mention a concern on his mind. Keep the request time short so you can spend time in prayer.

Bishop Phillip H. Porter Jr. is pastor of All Nations Pentecostal Center in Aurora, Colorado and chairman of the Promise Keepers board of directors.

Sunday, Week 36   **Accountability**

For Personal Study or Group Discussion

Real Life Application

Key Bible Verse: For where two or three come together in my name, there am I with them *(Matthew 18:20).* Bonus Reading: Matthew 18:15-19

Think and pray about these sentence starters on your own. Or, if you meet with other men, use them to trigger your discussion.

☐ The thing that keeps me from sharing private stuff in my life is . . .

☐ I think being accountable would help me to grow spiritually in the area of . . .

☐ Here's how my friends and I could upgrade our relationship to a "circle of safety". . .

Credits: Adapted from—Monday: *Dangers Men Face* (NavPress, 1997); Tuesday: Stephen Caldwell and Sean Womack, *Life@Work* (Vol. 1, No. 2); Wednesday: PKNet, Testimony of the Week (3/19/98); Thursday and Saturday: *Better Men* (Zondervan, 1998); Friday: *Preaching Today* (#57)

Dial 911

Key Bible Verse: In my distress I called to the Lord; I cried to my God for help. From his temple he heard my voice; my cry came before him, into his ears *(Psalm 18:6). Bonus Reading: Romans 8:26-27*

A couple of years ago in Minneapolis we came on line with the 911 emergency number. Dial those numbers, and you will almost instantly be connected to a dispatcher. That dispatcher will have a read-out that will list your telephone number, your address, and the name by which that telephone number is listed. Also listening in are the police, the fire department and the paramedics.

Someone might not be able to say what the problem is. It may be a woman whose husband has just suffered a heart attack; she is so out of control that all she can do is scream hysterically into the telephone. But the dispatcher knows where the call is coming from, and he can send help. When those numbers are hit, help is already on the way.

There come times in our lives when we in our desperation and pain run to God and dial our 911 prayers. Sometimes we're hysterical. Sometimes we don't know the words to speak. But God hears. He knows our number and he knows our name and he knows our circumstance. That help is already on the way; God has already begun to bring the remedy to us.

*—Leith Anderson,
Minnesota pastor*

Personal Challenge:
• *Do you insinctively turn to God when you run into trouble?*

Thought to Apply: The best prayers have often been more groans than words.

—JOHN BUNYAN (author of *Pilgrim's Progress,* 17th century)

Securing Your C³I

Key Bible Verse: The weapons we fight with are not the weapons of the world. On the contrary, they have divine power to demolish strongholds *(2 Corinthians 10:4)*. *Bonus Reading: Ephesians 6:12-18*

During Operation Desert Shield, Lt. Gen. Chuck Horner and his staff planned the most elaborate air campaign in the history of warfare. Its objective was to sever command and control of the Iraqi war machine. Without the ability to communicate, Iraqi units in the field would be incapable of sustaining a coordinated defense.

The strategy worked perfectly. After five weeks of intensive bombardment, the Iraqi Command, Control, Communications, and Information (C³I) resources were devastated. Their field elements were operating without "eyes" and "ears."

The analogy with our own spiritual life is obvious. Wearing the full armor of God, described in Ephesians 6, is not enough. If I am disconnected from my heavenly Commander-in-Chief, I am struggling against spiritual forces without His divine wisdom and strength. Thus, Paul concludes the passage with this command: "Pray in the Spirit on all occasions . . . be alert" (Ephesians 6:18).

I must not let the devil separate me from my spiritual C³I! I need to unceasingly communicate with my Master.

—*Colonel Mike Lane, U.S. Air Force, retired*

Personal Challenge:

• *Are you in daily contact with your Commander-in-Chief for orders?*

Thought to Apply: The Christian life is not a playground; it is a battleground.

—WARREN WIERSBE (pastor, broadcaster)

Blunt Terms about Prayer

Key Bible Verse: Very early in the morning, while it was still dark, Jesus got up, left the house and went off to a solitary place, where he prayed *(Mark 1:35).*
Bonus Reading: Colossians 4:2-4

After my ordination, I probably prayed as much as any young priest. But in the mid-1970s I was very busy and fell into the trap of thinking that my good works were more important than prayer.

One evening I spoke to three priests—all younger than I. I told them that I was finding it difficult to pray and asked if they could help me.

"Do you really want to turn this around?" they asked.

What could I say?

In blunt terms they helped me realize that I was urging a spirituality on others that I was not fully practicing myself. That was a turning point in my life. These priests helped me understand that you have to give quality time to prayer. It can't be done "on the run." After all, if we believe that the Lord Jesus is the Son of God, then of all persons to whom we give of ourselves, we should give Him the best we have.

I decided to give God the first hour of my day, no matter what, to be with Him in prayer and meditation to open the door even wider to His entrance. This put my life in a new and uplifting perspective.

—Joseph Bernardin, late archbishop of Chicago

Personal Challenge:
• *Have you given the Lord Jesus the gift of regular quality time with Him?*

Thought to Apply: The great tragedy of life is not unanswered prayer, but unoffered prayer.

—F.B. MEYER (British preacher, early 20th century)

Nobody Else Can Get That Time

Key Bible Verse: Come near to God and he will come near to you *(James 4:8). Bonus Reading: Matthew 26:36-46*

I promised God that I would give the first hour of each day to prayer [and] have kept [this promise] for nearly 20 years. This doesn't mean that I have not experienced the struggles that other people have faced. Quite the contrary.

But early on, I made another decision. I said, "Lord, I know that I spend a certain amount of that hour daydreaming, problem-solving, and I'm not sure that I can cut that out. I'll try, but the important thing is, I'm not going to give that time to anybody else. So even though it may not unite me as much with You as it should, nobody else is going to get that time."

I have found that the effect of that first hour keeps me connected to Him throughout the rest of the day as well. Frequently as I face issues, I think of my relationship to the Lord and ask for His help.

So two important points: Even if it's not used right, you shouldn't give that time to somebody else, you should just keep plugging away. And secondly, if you do give the time, little by little you become united with the Lord throughout your life.

—*Joseph Bernardin, late archbishop of Chicago*

Personal Challenge:
• *Have you, too, found that time focused on the Lord spills over into the rest of your day?*

Thought to Apply: One hour with God infinitely exceeds all the pleasures and delights of this lower world.

—DAVID BRAINERD (missionary to native Americans, 18th century)

A Cool Answer

Key Bible Verse: If you believe, you will receive whatever you ask for in prayer *(Matthew 21:22).*
Bonus Reading: Matthew 7:7-11

When my wife and I were at Dallas Seminary back in the early 1960s, we lived in an apartment since destroyed. In the summer the weather came inside; it was hotter than you can imagine. That hot fall we began to pray for an air conditioner. I remember through the cold, blowing winter we were praying for an air conditioner. We told nobody, made no announcement, wrote no letter; we just prayed.

The following spring, we visited my wife's parents in Houston. It was an unannounced, brief visit before we went back to seminary. One morning the phone rang. On the other end was a man I hadn't talked to in months.

Richard asked to speak to me. I said, "How are you?"

He said, "Great! Do you need an air conditioner?"

I almost dropped the phone. "Uh, yes."

"Well," he said, "we have just put in central air conditioning, and we've got this little three-quarter-ton air conditioner that we thought you might like to have. We'll bring it over and stick it in your trunk, if that's okay."

"That'll be fine, Richard. Bring it on over."

We put that thing in the window. It was so comfortable and cool!
—*Charles R. Swindoll, Dallas Seminary president*

Personal Challenge:
• *When did God clearly answer your prayers?*

Thought to Apply: We carry checks on the bank of heaven and never cash them at the window of prayer.
—VANCE HAVNER (late preacher and evangelist)

Up Close & Personal with Dick Eastman

Why Take Time to Pray?

Q. Why pray?

A. Because Jesus calls us to prayer. I had always believed God answers prayer, but my prayer life was never consistent. During a devotional transformation, I was gripped with the realization that Jesus asked His disciples only one question specifically related to prayer. During His intense experience in Gethsemane, Christ approached His sleeping disciples. Jesus asked, "Could you men not keep watch with me for one hour?" (Matthew 26:40).

Suddenly I realized Jesus was speaking to *me*. I, too, was a follower of Jesus. I was being challenged to make a daily sacrifice of at least one hour of my time specifically for prayer. It was my choice. No one would force me. I could either sleep or pray. I chose the latter—a decision I shall never regret. Although the battles have sometimes been difficult, the victories have always been sweet.

But how can anyone possibly pray an entire hour?

That was a question I, too, had to answer from the moment I determined to personally accept Christ's call to "watch" with Him daily for one hour.

Seeking an answer, I brought the matter before God in prayer. After all, if prayer really works in the first place, then to pray a prayer concerning "how to pray" ought to be the first order of business.

God answered my petition. He showed me how to structure my devotional hour into 12 scripturally-based aspects (described in *The Hour That Changes the World;* Baker,

1978). If an hour seems too lofty a goal—start with 12 minutes. Somehow, the simple act of prayer links a sovereign God to a finite man. When man prays, God responds. Difficult situations change. Unexplained miracles occur.

Dick Eastman is president of Every Home for Christ and originator of the Change the World School of Prayer.

Prayer Sunday, Week 37

For Personal Study or Group Discussion

Real Life Application

Key Bible Verses: Do not be anxious about anything, but in everything, by prayer and petition, with thanksgiving, present your requests to God. And the peace of God, which transcends all understanding, will guard your hearts and your minds in Christ Jesus *(Philippians 4:6-7). Bonus Reading: Philippians 1:9-14*

Think and pray about these sentence starters on your own. Or, if you meet with other men, use them to trigger your discussion.

☐ The time that works best for me to approach God in prayer is . . .

☐ What makes me want to pray is . . .

☐ One evidence that God responds to my prayers is . . .

Credits: Adapted from—Monday: *Preaching Today* (#48); Tuesday: *Command* (12/98); Wednesday and Thursday: *The Gift of Peace* (Loyola, 1997); Friday: *Preaching Today* (#50); Saturday: *The Hour That Changes the World* (Baker, 1978)

Runaway Horse

Key Bible Verses: I will counsel you and watch over you. Do not be like the horse or the mule, which have no understanding but must be controlled by bit and bridle or they will not come to you *(Psalm 32:9). Bonus Reading: Job 5:17-19*

Jess, today you had your first runaway.

It happened innocently enough. One moment we were loping slowly home from a morning's work.

Then gradually, like a drummer increasing tempo, I sensed your horse, Shogun, becoming excited. Suddenly he was stretched out and running with all his might. You tried to pull him in, but there was little your ten-year-old arms could do.

The fault was my own. That morning I had placed a bit on him that was his favorite, but it was the bit your mother and I use on him. We have the strength to pull him up. With you on his back, Jess, I should have put a more severe bit in his mouth.

There will be other runaways, Jess. But they may not happen on a horse.

The first time you fall in love. Your first car. Your first apartment. There may be a financial runaway or two. And certainly some spiritual ones.

But remember this: as we gallop through life's badlands, the runaways will always be more easily controlled if we allow the Lord to place a strong bit in our mouths during the early stages of our training.
—*John L. Moore, Montana rancher and author*

Personal Challenge:
• *How severe of a bit must God use with you to keep you in line with His will?*

Thought to Apply: A compass is narrow minded— it always points to the magnetic north. We must discipline ourselves, personally, to fight any deviation from the course Jesus set for us.   —BILLY GRAHAM (evangelist)

Tennis Bum

Key Bible Verse: Similarly, if anyone competes as an athlete, he does not receive the victor's crown unless he competes according to the rules *(2 Timothy 2:5).*
Bonus Reading: Philippians 3:12-18

In the early summer before entering seventh grade, I picked up a tennis racket for the first time . . . and I was hooked! I became a ten-year-old tennis bum. My memories of this and the summer that followed are of blistering black courts, hot feet, salty sweat.

That fall I determined to become a tennis player.

I was disciplined! I played every day after school and every weekend. When spring came, I biked to the courts where the local high school team practiced and longingly watched until they finally gave in and let me play with them. The next two summers I took lessons, played some tournaments, and practiced about six to eight hours a day—coming home only when they turned off the lights.

And I became good. Good enough, in fact, that as a twelve-and-a-half-year-old, one-hundred-and-ten-pound freshman I was second man on the varsity team of my large, 3,000-student California high school.

Not only did I play at a high level, I learned that personal discipline is the indispensable key for accomplishing anything in this life.

—R. Kent Hughes, author of Disciplines of a Godly Man

Personal Challenge:
• *Do you have a spiritual goal for which you are prepared to go all out to achieve?*

Thought to Apply: Man who man would be, must rule the empire of himself.

—PERCY BYSSHE SHELLEY (English poet, 19th century)

The Hunchback Prince

Key Bible Verse: Do not conform any longer to the pattern of this world, but be transformed by the renewing of your mind *(Romans 12:2a). Bonus Reading: Jeremiah 18:1-11*

You've come to the potter, and he wishes as Romans 12:2 says, to conform you to a better image.

It reminds of that fable of the Persian hunchback prince who would one day take the place of his stately father. Yet he was so deformed that even to imagine himself as a stately monarch was ludicrous.

One day he had an idea: he had the royal sculptor carve his statue exactly as he would look if there were no deformity. They set this statue of an erect, powerful and strong prince in the center of the court.

Each morning the prince took the shirt from his hunched back, backed up to his tall alter ego and tried as hard as he could in a pitiful comedy to throw his own shoulders back against the back of the statue. He worked at it. In discipline he gave himself to it. And there would come in the passing of years one magic day when this no-longer-deformed prince would find the thrill of cold marble touching his own shoulders.

Your gift to God is the discipline of getting the clay free from impurities so that God may better use it.

—*Calvin Miller,*
seminary professor and
author, Fort Worth, Texas

Personal Challenge:
• *Do you perceive any deformities in your life that the potter would want to smooth out?*

Thought to Apply: Do not be afraid of growing slowly, be afraid only of standing still.　　—CHINESE PROVERB

Rewards of Running

Key Bible Verse: Everyone who competes in the games goes into strict training. They do it to get a crown that will not last; but we do it to get a crown that will last forever. *(1 Corinthians 9:25) Bonus Reading: 1 Corinthians 9:24-27*

There was no fitness fad when I was in school. The "cool" athletes did as little as possible to stay in shape, as if to suggest their talent was so great they didn't need conditioning. Conforming to social pressure, I never tried to be a good runner. I trained only under the scrutiny of the coach.

As I ran tonight I thought about the years I had wasted because of rebellion.

As a runner, I am still an outcast. Cowboys aren't supposed to run. They are supposed to ride horses. Perhaps years ago people didn't need to exercise to stay in shape. Before machines, their work was hard and the hours long. Today few people work hard physically. Ranchers and farmers do much of their labor in pickups and tractors. They too easily grow broad of seat and soft of belly.

But running is more than exercise. It is a celebration of life. It is its own reward as you feel your limbs stretch with agility and power and know the freedom of challenging a distance and winning on your terms. It is the reward of subduing and conforming your body, of rewarding yourself with self-respect rather than with sweet foods and leisure.

—John L. Moore, Montana rancher and author

Personal Challenge:
• *Is there an area of your life where you may be going soft?*

Thought to Apply: Do not consider painful what is good for you.   —EURIPEDES (Greek playwright, 5th century)

A Soldier's Soldier

Key Bible Verse: Be diligent in these matters; give yourself wholly to them, so that everyone may see your progress *(1 Timothy 4:15). Bonus Reading: Psalm 119:97-100*

Lt. General William K. Harrison was the most decorated soldier in the 30th Infantry Division, rated by General Eisenhower as the number one infantry division in World War II. When the Korean War began, he served as Chief of Staff in the United Nations Command—and was ultimately President Eisenhower's choice to head the long, tedious negotiations to end the war.

General Harrison was also an amazing man of the Word. When a 20-year-old West Point cadet, he began reading the Old Testament through once a year and the New Testament four times. Even in the thick of war he maintained his commitment by catching up during the two- and three-day respites for replacement and refitting that followed battles, so that when the war ended he was right on schedule.

When, at the age of 90, failing eyesight no longer permitted his discipline, he had read the Old Testament 70 times and the New Testament 280 times! No wonder his godliness and wisdom were proverbial, and that the Lord used him for 18 fruitful years to lead Officers Christian Fellowship.

—*R. Kent Hughes, author of* Disciplines of a Godly Man

Personal Challenge:
• *Realize that working through God's Word allows His Word to work through you.*

Thought to Apply: Beware of saying, "I haven't time to read the Bible, or to pray"; say rather, "I haven't disciplined myself to do these things."

—OSWALD CHAMBERS (Scottish preacher, early 20th century)

Up Close & Personal with Mike Singletary

Why is teaching self-discipline so important? The kind of self-discipline we're teaching our children at home is no different than self-discipline on the football field or at the office or, for that matter, in any aspect of life. Each of us has tasks to carry out. Each of us gets the job done.

When the Chicago Bears were at a peak in the mid 1980s, winning the Super Bowl in 1986, we had an unbeatable defense not only because of the talent of the players but because we all carried out our given assignments. We didn't freelance. We didn't take a day off. We had a plan to execute, and we stuck with it. We demonstrated self-discipline.

Mike Singletary is a former Chicago Bears All-Pro middle linebacker.

For Personal Study or Group Discussion

Key Bible Verse: No discipline seems pleasant at the time, but painful. Later on, however, it produces a harvest of righteousness and peace for those who have been trained by it *(Hebrews 12:11). Bonus Reading: Hebrews 12:1-10*

Think and pray about these sentence starters.

☐ I feel spiritually out of shape in the area of . . .

☐ If I disciplined myself, I could . . .

Credits: Adapted from—Monday and Thursday: *Take the Reins* (Nelson, 1997); Tuesday and Friday: *Disciplines of a Godly Man* (Crossway, 1991); Wednesday: *Preaching Today* (#22); Saturday: with Russ Pate, *Daddy's Home at Last* (Zondervan, 1998)

Facing Death from AIDS

Key Bible Verse: In him we have redemption through his blood, the forgiveness of sins, in accordance with the riches of God's grace *(Ephesians 1:7). Bonus Reading: Psalm 103*

My nephew, I'll call him Kenneth, had AIDS; he was only 25. During a family reunion, Kenneth and I broke away for a walk.

"Kenneth, you are going to die any day," I said. "Do you have eternal life?"

Kenneth said, "I know God has forgiven me and I am going to heaven." Since his early teens, Kenneth had practiced homosexuality. He flaunted his lifestyle.

"How can you say that?" I replied. "You rebelled against God, made fun of the Bible, hurt your family, and now you say you've got eternal life . . . just like that?"

Kenneth looked me straight in the eye, "Luis, when the doctor said I had AIDS I realized what a fool I had been. I repented, and I know God has had mercy on me."

Several months later in excruciating pain, Kenneth went to be with the Lord. My nephew did not deserve God's grace. None of us do, but God's words [see Key Bible Verse] leave no doubt.

That forgiveness is final and freely available to everyone who accepts Christ. All the hanky-panky in your past is washed away through the blood of Christ on the cross.
—*Luis Palau, evangelist*

Personal Challenge:
• *Have you received Christ's redemption? If so, thank God for His undeserved grace to you.*

Thought to Apply: O Christ, the Ocean of forgiveness, allow me to wash off in You the dirt I am clothed in, so that I may become resplendent in the raiment of Your holy light.
—JOHN THE ELDER OF DALYATHA (spiritual writer, 8th century)

After I Pushed Too Hard

Key Bible Verses: Therefore, if you are offering your gift at the altar and there remember that your brother has something against you, leave your gift there in front of the altar. First go and be reconciled to your brother; then come and offer your gift *(Matthew 5:23-24). Bonus Reading: Matthew 18:21-35*

We're teaching our son Bryndan to drive. One morning Bryndan protested when I asked him to drive to take Holly and him to school. I was tired and under stress, so I pushed: "Son, *drive this car.* I'm not asking you, I'm *telling* you."

After I'd let the kids off and started on to my office, I became convicted. *I don't know why I acted that way,* I thought. I turned around and went back to Bryndan's school.

I went to the attendance office and asked if I could see my son. They paged him. When he saw me, I said, "Bryndan, that was terrible. I'm sorry. If you didn't want to drive the car, you didn't have to. I blew it, son. Would you please forgive me?"

Bryndan smiled and said, "Dad, you came all the way back here just to tell me that? That's no big deal."

We hugged right there. Bryndan said, "Look, man, have a good day."

He went off to class, I went to my office, and we *both* had good days.

—Crawford W. Lorrits, Jr., national director, Campus Crusade for Christ's Legacy Ministries

Personal Challenge:

* To whom can you pass on the forgiveness you have received in Christ?

Thought to Apply: Forgiveness needs to be accepted, as well as given, before it is complete.

—C.S. LEWIS (British scholar and writer, 20th century)

No More Nightmare

Key Bible Verse: You have been set free from sin and have become slaves of righteousness *(Romans 6:18)*. *Bonus Reading: Romans 6:11-23*

Picture yourself in a prison cell on death row, having been sentenced to death. A judge suddenly pardons you and orders your freedom. The cell doors open. But you decide to stay in prison. You are free. You will not be executed. But you do not leave and exercise your freedom. This is the picture of a believer who is free but chooses to continue letting sins invade his life.

The Living Bible paraphrases Romans 6:11: "So look upon your old sin nature as dead and unresponsive to sin, and instead be alive to God, alert to him, through Jesus Christ our Lord."

Act on the fact! The phrase "live in reality" reflects this truth. We all know of men who live in a dream world. But many men live in a nightmare world of captivity to sin. The nightmare is not real, but we can act as though it were, which leads to fear and incapacity.

We need to act on truth—the truth that we have died to sin in Christ. That is our position. We now need to live in accordance with our position as sons of God.

—Jerry White, president of The Navigators and a major general in the Air Force Reserve

Personal Challenge:
• *Thank God for the freedom He has made available.*

Thought to Apply: Sin forsaken is one of the best evidences of sin forgiven.
—JOHN CHARLES RYLE (Anglican bishop, 19th century)

Dragging an Inner Tube

Key Bible Verse: Therefore, since we are surrounded by such a cloud of witnesses, let us throw off everything that hinders and the sin that so easily entangles, and let us run with perseverance the race marked out for us *(Hebrews 12:1). Bonus Reading: Hebrews 12:2-3*

When I was in high school, about three o'clock in the morning a group of us decided to go swimming at the pool of an exclusive club at a hotel. We climbed over the gate, got to the pool unnoticed and had a great time swimming—for about five minutes.

Then one of the guys jumped off the high diving board sitting on a big inner tube. When he hit the water, he created a sound like a shotgun blast. It echoed against the side of the hotel; lights started going on everywhere. We all ran, except for this guy. When I looked backed, I saw him dragging the huge inner tube, sometimes tripping over it. I yelled, "Man, drop that dumb thing. You're going to get into bad trouble."

Our sin is like that inner tube; it hinders our running. Sin will always weigh you down; it will discourage you and make you depressed. Lying, adultery and stealing will do that. Greed, lust and bitterness will also do that. Whatever your sin, throw it away, purge it from you life.

—*Steve Brown, teacher and broadcaster*

Personal Challenge:
• *Is there a sin that is tripping you up? Ask God to purge it from your life.*

Thought to Apply: No sin is small. No grain of sand is small in the mechanism of a watch.

—JEREMY TAYLOR (Christian writer, 17th century)

"You Hurt My Heart"

Key Bible Verse: Be kind and compassionate to one another, forgiving each other, just as in Christ God forgave you *(Ephesians 4:32). Bonus Reading: Ephesians 4:30-5:2*

Walking to school with a few friends, all about 12 years old, we passed a factory that made chains for necklaces. Open boxes of their wares sat on the sidewalk. Overcome by mutual peer pressure and temptation, we scooped up a few handfuls and ran like crazy.

Over the next weeks, these friends stole several boxes of chains, were caught, and said I was part of their group. That evening the police came to our apartment. Confronted with the charges, I lied. But Pop made me open my dresser drawers; beneath my undershorts were those chains!

The officer said that the factory manager wanted to see us. My father drove us, made us own up, apologize and offer to pay. The manager graciously said that he wouldn't press charges.

When we got home, he did something worse than any spanking. Pop cried. He said, "Boy, if you wanted something, why didn't you ask me? You don't ever have to steal anything." Then came the clincher, Pop said, "You hurt my heart."

[From then on,] whenever I was tempted, I saw that tear trickling down my father's cheek.
—*Crawford W. Lorrits, Jr., national director, Campus Crusade for Christ's Legacy Ministries*

Personal Challenge:
• *Are you covering a sin that would make God the Father shed tears?*

Thought to Apply: It may well be that human sins afflict with grief even God himself.

—ORIGEN (theologian, 3rd century)

Up Close & Personal with Christoph Arnold

How to Find Full Forgiveness

Q. What would you say to people who don't feel forgiven?

A. Repentance has nothing to do with self-torment. We must be truly sorry for our sins, but we must also turn from them and look to God. If we look only to ourselves, we are sure to despair. Once we have cried our tears of remorse, we must stand back and allow the muddy waters of our hearts to clear—otherwise we will never see to the bottom of anything.

The grace that follows repentance is not just a feeling, it is a reality. Sins are forgiven and forgotten, never to be remembered or mentioned again. Suddenly, life is once again worth living.

Why is it so hard to forgive others?
Millions of Christians recite the Lord's Prayer every day. We ask God to "forgive us as we forgive our debtors," but do we really mean what we say? Too often, we repeat these holy words without a thought to their meaning: that when we recognize our own need for forgiveness, we will be able to forgive.

When we see how badly we need forgiveness ourselves, we will be filled with love and compassion for others. And when we realize how deeply we have hurt others, our own deep hurts will fade away.

What can forgiveness really do in our lives?
Forgiveness is power. It breaks the curse of sin, it frees us from our past, it overcomes every evil. It could change the world, if we would only allow it to flow through us unchecked.

We hold the keys to forgiveness in our hands, and we must choose whether or not to use them every day. Far too often we refuse to believe that He can work in others whom we deem unworthy—in our eyes, at least, they have sinned one time too many. We readily accept God's mercy for ourselves but refuse to extend it to others. We doubt that God can really change them.

Johann Christoph Arnold is senior elder of the Bruderhof, a Christian community movement in the northeastern U.S., and in England.

For Personal Study or Group Discussion

Real Life Application

Key Bible Verse: For Christ died for sins once for all, the righteous for the unrighteous, to bring you to God. He was put to death in the body but made alive by the Spirit *(1 Peter 3:18). Bonus Reading: 1 Peter 4:1-5*

Think and pray about these sentence starters on your own. Or, if you meet with other men, use them to trigger your discussion.

☐ I know my sins are forgiven by God because . . .

☐ I need to ask forgiveness from . . .

☐ I need to offer my forgiveness to . . .

Credits: Adapted from—Monday: *The Peter Promise* (Discovery House, 1996); Tuesday and Friday: *Never Walk Away* (Moody Press, Moody Bible Institute of Chicago, 1997); Wednesday: *Dangers Men Face* (NavPress, 1997); Thursday: *Jumping Hurdles* (Baker, 1992); Saturday: *Seventy Times Seven* (Plough, 1997)

Rag Doll

Key Bible Verse: This is love: not that we loved God, but that he loved us and sent his Son as an atoning sacrifice for our sins *(1 John 4:10). Bonus Reading: Isaiah 50:4-11*

Rosemarie was three. We had traveled from Britain to Australia as a family. A group had come to greet us. Among them was a lady who realized there was going to be a little girl arriving on a plane jet-lag silly, and brought a little rag doll made for the occasion.

When we got to Melbourne Airport, Rosemarie was quietly crying tears of exhaustion. The kind lady gave her the doll. Rosemarie was too tired even to say "Thank you," but immediately the rag doll went to her face to hide the tears. That night she went to bed still quietly crying, still hugging the doll. The next night the tears were gone, but not the doll. Nor the next week, month or year. She had other toys intrinsically far more valuable, none loved like the doll.

As years went by, it became more rag, less doll. If you tried to clean it, it became more ragged; if you didn't, it became dirtier. The sensible thing—to trash the rags—was unthinkable for anyone who loved my kid. It was part of a package.

Illogical? Maybe. But thank God it happens. Some things are loved because they're valuable; some are valuable because they're loved.

—Ian Pitt-Watson, pastor

Personal Challenge

• *Do you really believe you are valuable because you are loved by God?*

Thought to Apply: God carries your picture in his wallet.

—TONY CAMPOLO (Sociology professor and author)

In Spite of Ourselves

Key Bible Verse: We love because he first loved us *(1 John 4:19). Bonus Reading: Isaiah 52:13-53:12*

A friend told me about a boy who was the apple of his parents' eyes. Tragically, in his mid-teens, the boy's life went awry. He dropped out of school and began associating with the worst kind of crowds. One night he staggered into his house at 3:00 a.m., completely drunk. His mother slipped out of bed and left her room. The father followed, assuming that his wife was in the kitchen, perhaps crying. Instead he found her at her son's bedside, softly stroking his matted hair as he lay passed out drunk on the covers. "What are you doing?" the father asked, and the mother simply answered,

"He won't let me love him when he's awake."

The mother stepped into her son's darkness with a love that existed even though he did not yet love her back. So it is with God and us. He loves us often in spite of ourselves, even when we would reject Him. But in time, the knowledge of that wonderful, searching, forgiving, cleansing love sinks in. And once we are gripped by it, what can we do but [as our key verse says] love God in return?

—*Michael B. Brown in*
God's Man

Personal Challenge:
• *Recall a time when you have seen love prevail over indifference or rejection.*

Thought to Apply: Lord let me live long enough to see those fellows saved who killed our boys, that I may throw my arms around them and tell them I love them because they love my Christ.

—T. E. McCully (Father of Ed McCully, Ecuador missionary slain in 1956)

"He Gave His *Life* for Me"

Key Bible Verse: Greater love has no one than this, that he lay down his life for his friends *(John 15:3)*. *Bonus Reading: Psalm 22:1-21*

I remember the massive homecoming parade for Vietnam veterans in Chicago. One vet was interviewed on camera, standing by the mobile Vietnam Memorial Wall.

The newscaster asked why he had come all the way to Chicago to participate in this parade. The soldier, with tears flowing down his face, said, "Because of this man right here." He was pointing to the name of a friend etched on the wall. "He gave his *life* for me." As that news clip ended, the sobbing soldier continued to trace the name with his finger.

Soon you are going to come to a memorial service called Communion. We're going to say with wonder, "He gave His life for *me!* The sinless Son of God died in my place."

That's the central message of the Christian faith: "For God so loved the world. . ." People mattered so much to God that He provided His Son Jesus to die in the place of people who deserved to die eternally—as a payment for their sin, so that guilty, undeserving parties like you and me could go free.

—Bill Hybels, Illinois pastor

Personal Challenge:
• *Take a minute to thank God for His love demonstrated by Jesus' death.*

Thought to Apply: The love of God, with arms extended on a cross, bars the way to hell. But if that love is ignored, rejected, and finally refused, there comes a time when love can only weep while man pushes into the self-chosen alienation which Christ went to the cross to avert.

—MICHAEL GREEN (Anglican educator)

Solitary Confinement

Key Bible Verse: Who shall separate us from the love of Christ? Shall trouble or hardship or persecution or famine or nakedness or danger or sword? *(Romans 8:35).*
Bonus Reading: Romans 8:36-39

Benjamin Weir was held captive by terrorists in Lebanon for 18 months—15 in solitary confinement. They put him in a small room with a mattress on the floor and a radiator. One arm was always handcuffed to the radiator. The window had venetian blinds. There was no other furniture. An old stuffed bird sat in one corner. Where there had been a chandelier in the ceiling, three loose wires stuck down.

Ben said, "I began to use what was there to remind myself of the love of God. Those three wires reminded me of the way God's hand comes down and touches the hand of Adam in Michelangelo's Sistine Chapel ceiling. This meant God's gift of life." He counted the slats in the blinds to remind himself that he was surrounded by a cloud of witnesses. The bird he used to represent the Holy Spirit. The cracks in the walls, the places the plaster were marred—each he identified with some promise in Scripture. He would repeat to himself each day passages he had long ago hidden in his heart. Out of this focusing upon the love of God, he kept hold of himself for 15 months alone.

　　　　—Bruce Thielemann,
　　　　late Pennsylvania pastor

Personal Challenge:

• *Praise God for the bedrock of his love that we can cling to when everything else fails us.*

Thought to Apply: Love is the greatest thing that God can give us, for He is love: and it is the greatest thing we can give God.　　—JEREMY TAYLOR (Anglican writer, 17th century)

What Ruby Was Saying

Key Bible Verse: Jesus said, "Father, forgive them, for they do not know what they are doing" *(Luke 23:34).*
Bonus Reading: Matthew 5:34-47

In a speech given at Gordon-Conwell Seminary, Dr. Robert Coles, a child psychiatrist, related this story. He was in New Orleans when a federal judge ordered marshals to escort a six-year-old black girl named Ruby Bridges to integrate a public school.

Her parents could neither read nor write. At the time, her father had lost his job. To support her family, her mother scrubbed floors at night. Ruby entered and left school to the taunts and threats of a mob gathered outside.

Her teacher noticed her lips moving as she passed the mob and told Dr. Coles about it. When he asked Ruby what she was saying, she replied, "I wasn't talking to them, I was praying, 'God, please forgive them; they don't realize what they are doing.'"

Motivated by the love of Jesus Christ, this six-year-old loved her enemies with His love. Dr. Coles then said to his audience of seminarians, "You know a lot, but your goodness doesn't come from your knowledge. Goodness only comes from something deeper and more powerful." Our goodness comes *only* from the transforming power of God's love at work in us.

—Hudson Armerding,
president emeritus of
Wheaton College

Personal Challenge:
• *Think of one person you dislike whom you could begin to love as a response to Christ's love.*

Thought to Apply: Give me such a love for God and men as will blot out all hatred and bitterness.

—DIETRICH BONHOEFFER (German pastor hanged by Hitler)

Up Close & Personal with Chuck Colson

Feeling God's Love

In his book, *Loving God*, Charles Colson records an imagined dialogue between "Dave Chapman," an old out-of-state friend, and "Dr. Jack Newman," a well-known theologian:

Dave: Sometimes I don't know if I ever really felt the love of God. I just don't feel anything.
Jack: The fact that you really want to love God is a good sign. Let me ask you this. Do you love your wife?

Dave: Yes, very much. You don't stay married these days if you don't.
Jack: There ever come a time after you'd been married a while when you wondered whether you loved her at all?

Dave: Oh, sure. That's normal.
Jack: What changed things?

Dave: I don't know—just time mostly.
Jack: But you stayed faithful to your vows and to her, despite how you felt, right?

Dave: Yes, I've been lucky— never been tempted much.
Jack: I mean more than that, I mean you tried to love Kay as much as you could, despite your feelings.

Dave: Well, sure. It wasn't always easy though.
Jack: Right. Now what you need to learn is how to do the same thing with Christ. You promised Him something—to commit your life to Him and love

and obey Him. So you do that no matter how you feel. And the longer and more you do that—obey Him—then you'll begin to feel your love for Him and His love in return just like you did with Kay.

Charles Colson, president and founder of Prison Fellowship, is also a columnist and author.

God's Love

For Personal Study or Group Discussion

Real Life Application

Key Bible Verse: For Christ's love compels us, because we are convinced that one died for all, and therefore all died *(2 Corinthians 5:14). Bonus Reading: 2 Corinthians 5:15-21*

Think and pray about these sentence starters on your own. Or, if you meet with other men, use them to trigger your discussion.

☐ I couldn't feel the love of God when . . .

☐ I know God loves me because . . .

☐ When I think about how much God loves me, I feel motivated to respond by . . .

Credits: Adapted from—Monday: *Preaching Today* (#40); Tuesday: Don M. Aycock, *God's Man* (Kregel, 1998); Wednesday: *Preaching Today* (#43); Thursday: *Preaching Today* (#48); Friday: *Command* (12/98); Saturday: *Loving God* (Zondervan, 1983)

Learning Faith in the Duck Blind

Key Bible Verse: We did this ... in order to make ourselves a model for you to follow *(Philippians 4:9).*
Bonus Reading: Philippians 3:6-10

Chet Ellingson, a businessman in our town, often invited me to go hunting with him. On autumn mornings in the cold dark, I would climb into his Buick. A half-hour later, we would be in Pink Miller's duck blind in a marshy backwater of the Flathead River, waiting for the mallards to come in. I shivered there with my twelve-gauge Winchester, waiting, talking, feeling adult.

The "Christian thing"—his phrase—was implicit in our conversation but never seemed to be the explicit subject. Jesus and Spirit and Scripture were expressed in the shivering cold offhandedly. I can't remember him ever instructing me or giving me advice. There was no hint of condescension or authority. The faith was simply there, spoken and acted out in the midst of whatever else we were doing—shooting, rowing, retrieving; or, at other times, working or worshiping or meeting on the street.

He become a bridge on which I traveled from immaturity to maturity. He connected me with an adulthood that was virtually synonymous with "Christian." Through those confused and awkward years of adolescence, when I was with him I was, without being particularly conscious of it, an adult believer in Jesus.
—*Eugene H. Peterson,
writer, Bible translator*

Personal Challenge:
• *When you were young, who was a good example for you?*

Thought to Apply: A holy life will produce the deepest impression. Lighthouses blow no horns; they only shine.
—DWIGHT L. MOODY (evangelist, 19th century)

The Power of a Mentor

Key Bible Verse: Therefore I urge you to imitate me
(1 Corinthians 4:16). Bonus Reading: 1 Corinthians 4:14-17

I will never forget Brandt, a long-haired, bearded Christian who fit all the stereotypes of southern California's Jesus People.

I first noticed Brandt at lunchtime as he sat cross-legged among a circle of students on the lawn of the high school that I attended. Students had gathered around him, intent on discussing the Bibles open on their laps. Brandt had a zeal for evangelism and had adopted my high school as a mission field.

Soon I became a part of the lunchtime circle and got to know Brandt. One day, sensing my spiritual hunger, he asked if I would like to meet—just the two of us—for lunch once a week at a local restaurant.

I was flattered by his personal interest in me. So, week in and week out, throughout my senior year of high school, Brandt helped me to apply to daily decisions what I was learning about my faith. How often should I pray? How should I relate to my parents? What does it mean to stay sexually pure?

I graduated and lost touch with Brandt when I went on to college. But even though I had been only 16 when we were meeting together, Brandt's influence has stayed with me for more than 25 years.

—*Timothy Jones, writer*

Personal Challenge:
• *What do people see in you that draws them to Christ?*

Thought to Apply: Always do right. This will surprise some people and astonish the rest.

—MARK TWAIN (writer, 19th century)

The Seat-Belt Test

Key Bible Verse: In everything set them an example by doing what is good *(Titus 2:7a)*. *Bonus Reading: 2 Corinthians 1:12-14*

A father I know just finished wrestling with what some may consider an insignificant matter—wearing his seat belt. For years he had only bothered wearing it when traveling several hours or on busy freeways. But then something significant and scary happened. His oldest child, a daughter, began driver's education classes at school.

That's when he started wearing his seat belt every time he got in the car, recognizing that no matter what he *tells* his children, the life he *lives* communicates what he really believes. His desire to send a consistent message to his children was important enough that he decided to make a lifestyle change.

Modeling is at the heart of effective fathering, as we attempt to balance our internal commitments with external actions, to practice what we preach. Our children depend on that consistency.

Fathers have extraordinary power in modeling behavior they desire their children to emulate. A father who walks what he talks and leads by example will shape the next generation in a lasting way. But our words and deed must be in harmony.

—Ken Canfield, president National Center for Fathering

Personal Challenge:
• *What's one area where your stated and practiced beliefs match up?*

Thought to Apply: There is just one way to bring up a child in the way he should go and that is to travel that way yourself. —ABRAHAM LINCOLN (U.S. President during the Civil War)

"You Know What, Dad?"

Key Bible Verse: Whatever you have learned or received or heard from me, or seen in me—put it into practice. And the God of peace will be with you *(Philippians 4:9). Bonus Reading: 1 Peter 5:1-4*

A few weeks ago, I was in the car with my two boys. John is 16 and Josh is 13. We were stopped at a traffic light. As we waited, a woman crossed the street in front of us. She was wearing the minimum. And she wanted every guy at the intersection to notice.

A few minutes later, John said, "You know what, Dad? You never look."

"Look at what?"

"You never look at women."

"How do you know I don't look at women?"

"Because I watch you all the time. I've watched you on airplanes, I've watched you in restaurants, I've watched you at the beach, and I watched you back there at that intersection. And I have never seen you look. Not once."

"Well, John, I saw that woman, and so did you. But you have to train yourself to look away immediately when you see someone like that."

"That's what I mean, Dad. You look away. And that's what you tell those guys at your conferences to do. I've heard you tell them that for years. That's why I watch you so closely. I want to see if you will do what you say a man should do."

—*Steve Farrar, founder Men's Leadership Ministries Dallas, Texas*

Personal Challenge:
• *Do you look?*

Thought to Apply: Men best show their character by trifles, where they are not on their guard.

—ARTHUR SCHOPENHAUER (German philosopher, 19th century)

How I Became a Hero

Key Bible Verse: ... Set an example for the believers in speech, in life, in love, in faith and in purity *(1 Timothy 4:12). Bonus Reading: 1 Timothy 4:11-16*

Some 20 years ago, I was a big brother to a boy whose parents had divorced. Brian was figuring out his identity as a young man and a son. Dee and I were newly married with no children yet. Brian's mother was eager for me to spend some time with him.

Brian and I spent nearly every Saturday together, and I'll never forget the way he watched me and listened to everything I said. We never did anything extravagant— usually just shot baskets or hung out together. But that's when I realized that it's on God's heart to provide a male role model for the fatherless.

One day I sat down and wrote Brian a letter. It said something like:

Dear Brian,
I'm looking forward to getting together again with you this Saturday. I've enjoyed our time together, and I just want you to know that you're a great guy to be around.
Your big brother,
Ken

The next time I went to see Brian, my letter was proudly displayed on his wall with posters of the sports heroes of the day. When I saw it, I realized the impact I could have in Brian's life.

—*Ken Canfield, president of the National Center for Fathering*

Personal Challenge:
• *Is there someone for whom you could be a big brother or substitute dad?*

Thought to Apply: Of all commentaries upon the Scriptures, good examples are the best and liveliest.

—JOHN DONNE (Anglican pastor, poet, 17th century)

Up Close & Personal with Ken Canfield

Q. Why is consistency so important in shaping our children?

A. Children need to know what to expect. If you are inconsistent, they become lost in a large and frightening world.

A consistent father governs his moods. He is not affectionate one minute and angry the next. When he makes a promise, his children can count on his keeping it. If he preaches to his kids about lying, he doesn't turn around and cheat on his tax returns.

Ken Canfield is president of the National Center for Fathering and is the father of five children.

For Personal Study or Group Discussion

Key Bible Verse: And so you became a model to all the believers in Macedonia and Achaia *(1 Thessalonians 1:7).*
Bonus Reading: 1 Thessalonians 1:4-10

Think and pray about these sentence starters on your own. Or, if you meet with other men, use them to trigger your discussion.

☐ When I think about youngsters following in my steps, I feel motivated to work on . . .

☐ One way I've been able to model my faith is . . .

Credits: Adapted from—Monday: *Leap Over a Wall* (HarperCollins, 1997); Tuesday: *Decision* (12/98); Wednesday and Friday: *Spiritual Secrets of Faithful Fathers* (Beacon Hill, 1997); Thursday: *Anchor Man* (Thomas Nelson, 1998); Saturday: *The 7 Secrets of Effective Fathers* (Tyndale, 1992)

Sometimes God Allows It

Key Bible Verse: He who works his land will have abundant food, but he who chases fantasies lacks judgment *(Proverbs 12:11). Bonus Reading: Proverbs 14:23-24, 20:17-18, 27:23-24*

My friend Fred Smith was once approached by a businessman who had run a multi-million dollar business into the ground. Many people had lost their jobs, and there had been great financial loss to the investors.

This man said to Fred, "I don't know what God is trying to teach me."

Amazed but calm, Fred said, "God is teaching you that you have made some stupid decisions."

Fred says that pagans blame failure on luck and Christians blame it on God, but in the end there isn't much difference. Failure is failure, and sometimes God allows it.

But let me tell you something you ought to remember: God has no vested interest in the failure of His people. He would honor you that you might honor Him. Nevertheless, the Christian who ignores good business practices (or good relational dynamics or good educational philosophy or good church management), thinking God will clean up his or her mess, is in for a rude awakening. "Do not be deceived: God cannot be mocked. A man reaps what he sows" (Galatians 6:7).

—Steve Brown, broadcaster

Personal Challenge:

• *If you are in a mess, how is God allowing it to teach a lesson?*

Thought to Apply: We learn wisdom from failure much more than from success. . . . Probably he who never made a mistake never made a discovery.

—SAMUEL SMILES (Scottish writer, 19th century)

Failing Grade

Key Bible Verse: [He] redeems your life from the pit and crowns you with love and compassion *(Psalm 103:4)*.
Bonus Reading: Acts 15:36-40, 2 Timothy 4:11

When I entered the Air Force I embarked on a year of pilot training. In the final phase, in my formation check ride, I made an error on take-off that allowed the nose wheel to become "cocked" on the power run-up at the end of the runway. This caused me to fall behind the lead aircraft about 50 yards.

I got caught in its jet wash, and the plane suddenly banked in a dangerous way. I was shaken! The rest of the flight was a disaster.

On a recheck two days later I flew reasonably well, but the check pilot simply said, "You can fly it, but not well enough to fly four-ship formation." He gave me a failing grade, and I was out!

Up to this point in my life I had not failed in any significant way. Why be in the Air Force if I could not fly? So I asked God, and the Air Force, to give me an engineering assignment anywhere. I planned to serve my mandatory three years and get out.

God intervened and put me in the new space program. I could not have planned it better. But first God had to wound my pride.
—*Jerry White, president of the Navigators and a major general in the Air Force Reserve*

Personal Challenge:
• *Thank God for a time when you blew it but He turned things around for you.*

Thought to Apply: When it is dark enough, you can see the stars. —CHARLES A. BEARD (American historian, early 20th century)

Sore Muscles

Key Bible Verse: Restore us, O God; make your face shine upon us, that we may be saved *(Psalm 80:3).* *Bonus Reading: Matthew 26:69-75, John 21:15-19*

While it's always more fun winning than losing, every time I have ever run for something and lost, some type of "resurrection" has followed. When I lost my race for Congress, I was appointed state auditor. After I lost my race to stay in as state auditor, I ended up running for, and winning, the position of attorney general. In the '90s, my failure to be elected chairman of the Republican National Committee led to my successful race for the United States Senate.

We don't like the losses in life. They don't leave behind the sweet aftertaste of victory. Sometimes they leave us feeling nothing more than the sore muscles of defeat. But those sore muscles signify that growth is taking place, leading to something even better.

Here is what I learned from my dad: through the ups and downs of failure and success, we become better people, and as better people, God can call us to bigger jobs. As we travel through the peaks of acclaim and the valleys of rejection, we can take heart that it is the journey, not just the destination, that carries meaning and fulfillment.

—John Ashcroft, U.S. Senator and former Missouri governor

Personal Challenge:

• *How have you benefited from the "ups and downs of failure and success"?*

Thought to Apply: If you run into a wall, don't turn around and give up. Figure out how to climb it, go through it, or work around it.

—MICHAEL JORDAN (guard, Chicago Bulls)

A Sign You're Really Leading

Key Bible Verse He leads me beside quiet waters, he restores my soul *(Psalm 23:2b-3a).*
Bonus Reading: Psalm 23:1-6

Within six weeks I knew in my gut I had made a dreadful error. I had enthusiastically endorsed the hiring of a grossly incompetent staff member. We lost a small fortune, wasted three years and damaged our reputation before I could finally get him out.

Learning from failure is hard work. Learning from success is much more fun. But if I am leaning forward, taking the risks of visionary leadership, sometimes I will fail. Worst of all, sometimes those failures will not be just technical or planning failures; they may be failures of the spirit, failures of moral or ethical character, or even failures of sheer folly—like not waiting to check one more reference.

I admitted my failure to the staff, explained what I had learned from it, and requested forgiveness and support to keep leading.

My action set an important example. I made it plain that leaders must take reasonable risks and, in the process of leading, will sometimes fail. When they do, they must own it openly but not let it crush them.

—*Richard Kriegbaum,
consultant and former
college president*

Personal Challenge:
• *Have you moved on from failure by acknowledging it but then not letting it crush you?*

Thought to Apply: The God of redemption . . . buys back our blunders and sins and weaves them into the fabric of a beautiful future.

—Richard Kriegbaum

God Doesn't Want Our Success

Key Bible Verse: But he said to me, "My grace is suffi-cient for you, for my power is made perfect in weakness" *(2 Corinthians 12:9a). Bonus Reading: 1 Corinthians 2:1-5*

Waiting to speak in a prison chapel, the founder of Prison Fellowship, ex-White House staffer Chuck Colson, let his mind drift back:

"All at once I realized it was *not* my success God had used to enable me to help those in this prison, or in hun-dreds of others like it. My greatest humiliation—being sent to prison—was the beginning of God's greatest use of my life; He chose the one experience in which I could not glory for *His* glory.

"I understood with a jolt that only when I lost every-thing I thought made Chuck Colson a great guy had I found the true self God intended me to be and the true purpose of my life.

"It is not what we do that matters, but *what a sovereign God chooses to do through us*. God doesn't want our success; He wants us. The kingdom of God is a kingdom of paradox, where through the ugly defeat of a cross, a holy God is utterly glorified.

"Of course, our success-mad, egocentric culture can-not grasp that crucial truth. It is understandable only when the false values that obsess us are stripped away, sometimes in the midst of our most abject failures."

Personal Challenge:
• *How has God used a defeat in your life for His glory?*

Thought to Apply: It's the nature of God to make some-thing out of nothing; therefore, when anyone is noth-ing, God may yet make something of him.

—MARTIN LUTHER (Protestant Reformer, 16th century)

Up Close & Personal with John Block

Pulling Out of a Slump

Q. What was the low moment in your NBA career?

A. I was still a relatively young player with a relatively young team, the San Diego Rockets. I was a starter and one of the leading scorers. Then, during a game, I injured my back. After missing a few games and practices, I came back—but not 100 percent.

I was not one of those great players who could jump back into the game after an injury and play as if I'd never been gone. I had to gain confidence as I went along. But when the coach finally put me into the game during the last few minutes of the first half, I proceeded to make practically every mistake known to basketball. I stumbled, missed the ball, let my man score, traveled—it was horrible. I dragged myself into the locker room with the humiliating sounds of an arena-full of "boos" echoing in my ears.

We lost 16 of the next 17 games. Every time I took off my jersey or touched the basketball, the crowd booed. I had become their favorite scapegoat.

How did you pull out of this playing slump?

My coach came to me one day after practice and said, "John, we've got to turn this thing around or your career is going to end." Knowing that many athletes play well against certain teams, and that the team I played well against, the Cincinnati Royals, was coming to town, I told the coach, "Don't play me tonight. Let me wait and start against Cincinnati. The fans won't boo a starter." Looking back, I know now that my response was from the Lord.

I have always appreciated my coach's decision to go

along. Not only did our team start doing better, but I went on to enjoy a long and successful NBA career. Following God's leading, I moved from being stuck in depression and defeat to seeing a dream become a reality.

John Block played on the NBA 1972-73 All-Star team.

Dealing with Failure

For Personal Study or Group Discussion

Real Life Application

Key Bible Verses: And the God of all grace, who called you to his eternal glory in Christ, after you have suffered a little while, will himself restore you and make you strong, firm and steadfast. To him be the power for ever and ever. Amen *(1 Peter 5:10-11). Bonus Reading: Isaiah 43:1-7*

Think and pray about these sentence starters on your own. Or, if you meet with other men, use them to trigger your discussion.

☐ A lesson that a failure taught me is . . .

☐ If I were stuck in defeat, what would help me regain confidence is . . .

☐ What God has used to make me strong, firm and steadfast is . . .

Credits: Adapted from—Monday: *Jumping Hurdles* (Baker, 1992); Tuesday: *Dangers Men Face* (NavPress, 1997); Wednesday: *Lesson from a Father to His Son* (Thomas Nelson, 1998); Thursday: *Leadership Prayers* (Tyndale, 1998); Friday: *Loving God* (Zondervan, 1983); Saturday: Rosey Grier and Kathi Mills, *Winning* (Regal, 1990)

Stranglehold

Key Bible Verse: Having lost all sensitivity, they have given themselves over to sensuality so as to indulge in every kind of impurity, with a continual lust for more *(Ephesians 4:19). Bonus Reading: Ephesians 4:17-24*

How can a relatively normal adolescent be transformed into a person who rapes, kills, cuts up, cooks and eats boys? How can a Jeffrey Dalhmer get that sick? One pornographic image, one experience at a time. Sin never says "enough!"

As with any addiction, we build up tolerance, then need more of the substance to receive the same high. When someone looks at pornography, the chemical dopamine is released in the brain, bringing intense pleasure. That chemical, although internally produced, can become addictive. Reinforcing that experience with an orgasm makes it even more intense.

In leading support groups for sex addicts, I have observed a scary pattern. These men are moving from soft-porn to hard-porn to picking up prostitutes or molesting kids, and then on to more life-threatening behavior.

Don't give Satan a chance to do this in your life. Footholds in a believer's life can grow to strongholds. Unchecked, a stronghold ends up a stranglehold!
—Lew Gervais, director of Pressing Onward support groups

Personal Challenge:
• *What do you need to do to keep Satan from winning any footholds in your life?*

Thought to Apply: You cannot play with the animal in you without becoming wholly animal. . . . He who wants to keep his garden tidy doesn't reserve a plot for weeds.
—DAG HAMMARSKJOLD (United Nations secretary general in the 1950s)

Breaking the Pattern

Key Bible Verse: Finally, brothers, whatever is true, whatever is noble, whatever is right, whatever is pure, whatever is lovely, whatever is admirable—if anything is excellent or praiseworthy—think about such things *(Philippians 4:8). Bonus Reading: Ephesians 5:3-20*

A Christian leader told of his ten-year bondage to the sin of lust, which included a regular diet of pornography. The agony of his inner conflict finally became unbearable. To his horror he realized one day that such pleasures as a breathtaking sunset or the soft spray of an ocean breeze no longer excited him. His obsession with lust had dulled his appreciation of life's finest enjoyments and prevented the joy of fellowshiping with Jesus. Outwardly he had not engaged in adultery. Yet he had sinned against his wife. When he turned anew to God, he realized that a necessary step in the breaking of his lustful pattern was a long talk with his mate. The whole experience was painful and awkward, but the repentance was genuine.

She forgave him, and new love returned to their marriage.

C.S. Lewis said that "... a Christian is not a man who never goes wrong, but a man who is enabled to repent and pick himself up and begin over again after each stumble—because the Christ-life is inside him, repairing him all the time."
—Jerry White, president of The Navigators

Personal Challenge:
• *Are you allowing Christ to do his repairing work in your life?*

Thought to Apply: Sex involves the entire life and personality, and to misuse sex is to abuse oneself as well as one's partner.   —HAROLD P. WELLS (author)

Pulling Satan's Arm

Key Bible Verse: Do not offer the parts of your body to sin, as instruments of wickedness, but rather offer yourselves to God, as those who have been brought from death to life; and offer the parts of your body to him as instruments of righteousness *(Romans 6:13).*
Bonus Reading: Romans 6:1-14

I n college I took several semesters of martial arts. They drummed into us to use our opponent's weight to our advantage. They taught us, when he threw a punch, not to block his punch but to tug on his punching arm, throwing him off balance. The same principle holds in the spiritual dimension.

Some people play slot machines for 20 hours or more without stopping. What keeps them there is the occasional time when they win just a little. Our enemy is no different. When he tempts us and we give in to that temptation he will continue to use that temptation to make us fall.

But if every time our enemy tempts us to lust, that temptation causes us to immediately pray, Satan will soon quit tempting us in that area. Deciding to make Satan's temptation work like an alarm that drives us to the foot of the cross is like pulling on his arm when he throws a punch.

—Lew Gervais, director of Pressing Onward support groups

Personal Challenge:
• *Determine to use Satan's temptation as an opportunity to pray.*

Thought to Apply: There can never be peace in the bosom of a believer. There is peace with God, but constant war with sin.

—ROBERT MURRAY MCCHEYNE (Scottish pastor, 19th century)

Blinkers

Key Bible Verse: I made a covenant with my eyes not to look lustfully at a girl *(Job 31:1)*.
Bonus Reading: Proverbs 7:1-27

One of the more popular paraphrases [of the key Bible verse] says: ". . . how then could I ogle at a girl?" (MLB). You couldn't put it any more practically. The "eyegate" is a marvel, but it also opens to our experience a whole world of sensuality. When dealing with that kind of temptation, you've got to make that kind of covenant.

The Bible also mentions looking straight ahead and not turning to the right or the left. See Proverbs 4:25: "Let your eyes look directly ahead, and let your gaze be fixed straight in front of you."

In the oriental city of Naha on Okinawa, I used to take a little bus down to the place where a group of men in the military gathered for Bible study. I got off the bus at a particular corner and had to walk about six blocks, since this was as far as the bus would take us. Okinawa was unique—it had more bars per mile than any island in the South Pacific. There was just one sensual opportunity after another along the way. Each joint was an open door to lustful satisfaction.

I discovered that Proverbs 4:25 was literally the answer. I walked straight ahead, looking neither to the right nor to the left.

—Charles R. Swindoll,
seminary president

Personal Challenge:
• What do you need to deliberately avoid?

Thought to Apply: Our eyes, when gazing on sinful objects, are out of their calling and God's keeping.
—THOMAS FULLER (English pastor, 17th century)

The Broad Way

Key Bible Verse: But I tell you that anyone who looks at a woman lustfully has already committted adultery with her in his heart *(Matthew 5:28). Bonus Reading: Matthew 5:27-32*

John Piper, a Minnesota pastor, recalls his conversation with a husband and father who abandoned his family:

"I tried to understand his situation and I pled with him to return to his wife. Then I said, 'You know, Jesus says if you don't fight this sin with the kind of seriousness that is willing to gouge out your own eye, you will go to hell and suffer there forever.'

As a professing Christian he looked at me in utter disbelief, as though he had never heard anything like this in his life.'

". . . Many professing Christians have a view of salvation that disconnects it from real life, and that nullifies the threats of the Bible and puts the sinning person who claims to be a Christian beyond the reach of biblical warnings. I believe this view of the Christian life is comforting thousands who are on the broad way that leads to destruction (Matthew 7:13).

Jesus said, 'If you don't fight lust, you won't go to heaven.' Not that saints always succeed. The issue is that we resolve to fight, not that we succeed flawlessly."

Personal Challenge:

• *Have you discounted stern biblical warnings to excuse some behavior?*
• *Take some time to think this through.*

Thought to Apply: No man can be a true member of the church of God who is a stranger to moral righteousness.

—ANONYMOUS

Up Close & Personal with Jerry White

Q. What are some preventative measures against sexual sin?

A. 1. Daily time with God in His Word and a commitment to spiritual growth.

2. A commitment to the battle for winning the lost.

3. A committed accountability relationship with one or two other men.

4. A deepening marriage relationship with your wife.

5. A constant guard on your thought life and actions.

6. Determined and continually renewed commitment that you will not enter into sexual sin.

7. Defensive prayer.

Jerry White, president of The Navigators and a major general in the Air Force Reserve

---

For Personal Study or Group Discussion

Key Bible Verse: To the pure, all things are pure, but to those who are corrupted and do not believe, nothing is pure. In fact, both their minds and consciences are corrupted. They claim to know God, but by their actions they deny him *(Titus 1:15-16a). Bonus Reading: Titus 1:16b-2:14*

Think and pray about these sentence starters.

☐ One way that I am guarding against lust in my life is . . .

☐ One place or thing I have decided is "off limits" for me is . . .

Credits: Adapted from—Tuesday: *Dangers Men Face* (NavPress, 1997); Thursday: *Three Steps Forward, Two Steps Back* (Thomas Nelson, 1980); Friday: *Future Grace* (Multnomah, 1995); Saturday: *Dangers Men Face* (NavPress, 1997)

A Cause or Christ?

Key Bible Verse: Religion that God our Father accepts as pure and faultless is this: to look after orphans and widows in their distress and to keep oneself from being polluted by the world *(James 1:27). Philippians 3:7-11*

The world cannot understand the source of [the] power [of] A 70-year-old Albanian nun named Agnes Bojaxhiu—better known as Mother Teresa. Though her words sound naïve, something extraordinary happened wherever this little woman from the streets or Calcutta went. For *what* Mother Teresa did, whether in Washington or Calcutta, is what the Bible calls "religion ... pure and faultless." But *why* she did it is our point here.

A few years ago a brother in the order came to her complaining about a superior whose rules, he felt, were interfering with his ministry. "My vocation is to work for lepers," he told Mother Teresa. "I want to spend myself for lepers."

She stared at him a moment, then smiled. "Brother," she said gently, "your vocation is not to work for lepers, your vocation is to belong to Jesus."

Mother Teresa was not in love with a cause, noble as her cause is. Rather, she loved God and was dedicated to living His life, not her own. This is holiness. It is the complete surrender of self in obedience to the will and service of God.

—Charles Colson
founder, Prison Fellowship

Personal Challenge:
• *What is something worthy that threatens to take precedence over your relationship to Jesus?*

Thought to Apply: Our progress in holiness depends on God and ourselves—on God's grace and on our will to be holy. —MOTHER TERESA (late head of Missionaries of Charity, Calcutta)

Holiness-hostile

Key Bible Verse: Do not be surprised, my brothers, if the world hates you *(1 John 3:13)*.
Bonus Reading: 1 John 3:11-15

A few years ago a leading golfer on the professional tour was invited to play in a foursome with Gerald Ford, then president of the United States, Jack Nicklaus and Billy Graham. After the round, one of the other pros came up to the golfer and asked, "Hey, what was it like playing with the President and with Billy Graham?"

The pro unleashed a torrent of cursing, and said, "I don't need Billy Graham stuffing religion down my throat." He stormed off, heading for the practice tee.

His friend followed the angry pro. The pro took out his driver and started to beat out balls in fury. After a few minutes the anger of the pro was spent. His friend said quietly, "Was Billy a little rough on you out there?" The pro heaved an embarrassed sigh and said, "No, he didn't even mention religion. I just had a bad round."

Billy Graham is so associated with the things of God, that his very presence is enough to smother the wicked man who flees when no man pursues. The greater the holiness, the greater the human hostility toward it.
—*R. C. Sproul, theologian*

Personal Challenge:
• *Thank God for someone you know whose character challenges others.*

Thought to Apply: A holy life is a voice; it speaks when the tongue is silent and is either a constant attraction or a perpetual reproof.
—ROBERT LEIGHTON (English archbishop, 17th century)

Auto-pilot?

Key Bible Verse: No, I beat my body and make it my slave so that after I have preached to others, I myself will not be disqualified for the prize *(1 Corinthains 9:27). Bonus Reading: 1 Corinthians 9:24-27*

During a certain period in my Christian life I thought that any effort on my part to live a holy life was "of the flesh" and that "the flesh profits for nothing."

Just as I received Christ Jesus by faith, so I was to seek a holy life only by faith. Any effort on my part was just getting in God's way.

I misapplied the statement, "You will not have to fight this battle. ... see the deliverance the Lord will give you" (2 Chronicles 20:17), to mean that I was to turn it all over to the Lord and He would fight the sin in my life. In the margin of the Bible I was using during that period, I wrote alongside the verse, "Illustrations of walking in the Spirit."

How foolish this was. I misconstrued dependence on the Holy Spirit to mean I was to make no effort, had no responsibility. I mistakenly thought if I turned it all over to the Lord, He would make my choices for me and would choose obedience over disobedience. But this is not God's way. He makes provision for our holiness, but He gives us the responsibility of using those provisions.

—Jerry Bridges, author

Personal Challenge:

• *What is your role in cultivating a holy life? What is God's role?*

Thought to Apply: Holiness is not exemption from conflict, but victory through conflict.

—G. CAMPBELL MORGAN (English pastor, early 20th century)

Heartless Habit

Key Bible Verse: He said to them, "You are the ones who justify yourselves in the eyes of men, but God knows your hearts. What is highly valued among men is detestable in God's sight" *(Luke 16:15).*
Bonus Reading: 1 Samuel 16:7, 1 Chronicles 28:9

Our flight was making its way into Newark. I looked out the window, and there standing in the harbor was the great lady. Only this time she was shrouded with scaffolding. Scurrying around the scaffolding were welders, polishers and repairers. I began thinking that this grand lady had no capacity to take care of herself.

I know Christians who've become accustomed to living by the scaffolding. If my walk with God is not carefully maintained, there is that subtle drift to hollowness, where my Christianity becomes a heartless habit, often moving into hypocrisy.

Our walk with God is an inside-out reality. God works in our lives at the level of our hearts and is not impressed with the externals. When we live by the scaffolding, we are propped up, maintained and polished by a book, a tape, a pastor, a professor or a message, and we begin leaning on all those externals for the vibrancy of our Christianity.

—Joe Stowell,
president,
Moody Bible Institute

Personal Challenge:
• *What characterizes an internal faith?*

Thought to Apply: Holiness is not the laborious acquisition of virtue from without, but the expression of the Christ-life from within.   —J.W.C. WAND

Where's the Evidence?

Key Bible Verse: No one who is born of God will continue to sin *(1 John 3:9a). Bonus Reading: 1 John 3:4-10*

I recall a young man, a fairly new Christian, whose father was visiting him. He had not seen his father since he had become a Christian.

He was eager to share his newfound faith with his dad, and we prayed together that he might be an effective witness.

Several days later I asked him how it had gone. He told me his dad had claimed to have trusted Christ as his Savior when he "went forward" at age ten in an evangelistic meeting.

I asked the young man, "In all the years you were growing up, did you ever see any evidence that your father was a Christian?" His answer was "No."

What reason have we to put confidence in that man's salvation? He was almost 60 and had never once given his son any evidence that he was a Christian.

If we know nothing of holiness, we do not have the Holy Spirit dwelling within us.

—Jerry Bridges, author

Personal Challenge:
• *Is there evidence of practical holiness in my life? Do I desire and strive after holiness? Do I grieve over my lack of it and earnestly seek the help of God to be holy?*

Thought to Apply: He who gave His image to us must want to see His image in us. —ANONYMOUS

Men of Integrity is published in association with Promise Keepers by Christianity Today, Inc., 465 Gundersen Drive, Carol Stream, IL 60188. Printed in U.S.A. Canada Post International Publications Mail Sales Agreement No. 546526. **Staff:** Editors: Harry Genet, Ashley Nearn; Design Director: Doug Johnson. **Advisory Board:** Edgar D. Barron, Todd McMullen, Kevin A. Miller, Keith Stonehocker. **Subscriptions:** A one-year subscription to *Men of Integrity* is available for a suggested donation of $20 to Promise Keepers, P.O. Box 103001, Denver, CO 80250-3001. www.promisekeepers.org   Cover Photography © 1993 Ron Chapple/FPG

Credits: Adapted from—Wednesday and Friday: *The Pursuit of Holiness* (NavPress, 1978); Monday: *Loving God* (Zondervan, 1983); Tuesday: *The Holiness of God* (Tyndale, 1985); Thursday: *Preaching Today* (#45) Specified works copyrighted by authors of the readings unless otherwise specified.

Up Close & Personal with Jerry Bridges

Q. Some issues aren't mentioned in the Bible. How do you figure out if they're okay?

A. Years ago a friend gave me his "Formula: How to Know Right from Wrong":

• " 'Everything is permissible for me'—but not everything is beneficial" (1 Corinthians 6:12). **Question 1:** *Is it helpful—physically, spiritually, and mentally?*

• " 'Everything is permissible for me'—but I will not be mastered by anything" (1 Corinthians 6:12). **Question 2:** *Does*

it bring me under its power?

• "Therefore, if what I eat causes my brother to fall into sin, I will never eat meat again, so that I will not cause him to fall" (1 Corinthians 8:13).

Question 3: *Does it hurt others?*

• "So whether you eat or drink or whatever you do, do it all for the glory of God" (1 Corinthians 10:31).

Question 4: *Does it glorify God?*

Jerry Bridges is an author and Bible teacher with the Navigators.

For Personal Study or Group Discussion

Key Bible Verse: For it is God who works in you to will and to act according to his good purpose *(Philippians 2:13). Bonus Reading: Philippians 2:12-16*

Think and pray about these sentence starters.

☐ People could notice I belong to Jesus because . . .

☐ One "permissible" thing I can live without is . . .

Credit: Adapted from: *The Pursuit of Holiness* (NavPress, 800-366-7788, 1978)

Getting Out of an Affair

Key Bible Verse: Marriage should be honored by all, and the marriage bed kept pure, for God will judge the adulterer and all the sexually immoral *(Hebrews 13:4).*
Bonus Reading: 1 Corinthians 6:12-20

I attended the PK conference in the Los Angeles Coliseum —Bishop Kenneth Ulmer spoke, and it felt like he had prepared his message for me. I was at the time getting out of a six-month affair, and I had almost lost my marriage of more than five years.

Bishop Ulmer said, "You men in extra-marital affairs, stop, and turn it all over to God." And there I was with my dad and my brothers. They all knew what was going on in my life.

Bishop Ulmer gave an invitation for men to come forward and start a new life. I knew about the Lord when I was younger but did not have a relationship with Christ. I looked over to my dad, the rock, and saw tears rolling down his face. I asked him to go down with me. We walked down those steps arm-in-arm, just sobbing all the way to the ground floor.

That was the start. I am currently active in a PK group, and my wife and I are on the long road to recovery. If I learned anything from my mistakes, I learned that "I can do all things through him who gives me strength" (Philippians 4:13).
                    —A Los Angeles
                    promise keeper

Personal Challenge:
• *Who can help you keep or reclaim purity in your marriage?*

Thought to Apply: He who does not honor his wife dishonors himself.   —SPANISH PROVERB

G.I. Joe Mode

Key Bible Verse: Husbands, in the same way be considerate as you live with your wives, and treat them with respect as the weaker partner and as heirs with you of the gracious gift of life, so that nothing will hinder your prayers *(1 Peter 3:7). Bonus Reading: Matthew 5:23-24*

One morning before I left for class, Barbara said, "Why are you wearing that?" I took her comment as an attack and went into my G.I. Joe mode. I counterattacked.

I said, "Why are you always criticizing what I put on?"

She said, "I'm *not* always criticizing you."

I answered, "Yes you are! You do it all the time."

She replied, "I *don't* do it all the time." We continued to exchange comments with increasing volume. I thought, "Hey, I don't have to put up with this," and remained aloof [for three weeks].

Finally I said, "Barbara, I really need to talk with you" She said, "Sure." I explained in detail how I had been offended by her responses to me. Barbara waited patiently until I was finished. Then she said, "Honey, I never said those words that you said I said."

Normally Barbara would "give in" first, but it didn't happen this time. So that morning I said, "God, what am I going to do? I believe I'm right... Then He asked me the question, "Do you want to be right, or do you want to be reconciled?"

As much as I hated the question, I knew the answer.
—*Joseph L. Garlington in* Right or Reconciled?

Personal Challenge:
• *Confess your pride and let go of your need to be right.*

Thought to Apply: A happy marriage is the union of two good forgivers.   —ROBERT QUILLEN (writer)

Weeds in Your Marriage Garden

Key Bible Verse: In the same way, husbands ought to love their wives as their own bodies. He who loves his wife loves himself *(Ephesians 5: 28).*
Bonus Reading: Ephesians 5:25-33

In marriages, we often see relationships reduced to a minimal necessity—functional communication, a moderate amount of argument, some level of tension, obligatory sexual activity, and public togetherness. Love is still there. Commitment remains. Yet something has left the relationship. We stop growing. In fact we regress.

Mary and I have seen that tendency several times in our marriage. When the children were young it seemed that we lived in separate worlds, meeting at the point of crisis or necessary decisions. I was intent on work, career—she on child rearing. We sensed stagnation in our relationship. Recognition, and some conflict, helped us work through it to keep growing.

But the problem repeats itself. It is like growing a garden. It takes constant attention or it dies or becomes choked with weeds. We have found that we regularly, at least yearly, need to assess where we are in our relationship. We have tried to take time apart together just to talk and rebuild our relationship.

The danger occurs when a couple allows the stagnation to settle in and become the norm.

—Jerry White in
Dangers Men Face

Personal Challenge:
• *When was the last time you "weeded the garden" of your marriage? Set aside time for that.*

Thought to Apply: Try praising your wife, even it it does frighten her at first.—BILLY SUNDAY (Pro baseball player and evangelist)

Remembering Romance

Key Bible Verse: All beautiful you are, my darling; there is no flaw in you *(Song of Songs 4:7).*
Bonus Reading: Song of Songs 4:1-15

Years ago, in the Midwest, a farmer and his wife were lying in bed during a storm when the funnel of a tornado suddenly lifted the roof right off the house and sucked their bed away with them still in it. The wife began to cry, and the farmer called to her that it was no time to cry. She called back that she was so happy, she could not help it—it was the first time they had been out together in 20 years!

Psychology Today once did a survey of 300 couples, asking them what keeps them together. One of the major "staying" factors was time spent together. Make sure you maintain this priority. Your calendar reveals what is important to you, so write her calendar into yours. Schedule weekly times together that do not just "happen." Be creative. Date! Surprise her. Be extravagant.

Men, when was the last time you opened the door for her ... said "I love you"... complimented her ... wrote her a loving note ... sent her flowers ... "dated" her ... gave her extra special attention?
—*R. Kent Hughes in* Disciplines of a Godly Man

Personal Challenge:
• *Plan something special for your wife this week or next.*

Thought to Apply: Chains do not hold a marriage together. It is threads, hundreds of tiny threads, that sew people together through the years.

—SIMONE SIGNORET (actress)

A High Honor

Key Bible Verse: Lord, who may dwell in your sanctuary? Who may live on your holy hill? He . . . who keeps his oath even when it hurts *(Psalm 15;1,4b).*
Bonus Reading: Psalm 15

In March 1990, Dr. Robertson McQuilkin, president of Columbia Bible College, announced his resignation:

"My dear wife, Muriel, has been in failing mental health for about eight years. So far I have been able to carry both her ever-growing needs and my leadership responsibilities at CBC. But recently it has become apparent that Muriel is contented most of the time she is with me and almost none of the time I am away. She is filled with fear—even terror—that she has lost me and always goes in search of me when I leave home. So it is clear to me that she needs me now, full-time. ...

"The decision was made, in a way, 42 years ago when I promised to care for Muriel 'in sickness and in health ... till death do us part.' Integrity has something to do with it. But so does fairness. She has cared for me fully and sacrificially all these years. Duty, however, can be grim and stoic. But there is more; I love Muriel. She is a delight to me. I do not *have* to care for her, I *get* to! It is a high honor to care for so wonderful a person."

Personal Challenge:
• *Thank God for the honor of caring for the people you love.*

Thought to Apply: The sum which two married people owe to one another defies calculation. It is an infinite debt, which can only be discharged through all eternity.

—GOETHE (German poet, 19th century)

Up Close & Personal with Louis and Melissa McBurney

Becoming a Team without Losing Me

Q. ■ **How can my wife and I move toward a shared purpose without sacrificing our individuality?**

A. You need to do three things:

1. Check out your expectations. Each person has come into the marriage with well-formed but ill-understood expectations. Each of you should sit down with a pencil and paper and write out what your expectations of marriage and your mate were when you married. It's important to discuss individual roles, financial management, parenting philosophy, affection, sexual interaction, leisure time activities, orderliness, spiritual sharing, and relationships with parents.

As you go over your lists together, try to hear each other with compassion and understanding rather than defensiveness. Try to verbalize what it must have felt like to your mate to live with your expectations. You'll come to appreciate each other's frustration when you can stop seeing your own ideas as "right."

2. Listen to each other's goals. Ask each other: what do you envision for our marriage in the next year? The next five years? In 20 years, where would you like for us to be emotionally and relationally? What are your private dreams? What role, if any, do you see for me in your dream?

Try to listen without editorializing, judging, or embellishing your mate's ideas. A dream is a fragile, private creation, easily broken.

3. Create common goals. Look together at short-term relational goals. What would you like for your marriage in the next six months or a year? Perhaps you can each give enthusiastic support to the goal of having better communication by your next anniversary. Maybe things have settled into a boring routine and you'd like to renew your romance through courtship. Set a goal of having a date once a week and put your creativity to work, infusing your marriage with a little mystery and fun.

Dr. Louis and Melissa McBurney counsel clergy at Marble Retreat in Marble, Colorado.

Marriage   Sunday, Week 45

For Personal Study or Group Discussion

Real Life Application

Key Bible Verse: He who finds a wife finds what is good and receives favor from the Lord *(Proverbs 18:22).* *Bonus Reading: Genesis 2:18-24*

Think and pray about these sentence starters on your own. Or, if you meet with other men, use them to trigger your discussion.

☐ Some specific ways I have experienced the Lord's favor through my wife are . . .

☐ I could better care for my wife by . . .

☐ One thing I really need to tell my wife is . . .

Credits: Adapted from—Monday: *The Promise Keeper*; Tuesday: *Right or Reconciled?* (Destiny Image, 1998); Wednesday: *Dangers Men Face* (NavPress, 800-366-7788, 1997); Thursday: *Disciplines of a Godly Man* (Crossway, 1991); Friday: *Christianity Today* (10/8/90); Saturday: *Marriage Partnership* (11/12/87)

Killer Whales

Key Bible Verse: Do not be quickly provoked in your spirit, for anger resides in the lap of fools *(Ecclesiastes 7:9). Bonus Reading: Genesis 4:2b-12*

The ice-cold water hit me in the face. The killer whale had splashed water from his tank up 14 rows! As I dried, I marveled at the relationship the human trainers had developed with each of their whales. Joy at working together was written all over their faces.

As I left at the end of the show, I noticed the largest whale far behind the stage in its own tank. Later, I learned this whale had suddenly turned on his trainer and killed him. I tried to imagine what would change the loving, passionate relationship I witnessed between trainer and animal into murder.

As men, we feel this sudden change of natures within us every day. It is like a lightning-fast ambush appearing out of nowhere. One moment, we are sane, civilized, Christian examples of manhood. The next moment, provoked by sometimes the most trivial event, we become raging, vicious animals.

Society tells us we can be just a little bit bad. But the dividing line between good and evil, between walking in the Spirit and walking in the flesh, is very fine. One minute we are working harmoniously with our God, the next we betray Him.

— *Bruce Hennigan*
in God's Man

Personal Challenge:
• *When has your temper controlled you? Confess your sin and ask God to heal you.*

Thought to Apply: Control yourself! Anger is only one letter short of danger.   —ANONYMOUS

Angry Young Man

Key Bible Verse: Like a city whose walls are broken down is a man who lacks self-control *(Proverbs 25:28).* *Bonus Reading: Proverbs 14:17, 19:19, 29:22*

I see a lot of angry kids in my work, but none can match the anger of a boy I knew years ago. He was the second-youngest of six children; his father was a coal miner. He lived about a block and a half from the mouth of the mine. As a child, no more than three years old, he used to wait for his father to come up from the mine after his shift.

Then one day, his father was gone. His long bouts of illness had grown worse, and he was taken away to a mental institution. The shame of that sort of thing was strong in those days. The little boy was never told where his father went; he never saw him again.

Without his father around, the boy's life went downhill. His idleness led to throwing rocks in the pond, pretending the rocks were aimed at his father. When he grew up, he left school before graduating and fathered a child with a girl he had no intention of marrying. To run away, he joined the Army, began using drugs and ended up in prison.

That angry young man is someone I knew well. He was me.

—*Dr. Charles A. Ballard* in Say Amen

Personal Challenge:
• *Don't let the hurts of the past sour the present. Let God carry the pain for you and soften your heart.*

Thought to Apply: No man can think clearly when his fists are clenched. —GEORGE J. NATHAN (editor and critic)

Handball Hotheads

Key Bible Verse: A fool gives full vent to his anger, but a wise man keeps himself under control *(Proverbs 29:11).* *Bonus Reading: Romans 12:17-21*

I still play handball. As in most competitive sports I see a lot of anger. In frustration men slam fists into the wall, swear at themselves, or argue over a shot or a foul. Usually their temper is their undoing in a game. Only a very few play the game better when they are angry.

Most of us who play handball tolerate some degree of anger in others and in ourselves. But there are some people with whom no one likes to play. Their temper and conduct on the court are unbearable and inexcusable. I have seen yelling matches that are just short of physical blows. There are some who become sullen and give up, ruining the game by not playing to the best of their ability.

When the game is over they leave in their business suits or go back to being a lawyer, teacher, engineer, businessman, or stockbroker—seemingly normal people.

Emotional boundaries exist even in a game. The line is crossed when anger overtakes and controls. Then everyone becomes uncomfortable. Angry outbursts cause the person to lose respect whether or not he wins or loses the game.

So it is in life. Anger, out of bounds, never brings approval.
—*Jerry White in* Dangers Men Face

Personal Challenge:
• *In what situations are you apt to cross emotional boundaries? What steps can help you stay under control?*

Thought to Apply: Anger is often more hurtful than the injury that caused it.   —AMERICAN PROVERB

Use It. Don't Lose It

Key Bible Verses: Everyone should be quick to listen, slow to speak and slow to become angry, for man's anger does not bring about the righteous life that God desires *(James 1:19-20). Bonus Reading: Psalm 4*

Every time anger explodes inside me, I see myself ten years old, writhing on the ground, pounding my fists in the grass, crying and screaming. My team had just lost a game of pickup football, and my anger was totally out of control. My dad walked across the field to me and firmly reprimanded me.

"You lose your temper sometimes," I shot back.

There was a pause of awful silence during which I finally came to my childish senses.

Dad spoke in a measured tone. "We are both wrong to waste our energy by losing our tempers. I will work at controlling mine if you will learn to control yours."

In relief I nodded.

My dad was a passionate leader. Anger is the ready passion of those who care intensely and expect much from themselves and others. But releasing uncontrolled anger inevitably turns a person into a fool.

My dad's anger was just as strong after that event as before, but he increasingly demonstrated to me and to others what it meant to use it rather than lose it. We kept the covenant we made with each other that afternoon.

—Richard Kriegbaum in
Leadership Prayers

Personal Challenge:
• *Whom can you covenant with to help you use anger properly?*

Thought to Apply: When angry, take a lesson from technology; always count down before blasting off.

—UNKNOWN

That's Just the Way You Look

Key Bible Verse: A patient man has great understanding, but a quick-tempered man displays folly *(Proverbs 14:29). Bonus Reading: Galatians 5:16-26*

Even though I had become a Christian while in college, I still had a terrible temper. I was ready to fight anytime, anywhere. Until the Lord let me see myself as others saw me.

I was out on the practice field going through one-on-one drive-block drills with the rest of the Los Angeles Rams, when I noticed a problem developing between two players.

A young guard was blasting a long-time veteran so hard he was driving him right off the board. After this had happened several times, the veteran got mad and started throwing punches. Before the young guard could fight back, however, it was broken up.

I watched the young guard storm off the field and stand along the sidelines, seething with rage. "That's you, Jackie," the Lord seemed to say to me. "That's just the way you look when you lose your temper." I knew it was true. I decided I didn't like what I was seeing.

Right then and there, I resolved to seek the Lord's help each and every time I felt myself beginning to lose control to my anger. As long as I have remembered to do that, He has never let me down.

—Jackie Slater in Winning

Personal Challenge:
• *What do you look like to other people?*

Thought to Apply: People who fly into a rage always make a bad landing.   —WILL ROGERS ("cowboy philosopher")

Up Close & Personal with Jerry White

Q. What is the one consistent emotion men express?

A. Anger. Men's anger usually comes explosively without early warning signals.

When is anger wrong?
Anger toward injustice, evil in our community, or sin in our lives is appropriate. When I am angry at not getting my way, at others for not performing up to my expectation, at my wife when we are in conflict, or at my children when they disobey—then I cross that line into sin.

Usually when a person expresses his anger in a hurtful way, he feels almost immediate regret. Then an apology is in order. Many times I have had to ask for forgiveness from my family and others.

When does anger become dangerous?
When it is persistent, repeated, and unresolved.

Jerry White is president of The Navigators and a major general in the Air Force Reserve.

For Personal Study or Group Discussion

Key Bible Verse: Get rid of all bitterness, rage and anger, brawling and slander, along with every form of malice *(Ephesians 4:31). Bonus Reading: Ephesians 4:17-5:2*

Think and pray about these sentence starters.

☐ Things that make me angry are . . .

☐ I commit to changing the way I deal with anger by . . .

Credits: Adapted from—Monday: Don M. Aycock, editor, *God's Man* (Kregel, 1998); Tuesday: "Prodigal Dad," *Say Amen* (Spring 1998); Wednesday & Saturday: *Dangers Men Face* (NavPress, 800-366-7788, 1997); Thursday: *Leadership Prayers* (Tyndale, 1998); Friday: Rosey Grier and Kathi Mills, *Winning* (Regal, 1990)

Not Swearing in Court

Key Bible Verse: When a man makes a vow to the Lord or takes an oath to obligate himself by a pledge, he must not break his word but must do everything he said *(Numbers 30:2). Bonus Reading: Matthew 5:33-37*

Historically Quakers have resisted being sworn in before testifying in court. Their rationale is simple. If they have to promise to be honest for the next few minutes, the obvious implication is that they are dishonest the rest of the time. And if such is the case, why should anyone trust the oath they make?

A person's integrity should be such that no one would ever ask whether she or he will speak "the truth, the whole truth, and nothing but the truth." Indeed, it would never occur to anyone to suspect that the person would do otherwise. In this way, the Quakers make a strong point about character and integrity.

Jesus made the same point in Matthew 5:37 when He told His listeners, "Simply let your 'Yes' be 'Yes,' and your 'No,' 'No.'" In other words, be a person of such integrity that when you speak, the community will never have reason to doubt what you say. Moses emphasized the same truth to "the heads of the tribes of the people of Israel" [in our Key Verse].

Integrity, honesty, and trustworthiness: whatever else we have, we remain impoverished if we lose any of these virtues.

—*Michael B. Brown in God's Man*

Personal Challenge:
• *Commit yourself to speak the truth in all situations.*

Thought to Apply: Some people strengthen the society just by being the kind of people they are.

—JOHN W. GARDNER (writer and educator)

Dads Showing Their Stuff

Key Bible Verse: The righteous man leads a blameless life; blessed are his children after him *(Proverbs 20:7)*. *Bonus Reading: Psalm 24*

I was invited to a home to talk with a father about his son. As he described the circumstances, he said, "The thing that bothers me most is that drugs have made him a liar."

The phone rang and his wife went to answer it. She came back and said, "So-and-so is on the phone and wants to talk to you."

His immediate answer was "Tell him I'm not home."

[In contrast to that, a] friend told me about the summer his sister was looking for employment. She had two job possibilities. One she wanted very much and the other she didn't but would take as a second choice. The second-choice job was offered. She didn't know if the other was going to come. So she went ahead and accepted [her second choice]. A few days later the other job became available. She very much wanted to quit the first and go to the second. So she went to her father.

"Dad, I have a problem." She described it to him.

He looked her straight in the eye and said, "Did you take the first job?"

"Yes."

"Did you promise you would work there this summer?"

"Yes."

He said, "Why are we having this conversation?"

—*George Munzing, pastor*

Personal Challenge:
• *Where are you most tempted not to be honest or consistent?*

Thought to Apply: A crooked stick will have a crooked shadow.   —PROVERB

Before the Label Goes On

Key Bible Verse: Make a tree good and its fruit will be good, or make a tree bad and its fruit will be bad, for a tree is recognized by its fruit *(Matthew 12:33).*
Bonus Reading: Matthew 12:34-35, 15:10-20

I accepted a pastorate in California [with] only the unfinished shell of a building. We tried to remodel with volunteer labor, small amounts of cash, and donated or used materials. We did have a few craftsmen. One was Paul.

Paul's final task was to put a wooden veneer on the wall behind the pulpit. The rest of us were awed by the difference his exquisite work made. So it came as a shock when he took me aside and asked me not to tell anyone he had done the woodwork.

"Why?" I asked. "I want to tell everyone what a great job you've done."

"Please don't," he reiterated. "I'll show you why." He proceeded to show me where the wood grain did not match exactly, where the miter was not perfectly joined, and the levels were off a fraction of an inch.

"I was glad to help," he said. "However, this work is not up to my standard. I could have done a better job if the material had been of better quality."

I never forgot that lesson: The quality of the product depends on the quality of the material used. A "real man" is real in every area of life.

—*Edwin Louis Cole*
in Real Man

Personal Challenge:
• *How high are your standards? Do you want people to see up close the quality of your work?*

Thought to Apply: You can't make a good cloak out of bad cloth. —SPANISH PROVERB

NFL Strike Breaker

Key Bible Verse: When you make a vow to God, do not delay in fulfilling it. *(Ecclesiasties 5:4). Bonus Reading: Isaiah 33:13-16*

In 1984, some players in the National Football League went on strike for more money and better contracts. I received a call from a Christian player. He had continued going to practices, but fellow players were accusing him of being a strike breaker. He couldn't decide if he should be loyal to the players' union or the owners.

"Who did you sign a contract with?" I asked.

"Obviously, I signed with the owner," he replied. "But I also signed an agreement with the union that they could represent me in contract disputes."

"Do you have a dispute?"

"Not really, but that's what the union is saying. Their contract with the NFL is running out, and they want the players' support to renegotiate."

"Well, you can't have two authorities in this issue. Who pays your salary?"

"The team owner," he replied.

I reminded him of what Solomon wrote about keeping vows [see the Key Verses].

He continued to show up for practice even though the owners refused to pay him his due salary. He went on to become the league's most valuable player and broke virtually every NFL record.

—*Larry Burkett, financial adviser*

Personal Challenge:

• *Take some time to sort through your loyalties. Who is your primary authority?*

Thought to Apply: If one can be certain that his principles are right, he need not worry about the consequences.

—ROBERT E. SPEER (leader in American missionary movement)

Selling the Junker

Key Bible Verse: Love does no harm to its neighbor. Therefore love is the fulfillment of the law *(Romans 13:10). Bonus Reading: Romans 13:8-10*

The VW camper had seen better decades. It had a terrific sound system, but compression was low in three cylinders, and the body was a rust bucket.

I set a price I thought was fair and put a FOR SALE sign in the window.

One serious buyer showed up. As we circled the camper together and poked and revved, I learned that he was a student at a local Bible college and dating a young woman down the street. I discovered that I also knew his father.

Why did my palms suddenly get sweaty? Maybe deep down I'd hoped some stranger would take it off my hands and never be seen again. This young man was almost a neighbor.

Perhaps he could be talked out of it. "You good at body work? Needs an overhaul, too. Hmm, is that clutch slipping?"

He was undaunted.

I was relieved when I encountered the fellow a year later and learned he was still happy with his purchase. If he had been a stranger, I probably wouldn't have cared.

Real neighborliness means showing mercy and acting with compassion when there is no conventional social obligation to do so.

—*Wally Kroeker*
in God's Week Has 7 Days

Personal Challenge:
• *How would my dealings be different if every needy person were my neighbor and the whole world my neighborhood?*

Thought to Apply: If the deal isn't good for the other party, it isn't good for you.

—B. C. FORBES (magazine and book publisher)

Up Close & Personal with Howard Hendricks

Being Honest to God

Q. **If you had only one thing to give your four children, what would it be?**

A. Honesty. You show me a person who is honest with God, who is honest with other people, and most of all, who is honest with himself, and I will show you a man of integrity.

Honesty is adherence to truth, and truth is always a return to reality. Unbelievers do not expect Christians to be perfect. (I hope you're not trying to pull that off.)

Occasionally people come to me and say, "Hey, Hendricks. Would you recommend a church?" I always ask, "What kind of a church are you looking for?" After they give me the specifications, I say, "You're looking for a perfect church. I don't know of a church like that,

but if you find one, don't join it because you'll ruin it."

How can men of Christian character make an impact?

We need a larger corps of guys who are men of integrity, who will penetrate the companies of the United States.

John Gardner is one of my favorite writers, particularly his book entitled *Excellence*, in which he says, "The society that scorns excellence in plumbing, because plumbing is a humble activity, and honors philosophy because it is an exalted activity, will have neither good plumbing nor good philosophy. Neither its pipes nor its theories will hold water."

In Colossians 3:17, Paul writes, "Whatever you do, whether in word or deed, do it all in the name of the Lord

Jesus, giving thanks to God the Father through him." And again: "Whatever you do, work at it with all your heart, as working for the Lord, not for men, since you know that you will receive an inheritance from the Lord as a reward. It is the Lord Christ you are serving."

Howard Hendricks is a professor at Dallas Theological Seminary and chairman of its Center for Christian Leadership.

For Personal Study or Group Discussion

Real Life Application

Key Bible Verse: For we are taking pains to do what is right, not only in the eyes of the Lord but also in the eyes of men *(2 Corinthians 8:21). Bonus Reading: Philippians 4:8-9*

Think and pray about these sentence starters on your own. Or, if you meet with other men, use them to trigger your discussion.

☐ Characteristics I most want people to see in my life are ...

☐ An area where I struggle is ...

☐ Character strengths I have are ...

Credits: Adapted from—Monday: Don M. Aycock, editor, *God's Man* (Kregel, 1998); Tuesday: *Preaching Today* (32); Wednesday: *Real Man* (Nelson, 1992); Thursday: "True to Your Word," *The Christian Businessman* (9-10/98); Friday: *God's Week Has 7 Days* (Herald, 1998); Saturday: *A Life of Integrity* (Multnomah, 1997)

I Got Clobbered!

Key Bible Verses: Your enemy the devil prowls around like a roaring lion looking for someone to devour. Resist him, standing firm in the faith *(1 Peter 5:8-9).* *Bonus Reading: Revelation 12:10-12*

A Wycliffe Bible translator writes: "I went to the Amazon jungle in 1963 among the Apurina people. I was the first to challenge Satan's dominion over this people. My purpose was to transfer them from the kingdom of darkness to the kingdom of light.

"Unfortunately, in spite of a Master of Theology degree, I was not aware of these truths [about spiritual warfare]. I got clobbered! Satan wiped the floor with me. I didn't understand what was happening. I knew that Satan and demons exist; the Bible is clear on that score. But I knew very little about how they operate and virtually nothing about the use of our weapons, whether for defense or offense. My professors transmitted the idea that demonic attack wouldn't be a problem for us."

[But] the warnings in the New Testament about conflict with Satan and demons are all addressed to believers. We are involved whether we want to be or not. And the stakes are high—the glory of God. Our enemy is committed to making us ineffective in our personal lives and in our ministries.

—Timothy M. Warner in Spiritual Warfare

Personal Challenge:

• *What role might Satan be playing in the struggles you face? Ask God for greater awareness of Satan's schemes.*

Thought to Apply: In war there is no substitute for victory.
—DOUGLAS MACARTHUR (U.S. general, World War II)

Use Your Weapons

Key Bible Verse: The weapons we fight with are not the weapons of the world. On the contrary, they have divine power to demolish strongholds *(2 Corinthians 10:4)*. *Bonus Reading: Psalm 27:1-3*

The ability and the will to use weapons is what warfare is all about. Passivity is what the devil wants from us.

The skill of the soldier in hitting the bull's-eye on the practice range is not enough. Let me quote from the book *Men against Fire* by S.L.A. Marshall: "Only five infantry companies (on Omaha Beachhead, June 6, 1944) were tactically effective. In these companies, one-fifth of the men fired their weapons during the day-long advance —a total of not more than 450 men firing consistently." On another front, "The best showing that could be made by the most spirited and aggressive companies was that one man in four had made some use of his firepower."

In the warfare of the church on earth, if three-fourths of those on church membership rolls are so uncertain and confused about their role in the conflict or so paralyzed by fear that they do not use their weapons, then victory will obviously be that much longer in coming. The gospel moves at a slow and timid pace when the saints are not at their prayers early and late and long.

—*R. Arthur Mathews
in* Born for Battle

Personal Challenge:
• *What weapons do you have to fight against Satan? What keeps you from using them?*

Thought to Apply: On the battlefield the real enemy is fear and not the bayonet and the bullet.

—ROBERT JACKSON (chief U.S. prosecutor, Nuremberg war crimes tribunal)

Where the Cross Was Won

Key Bible Verse: Submit yourselves, then, to God. Resist the devil, and he will flee from you *(James 4:7)*. *Bonus Reading: 2 Timothy 2:3-5*

It has been said that "the battle of Waterloo was won on the playing fields of Eton." Had there been no soccer-field discipline, there could have been very different results. The schoolboy playing for his school learns that [his] will must be subservient at all times to the will of his captain. He plays to give all that he has for the glory of his side, not just to win a name for himself.

[Similarly,] the battle of the Cross was won on the praying field of Gethsemane. His will was assailed at every point. "His sweat was like drops of blood falling to the ground." In his Gethsemane struggle the Lord Jesus teaches us two important things: "submit to God" and "resist the devil." God's warfare against Satan is carried on by his submissive people actively resisting Satan by insisting at all costs, "Your will be done on earth as it is in heaven."

The will of God is not an inexorable omnipotence overriding or ignoring the will of man. God has willed that His hand be held back while He seeks for a man to plead "Your will be done" in this or that specific situation.

—*R. Arthur Mathews*
in Born for Battle

Personal Challenge:
• *Thank God that "the one who is in you is greater than the one who is in the world"* (1 John 4:4).

Thought to Apply: You cannot fight hard unless you think you are fighting to win.

—THEODORE ROOSEVELT (26th U.S. president)

We Shall Overcome

Key Bible Verse: The God of peace will soon crush Satan under your feet *(Romans 16:20). Bonus Reading: Colossians 2:13-15*

There was a confidence, a joyous abandon about the early Christians that had the flavor of adventure. They really did believe that no weapon formed against Christ, and therefore against them, could ultimately prosper. They were prepared to follow Him to the cross If need be, confident that they would share in His resurrection.

If we asked those early Christians for the secret of their confidence and expectancy, they would take us back to Calvary. There all the forces of evil had concentrated their assault on the Son of God, and had been broken by His obedient and sacrificial death. They never tired of reminding Satan that he was a beaten foe.

I remember reading advice on what to do if you should find a prairie fire bearing down on you. You should light a fresh fire at your feet, allow the wind to drive it away, and then stand on the burnt ground as you begin to be enveloped by all the savagery of the prairie fire. The early Christians did not flinch in the face of all the problems unleashed against them. They stood on the burnt ground of Calvary, and the fire could not touch them there.

—*Michael Green in* Exposing the Prince of Darkness

Personal Challenge:
• *Where is the "prairie on fire" in your life? Take a risk in faith, knowing you are already protected from harm.*

Thought to Apply: I have read a fiery gospel writ in burnished rows of steel.

—JULIA WARD HOWE (in "Battle Hymn of the Republic")

Birth-Certificate Surprise

Key Bible Verse: Now if we are children, then we are heirs—heirs of God and co-heirs with Christ *(Romans 8:17a). Bonus Reading: Galatians 4:1-7*

When I adopted our two older children (a girl and a boy), I went before a judge who said, "Do you understand that these children must be equally your heirs with any children who may be born to you and your wife?" My ready reply was, "I understand that, sir, and gladly accept it." So these two children have as much right to my name and resources as the two born into our family.

Our adoption into the family of God brings us into the same relationship with Him. Because we are God's children we are "heirs of God and co-heirs with Christ." One of Satan's chief tactics is to keep us from understanding the implications of this new relationship with our Heavenly Father. Through the Cross, Satan's claim on us is completely canceled.

When my son and daughter's new birth certificates came, I was surprised. They make no mention of their biological father but list me alone as their father. Just so, we are spiritually children of God alone. With the resources of God at my disposal, I am more than a match for the enemy in his attempts to bring me into bondage to him again.

—*Timothy M. Warner*
in Spiritual Warfare

Personal Challenge:
• *Thank God because He became your Dad—for keeps.*

Thought to Apply: The harder the conflict, the more glorious the triumph.

—THOMAS PAINE (colonial author of "Common Sense")

Up Close & Personal with Roger Barrier

How to Fight for Christ

Q. ▪ **What do you do when you suspect a spiritual attack?**

A. James 4:7 gives a simple formula: "Submit yourselves to God. Resist the devil, and he will flee from you."

Submitting to God involves, for me, three things:

1. *Confessing that the area is out of control and needs help;*
2. *Consciously yielding the area to God;* and
3. *Considering myself dead, according to Romans 6, to the sin in that area.*

If these three activities provide freedom, then I thank God the problem was only a sin of the flesh.

What if the struggle persists? I consider that I may be experiencing a spiritual attack. The second half of James 4:7 then comes into play.

"Resisting the devil" involves four things:

1. *Declaring that I have forsaken and confessed my sin to God so the forces of evil no longer have a foothold;*
2. *Renouncing the attacking forces ("In the name of Jesus Christ, depart and leave me alone. I rebuke you and your attacks against me. I want nothing to do with you");*
3. *Asking for the filling of the Holy Spirit;* and,
4. *Imploring the Holy Spirit to build a hedge of protection around me from future attacks.*

How can you get prepared for spiritual conflict? Every day I specifically pray for	the spiritual armor of Ephesians 6:10-17.

Roger Barrier is pastor of Casas Adobes Baptist Church in Tucson, Arizona, and author of Listening to the Voice of God.

For Personal Study or Group Discussion

Real Life Application

Key Bible Verse: Put on the full armor of God so that you can take your stand against the devil's schemes *(Ephesians 6:11). Bonus Reading: Ephesians 6:10-17*

Think and pray about these sentence starters on your own. Or, if you meet with other men, use them to trigger your discussion.

☐ A place in my life Satan attacks me is . . .

☐ Jesus protects me by . . .

☐ Pieces of the armor of God I need to put on are . . .

Credits: Adapted from—Monday & Friday: *Spiritual Warfare* (Crossway, 1991); Tuesday & Wednesday: *Born for Battle* (Harold Shaw Publishers, 1978); Thursday: *Exposing the Prince of Darkness* (Servant, 1981); Saturday: *Listening to the Voice of God* (Bethany, 1998)

Pocket-Knife Payoff

Key Bible Verse: His master replied, "Well done, good and faithful servant! You have been faithful with a few things; I will put you in charge of many things. Come and share your master's happiness!" *(Matthew 25:21).* *Bonus Reading: Matthew 25:14-30*

Its blades glistened under the glass of the display case: the prettiest pocket knife my six-year-old eyes had ever seen. The only problem was that I didn't have even a dime, much less the considerable sum of two dollars, for my pearl-handled prize. So I stood there with my face almost touching the glass and wished.

My dad sized up the situation and proposed a deal: I would dry the dishes each night for two weeks and earn the money. Deal! For the next two weeks I stood by my mother in the farmhouse kitchen and dried dishes, handling the dinner plates carefully, pushing the towel into the glasses, sorting the silverware.

Two Saturdays later I walked into the hardware store, placed my two dollars on the countertop and watched almost without breathing as the owner put the sleek penknife in my hand.

I was the proudest boy in the county! It was the first possession in my life that was truly *mine*, something I had worked for.

There is a payoff for faithfulness, a reward for serving with integrity and selflessness.
—*Dennis Hillman*
in *God's Man*

Personal Challenge:
• *When did you feel proud for doing a job well?*

Thought to Apply: The reward of a thing well done is to have done it.
—RALPH WALDO EMERSON (poet and essayist, 19th century)

How I Lost My Money

Key Bible Verse: Do not defraud your neighbor or rob him *(Leviticus 19:13). Bonus Reading: Proverbs 10:4-5*

I lost some money recently. I gave it to a thief!

I hired the owner of a small company to do some work on my house. He required me to pay a third of the cost up front.

I checked this fellow out. He seemed to be a good guy. But when he got the check, he disappeared. I finally had to take him to court to recover my money. But I was too late; the IRS got him first.

So much of our lives depend on trusting others. An honest person will do right no matter what. A crook will cheat you no matter how many references you find on him.

This is no less true in relationships with our fellow employees. Some pull their share and do what is expected of them. Others will go beyond the minimum and give an extra effort. But another group believes they are somehow exempt from work, that they are paid to hold down a chair.

Leviticus 19:13 reminds us not to "defraud" our neighbor. You don't have to use a gun or fraud to rob someone; you can do it by being lazy and uncaring on the job. At our place of employment, we depend on each other, so let's give what is due.

—*Don M. Aycock*
in God's Man

Personal Challenge:
• *What can I do to better please God and serve others through my work?*

Thought to Apply: The number of people who are unemployed isn't as great as the number who aren't working.

—Frank A. Clark (author)

Power of the Postal Worker

Key Bible Verse: Now it is required that those who have been given a trust must prove faithful *(1 Corinthians 4:2). Bonus Reading: Ephesians 6:5-8*

Peter Epp spent nearly a year in a Soviet prison [and] was sent to a labor camp for a decade, cut off from family. My late grandfather had talked of kinfolk who hadn't made it out of Russia. Peter was one.

Thanks to the Gorbachev reforms, now, in his late 60s, he was here in Canada to meet his extended family.

What a wonderful visit—made possible by some civil servant who went to extra effort to do the job right.

Peter had been at a loss as to how to track down his missing family. He wrote a letter to my maternal grandmother, not knowing she had passed away ten years earlier. He addressed it to "Margaret Epp, Steinbach, USA."

Right town. Wrong country. Not many American postal clerks have ever heard of Steinbach. None of the 50 states has a Steinbach. Someone, however, must have cared enough to check another country. The letter arrived in the right town, where the name Epp is well-known.

So now we have a bigger family, a new store of precious memories. We also have enduring gratitude for some anonymous friend in a postal station somewhere.

—*Wally Kroeker in God's Week Has 7 Days*

Personal Challenge:
• *How could you care about the "stranger" through extra effort at work?*

Thought to Apply: Every calling is great when greatly pursued.

—OLIVER WENDELL HOMES, JR. (associate justice, Supreme Court)

Unforgiving Employer

Key Bible Verses: If I have denied justice to my menservants and maidservants when they had a grievance against me, what will I do when God confronts me? What will I answer when called to account? *(Job 31:13-14). Bonus Reading: Matthew 18:21-35*

Supervisor John Towns had suspicions that several workers were slacking off in their jobs. They would take their breaks and return later than allowed. He spoke to the men about this; they said that it would not happen again. John did not report the incident to his plant manager. Later, the men with whom he had talked were caught distributing drugs to other plant workers.

During an inquiry, the president reprimanded John severely for not reporting the men, and John was fired on the spot. John asked the president to have mercy, but he was unable to forgive John for a seemingly small mistake.

Have you been unable to forgive someone you employ or with whom you work for a mistake he has made? If so, look at [today's key verses]. The writer said that if he had been unfair to his servants or had refused to hear their complaints, he would be unable to face God when questioned by Him for his actions.

In your relationships with your coworkers, learn to understand the reasons for their action. Then, discern through prayer and God's leading what you should do.

—*Harold Hawkins*
in God's Man

Personal Challenge:
• *How can you show mercy to coworkers who have made mistakes?*

Thought to Apply: If God were not willing to forgive sin, heaven would be empty. —GERMAN PROVERB

What Work Won't We Do?

Key Bible Verse: So whether you eat or drink or whatever you do, do it all for the glory of God. *(1 Corinthians 10:31). Bonus Reading: 1 Corinthians 10:23-11:1*

A pharmaceuticals executive is proud of his work with heart medications, but fears his company may venture into "home abortion" drugs. In that case he will be obliged, for reasons of conscience, to leave his job (and its six-figure salary).

The early church faced the same issue. Many converts in the first and second century left the army when they accepted Jesus as Lord. Silversmiths changed occupations rather than make pagan idols.

Not all Christians agree on issues of liquor production, abortion, pollution, and military service. Richard Foster makes a simple proposal in his book *Money, Sex and Power:* "As believers we affirm work that enhances human life and shun work that destroys human life."

Well, it sounds simple. Deciding what exactly is life-enhancing and life-destroying is more complex. He suggests prayer groups and "clearness meetings" to help believers find their place in the world of work.

Foster is right. The issue should be talked about in the discerning community. For many Christians, the issue is too big to handle alone.

—Wally Kroeker in God's Week Has 7 Days

Personal Challenge:
• *What kind of work won't you do?*
• *Where do you draw the line between good work and bad?*

Thought to Apply: Most of us follow our conscience as we follow a wheelbarrow. We push it in front of us in the direction we want to go. —BILLY GRAHAM (evangelist)

What Would You Do?
Rudy's Magazine Distribution

As you read the following situation, consider what you would tell Rudy, and what you would do in his situation:

Rudy talks openly about his faith. He says it "remains an important part of my life today." Some fellow believers were dismayed to learn that his vast business holdings included a magazine distribution company which handles *Playboy* and *Penthouse*. The adult men's magazines account for 1 percent of total unit sales.

Some of Rudy's detractors say that since he profits from the offensive magazines, he shares the blame for "this pernicious influence in our midst."

Rudy offers his defense.

• It would be difficult selectively to weed out particular periodicals because they come as part of a larger package along with wholesome magazines.

• Refusing to distribute certain periodicals would be a form of censorship. By selling all kinds of material, he is helping preserve freedom of expression.

• He is only one link in a distribution network that includes advertisers, publishers, international distributors, customs officials who let the material into the country, trucking firms, wholesalers, retailers, and customers. No matter what he does, the other links will continue to operate.

• By working within the system, he can help improve it. Selling the company is no solution, he says.

How, his critics ask, is he influencing the magazine distribution business for the good?

Rudy responds that he helped his province set up a review agency. "My reviewers," he explains, "screen the so-called adult magazines. They keep the worst of them off the racks."

One local pastor has said, "Rudy couldn't criticize the business if he weren't in it. He has to take the harder road. If he opts out, he will lose the ability to help bring about change."

(Use the Scriptures and questions on Sunday to further consider this situation.)

Wally Kroeker edits The Marketplace *magazine from Winnipeg, Manitoba, Canada.*

Sunday, Week 49   **Work**

For Personal Study or Group Discussion
Real Life Application

Key Bible Verse: So then, each of us will give an account of himself to God *(Romans 14:12). Bonus Readings: Matthew 9:9-13; Romans 14:1-13; 1 Corinthians 5:9-11; 2 Corinthians 6:14-15; Acts 16:16-19; Acts 19:23-41*

Questions to Consider

☐ Does Rudy seem to be separating his business from his faith? Where else do Christians exhibit the same tendency?

☐ How valid is the defense that "Rudy couldn't criticize the business if he weren't in it"? In what other kinds of work are we likely to hear the same argument?

Credits: Adapted from—Monday, Tuesday, Thursday: Don M. Aycock, editor, *God's Man* (Kregel, 1998); Wednesday, Friday: *God's Week Has 7 Days* (Herald, 1998); Saturday & Sunday: Kroeker with Ben Sprunger & Carol J. Suter, *Faith Dilemmas for Marketplace Christians* (Herald, 1997)

Can't Brush Them Off

Key Bible Verse: But I am among you as one who serves *(Luke 22: 27b). Bonus Reading: Philippians 2:1-11*

I was coming back from Ridgecrest [conference center]; there had been three thousand students. They show up everywhere—in your shower—for a whole week!

Finally you're on the plane, and you pull [the Bible] up around your face. Everybody will leave you alone.

I became aware of a young man crying in the seat beside me. I said, "Lord, he's not mine. My sinners are all on the ground in Omaha." He kept crying. Finally I said, "Son, I don't know what the matter is, but if I can help you, I'd like to."

He told me that his mother, father, and little sister had been killed in a car accident the day before. Suddenly, my heart grew very still. I said, "I don't know what you're feeling, but I know Someone who understands perfectly." I took the Bible behind which I'd been hiding, shared with him about Jesus, and led him to Christ.

I got off the plane, called someone I knew and asked him to meet him at the plane where he was going to land. He needed help that day.

I can't brush off somebody because I don't know him. If [Jesus] is a servant, then we are servants.

—Calvin Miller, professor and author

Personal Challenge:

• *Are times when staying in your comfort zone keeps you from obeying God's demands on your life?*

Thought to Apply: O Lord, baptize our hearts into a sense of the conditions and need of all men.

—GEORGE FOX (English founder of the Quakers, 17th century)

Hugged by Truckers

Key Bible Verse: Be devoted to one another in brotherly love *(Romans 12:10a). Bonus Reading: Colossians 3:12-14*

Linda was traveling up the rutted AlCan Highway from Alberta to the Yukon, alone in a rundown Honda Civic, where only four-wheel drives normally venture.

The first evening she found a room and asked for a 5 a.m. wakeup call. The clerk looked surprised. As she awoke to fog shrouding the mountain tops, she understood [why. When] she went to breakfast, two truckers invited Linda to join them.

"Where are you headed?" one asked.

"Whitehorse."

"In that little Civic? No way! This pass is dangerous in weather like this."

"Well, I'm determined to try," was Linda's gutsy, if not very informed, response.

"Then I guess we're just going to have to hug you," the trucker suggested.

Linda drew back.

The truckers chuckled.

"Not like that. We'll put one truck in front of you and one in the rear."

All that foggy morning, Linda followed two red dots, reassured by the big escorts as they made their way through the mountains.

In our dangerous passage through life, we need to be "hugged"—with Christians who know the way ahead of us; with others behind, gently encouraging us.

—*Don Graham in* Leadership

Personal Challenge:
• *Who do you know who might need a "hug" to get through the fog?*

Thought to Apply: Too many people don't care what happens so long as it doesn't happen to them.

—WILLIAM HOWARD TAFT (27th U.S. president)

The Gerber Boy

Key Bible Verse: This is what the Lord almighty says: "Administer true justice, show mercy and compassion to one another" *(Zechariah 7:9). Bonus Reading: Matthew 9:35-36*

In 1975 Raymond Dunn, Jr., was born with a skull fracture and oxygen deprivation that caused severe retardation. As Raymond grew, the family discovered further impairments. His twisted body suffered up to 20 seizures per day. He was blind, mute, immobile. Severe allergies limited him to only one food: a meat-based formula made by Gerber Foods.

In 1985, Gerber stopped making the formula that Raymond lived on. His mother scoured the country to buy what stores had in stock, accumulating cases and cases, but in 1990 her supply ran out. In desperation she appealed to Gerber for help.

In an unprecedented action, employees of the company donated hundreds of hours to bring out old equipment, set up production lines, obtain special approval from the USDA and produce the formula—all for one special boy.

In January 1995, Raymond Dunn, Jr., known as the Gerber Boy, died from his physical problems. But during his brief lifetime he called forth a wonderful thing called compassion.

—*Larry A. Payne in Fresh Illustrations for Preaching and Teaching*

Personal Challenge:
• *To what lengths are you willing to go when you are confronted with someone's need?*

Thought to Apply: Every act of kindness and compassion done by any man for his fellow Christian is done by Christ working within him.

—JULIAN OF NORWICH (English recluse, 14th century)

I Said Virtually Nothing

Key Bible Verses: Praise be to … the Father of compassion and the God of all comfort, who comforts us in all our troubles, so that we can comfort those in any trouble with the comfort we ourselves have received from God *(2 Corinthians 1:3-4). Bonus Reading: 2 Corinthians 2:3-11*

My phone rang on a Monday morning. A good friend tried to speak, but his voice broke. He wanted to meet with me … my counsel was vital … it couldn't wait.

I dropped everything. We met in my study. He stumbled in, weeping audibly as we embraced. I sensed immediately that Clifford (not his real name) was in no condition for high-powered advice. Between sobs and lengthy pauses, I said virtually nothing.

Cliff's wife had just returned from seeing her physician. A battery of diagnostic exams [had confirmed that] she has a malignancy of the lymph glands—the kind that has a very bleak prognosis.

For almost an hour he poured out his anguish, fears, confusion. He needed a listening ear, plain and simple.

Funny thing, as Cliff left he embraced me again and thanked me for my counsel. I don't believe I said ten sentences the entire time.

When you have friends going through valleys, they will appreciate the fact that you care. Your presence, a warm embrace—these best show your love. Sitting beside them and crying with them often helps the most.

—Charles R. Swindoll in Three Steps Forward, Two Steps Back

Personal Challenge:
• *When people are hurting, how good are you at listening?*

Thought to Apply: Hearin' is one thing and listenin' is another.   —WILLIAM FREND DEMORGAN (English novelist)

Confused Sheep

Key Bible Verse: The King will reply, "I tell you the truth, whatever you did for one of the least of these brothers of mine, you did for me *(Matthew 25:40).* *Bonus Reading: Matthew 25:31-46*

In Matthew 25, the sheep are as confused as the goats. It seems that judgment will be based on the acts of kindness we hardly think about. I picture myself standing before that King.

"Robinson, did you bring your date book?"

"Yes, Lord. Right here."

"Look up March 6, 1996."

"Oh yes. That's when *Newsweek* said I was a top communicator."

"I never read news magazines. After class, a young woman was at the back. She said her father had died and, the month before, her brother. You sat and talked to her. Do you remember?"

"I guess so, Lord."

The King will say, "I remember. When you talked to her, you were talking to me. Look up November 17, 1984."

"Yes, Lord, that's when I presented a paper at the theological society."

"I found those meetings stuffy. No, do you remember that morning your wife told you about a couple at the seminary having a hard time, and you put some money in an envelope and dropped it in their box?"

"I don't remember."

The King will say, "What you gave to that couple you gave to me. I've never forgotten."

—*Haddon Robinson, Gordon-Conwell Seminary professor*

Personal Challenge:

• *What would the King say to you about the way you treat His brothers?*

Thought to Apply: Nobody cares how much you know —until they know how much you care.   —JOHN CASSIS

Up Close & Personal with Haddon Robinson

What It Takes to Be a Good Neighbor

Q. ▪ We know we're supposed to help our neighbor. What does "neighbor" mean?

A. In Jesus' story in Luke 10, the answer of the man who had been beaten up by muggers and left to die would be: "Just about anybody coming down the road who's willing to stop and lend a hand!" Your neighbor is anyone whose need you see and whose need you're in a position to meet.

Why do good people sidestep that definition?
The priest's reasons were religious. The law said that if a priest touched a dead body, he would become ceremonially defiled.... In the name of holiness, we withdraw from people on the Jericho road who need our help.

The Levite may have indulged in a kind of arithmetic that is always interested in reaching the masses but somehow never gets down to a man or a woman. [It] talks about winning the world for God but doesn't think much about winning a neighborhood for God.

Why are neighbors so hard to love?
Your neighbor may be someone who is:

Unknown. There's no evidence that this Jew and Samaritan ever met each other before.

Unfriendly. The Jews and Samaritans were deep and long-standing enemies. You may find your neighbor is somebody who doesn't appreciate you, and slams the door when you try to visit.

Unlovely. There's nothing attractive about a man lying in a pool of blood. You may have a neighbor whose lifestyle you don't approve, whose whole way of operating turns your thermostat down.

Unrewarding. There's no evidence that that Jew was ever able to pay the Samaritan back for what he'd done.

What does it take to be a neighbor? Willingness to be involved, to lend a hand, and to give time. Like most of you, I live a hectic, hurried, and somewhat harassed life. The hardest thing to give to people is time. It [also] costs money. This Samaritan laid out two silver coins (roughly two days' wages) on the counter and then became surety for anything else that was left.

Haddon Robinson is a writer and professor at Gordon-Conwell Theological Seminary in South Hamilton, Massachusetts.

Caring for Others   Sunday, Week 50

For Personal Study or Group Discussion

Real Life Application

Key Bible Verse: Jesus told him, "Go and do likewise" *(Luke 10:37b). Bonus Reading: Luke 10:25-37*

Think and pray about this sentence starter on your own. Or, if you meet with other men, use it to trigger your discussion.

☐ Write the name of one person you'd like to help this week:

Credits: Adapted from: Monday: *Preaching Today* (35); Tuesday: *Leadership* (Vol. 9, No. 1); Wednesday: Edward K. Rowell, *Fresh Illustrations for Preaching and Teaching* (Baker, 1997); Thursday: *Three Steps Forward, Two Steps Back* (Nelson, 1980); Friday: *Preaching Today* (186); Saturday: *Preaching Today* (102)

Monday, Week 51   This Week's Theme: **Fathering**

Determined to Be a Good Dad

Key Bible Verses: For I am the Lord your God, who takes hold of your right hand and says to you, Do not fear; I will help you *(Isaiah 41:13). Bonus Reading: Psalm 37:23–24*

Eight years ago, I went through a terrible divorce. I made many awful mistakes, and I left two kids behind. Since my divorce, I have re-married a wonderful woman with three kids.

Two years ago, all was not well, and the step-father thing was not working. During that year, I attended the Memphis Promise Keepers conference. As soon as I walked into the stadium and heard about 50,000 men singing praises to the Lord, I was broken. The main thing I remember is that I cried for the entire weekend. I cried over leaving my two kids in my first marriage; I cried over the tough time I was having with my step-kids; and I cried because I knew I was not much of a husband, a father, and a man.

When I got home, I was determined to be a dad to all of my kids. The two years since then have been awesome. All five of my children are doing well. I have a relationship with each of them. God has given me a family, and I love them very much. It feels so good to do the right thing.

I still have a lot to learn, but, trust me, I thank God daily for what I have now.

—A promise keeper from Arizona

Personal Challenge:
• *What is God asking of you as a Dad?*

Thought to Apply: Children want to feel instinctively that their father is behind them as solid as a mountain, but like a mountain, is something to look up to.

—DOROTHY THOMPSON (journalist)

"I Rely Upon God"

Key Bible Verse: God has said, "Never will I leave you; never will I forsake you." So we say with confidence, "The Lord is my helper; I will not be afraid. What can man do to me?" *(Hebrews 13:5b). Bonus Reading: 1 John 3:1-3*

David Roseboro never thought he would be a single parent, but he gained custody of his small children after a divorce six years ago. "I wanted to give my boys the same stability I had as a kid," said the Atlanta father of David, 8, and Micah, 7. "I wanted them to know that I would always be there for them."

David's decision to be the best father he could be to his children signaled the beginning of a challenging yet rewarding journey. Being a single parent is not God's plan, said David, but the anointing and wisdom of God always kick in when needed.

"I rely upon God," said David, a systems analyst whose job sometimes calls for long hours. "Even when I need someone to look after the kids, I pray about it and God always sends someone to help. I've put it all in His hands."

The sacrifices and adjustments David and other single fathers make are worth the benefit of spending more time with their children, and for the children, the time spent with their fathers is priceless.

—Charlene Fain
in Say Amen

Personal Challenge:
• *Think of specific ways to devote your time to your family.*

Thought to Apply: The kind of man who thinks that helping with the dishes is beneath him will also think that helping with the baby is beneath him, and then he certainly is not going to be a very successful father.

—ELEANOR ROOSEVELT (wife of President Franklin D. Roosevelt)

Negotiate or Direct?

Key Bible Verse: He who spares the rod hates his son, but he who loves him is careful to discipline him *(Proverbs 13:24). Bonus Reading: Proverbs 23:13-14; 29:15, 17*

Adam caught our attention as we watched the seals in San Francisco Bay. His mother repeatedly begged the child, about six years old, to leave the slimy sand in which he was digging.

Finally, his mother threatened, "Come now! Or Dad will get you." Sure enough, Dad soon arrived. "Okay, Adam," he whimpered, "please come." Adam, digging and filthy, paid no heed. Dad's second approach demonstrated what was really wrong: "Okay, Adam, let's negotiate. What will it take to make you leave?"

Negotiate! That scene was a far cry from the role God originally intended for fathers. The Lord has called fathers to demonstrate godly leadership.

Negotiation gives children executive equivalency, whereas direction teaches them to respect authority and to be responsible in their actions.

A father and son on a mountain climb came to a particularly treacherous place. The father paused to consider which way to go, and the lad called out trustingly, "Choose the right path, Daddy. I'm following right behind you." God calls us to be stewards of our own souls and the souls of our families. May we do it well for both Christ's sake and theirs.

—*Robert Leslie Holmes*
in God's Man

Personal Challenge:
• *Which comes easier for you: negotiating or directing?*

Thought to Apply: A permissive home is a home where you don't love enough to exercise the authority that Christ gave you. —BEN HADEN (pastor)

Coaching Clinic

Key Bible Verse: Fathers, do not embitter your children, or they will become discouraged *(Colossians 3:21).*
Bonus Reading: Ephesians 6:1-4

When I was young, baseball was my life. You can imagine the excitement I felt when my oldest son began playing. This game would be one of our main bonding mechanisms. If my son would just listen, I could help him be a great baseball player. Learning to read curve balls, shift his body weight with the swing, steal bases, turn double plays—these things separate the amateurs from the pros.

A pattern developed in our relationship. Because of my familiarity with the game, I saw every mistake my son made. In addition, I knew how to correct them. So post-game drives home became a critique of how to improve his game. It soon got old for my son. One night he finally said, "Dad, could you not start by telling me everything I did wrong. Tell me what I did right first."

My mobile coaching clinic wasn't helping. My son had become discouraged. I was anxious to help, but I had become a hindrance. He was becoming bitter toward me. It caused me to think. Was my childhood obsession with baseball risking a relationship with my son? It was time to de-emphasize a game and refocus on the person.

—Jim Burton
in God's Man

Personal Challenge:
• *Are you more a coach or critic with your kids?*

Thought to Apply: Children have more need of models than of critics. —JOSEPH JOUBERT (French moralist, 18th century)

I Showed Up

Key Bible Verse: If you, then, though you are evil, know how to give good gifts to your children, how much more will your Father in heaven give good gifts to those who ask him! *(Matthew 7:11). Bonus Reading: Psalm 15*

I just love hanging out with my children. We do things together. It's part of my schedule.

When Bryndan was eleven years old he wanted to play football. That fall I was scheduled to travel a great deal, but I made a commitment to him that I would be at all of his games.

One weekend I was speaking on the West Coast on Friday, Bryndan had a game on Saturday, and I was scheduled to speak at a banquet in the Washington, D.C., area on Saturday night. In order to keep my word, I had to fly all night from Los Angeles back to Atlanta for his game.

When I got there, rain was pouring down. There were only half a dozen parents in the stands. But there I was, in the stands with my umbrella up, rooting on this little guy of mine and his friends at their football game. Afterward Bryndan said to me, "Dad, I know you said you'd be at all my games, but you didn't have to come today. Nobody else was there."

I said, "Buddy, I promised you that I would be there, and I wanted to make sure that I showed up."

—*Crawford W. Loritts, Jr.,*
in Never Walk Away

Personal Challenge:
• *Have you made a promise you need to keep?*

Thought to Apply: The best gift a father can give to his children is the gift of himself—his time. For material things mean little if there is not someone to share them with.

—C. Neil Strait (writer)

Up Close & Personal with Crawford Loritts

Q. **How did your dad form accountability in you?**

A. Pop knew that we needed to internally embrace the difference between right and wrong. Often, when I was a teenager on my way to go out, my father wasn't really sure about what I might be "getting into." So he would say: "Do right. Son, do right." I can't tell you the number of times that expression bailed me out of potentially devastating situations when I could have compromised my behavior.

The expression "Do right" was Pop's way of letting me know that he trusted me, but also it was a warning not to violate that trust. "Do right" was based on our relationship with Pop— and that's the key.

Crawford W. Lorrits, Jr., is the national director of Campus Crusade for Christ's Legacy Ministries.

For Personal Study or Group Discussion

Key Bible Verse: For I have chosen him so that he will direct his children and his household after him to keep the way of the Lord by doing what is right and just *(Genesis 18:19a). Bonus Reading: 1 Thessalonians 2:10-12*

Think and pray about these sentence starters.

☐ Something valuable I learned from my father is . . .

☐ A lesson I've learned from dealing with children is . . .

Credits: Adapted from—Monday: PKNet Testimony of the Week (5/28/98); Tuesday: *Say Amen* (Spring 1998); Wednesday & Thursday: Don M. Aycock, *God's Man* (Kregel, 1998); Friday & Saturday: *Never Walk Away* (Moody Bible Institute of Chicago, Moody Press, 1997)

Harvest Workers

Key Bible Verse: Then he said to his disciples, "The harvest is plentiful but the workers are few" *(Matthew 9:37). Bonus Reading: Romans 10:6-17*

When Dawson Trotman, founder of The Navigators, was recruiting counselors for a Billy Graham Crusade in a large city, he made numerous phone calls to the supporting churches. He would ask, "Could we have the names of the men and women in your congregation who know their Bibles well enough to lead someone to Christ?"

After a long pause, the church secretary of one of the larger churches replied rather wistfully, "You know, we did have a man like that in church once, but he moved away."

The analysis of Jesus of His own time [see the Key Bible Verse] is still the case. Spiritually qualified workers—disciples who labor hard to make other disciples—are rare.

I was raised on a farm in Iowa. We always had tons of work to do. Fences had to be fixed. Roofs needed repair. We had to vaccinate the pigs, mow the weeds, go to town for new tires for the tractor.

But [when] it was time for the harvest, we dropped our other work and became *harvest workers.* Jesus was talking about "harvest workers."

—Leroy Eims in The Lost Art of Disciple Making

Personal Challenge:
• *What does a person need to know to accept Christ?*

Thought to Apply: These early Christians [in the Book of Acts] were led by the Spirit to the main task of bringing people to God through Christ, and were not permitted to enjoy fascinating sidetracks.

—J. B. PHILLIPS (British pastor and New Testament translator)

A Whole New Deal

Key Bible Verse: "One thing I do know. I was blind but now I see!" *(John 9:25b). Bonus Reading: Acts 22:14-16*

I'd been racing 10 or 15 years when I married. After four years, I left racing to start a business. Money got tight; it bothered my wife. Finally, she said, "I'm leaving." I couldn't handle it. I tried to commit suicide three times.

[When] I went to work for Phil Parsons, I told him, "I need help." Phil put me in touch with [Motor Racing Outreach chaplain] Max Helton. MRO was having its yearly conference that weekend in Hilton Head; so Max said, "Why don't you come?"

I went. I accepted Christ that Friday night. To be nowhere before and all of a sudden to be at the top— this was a whole new deal!

On Sunday we went to the nearby Parris Island Marine artillery range. I saw all these bald-headed recruits coming up. I thought, *Maybe what I've been through will mean something to these kids.* I asked their chaplain, "Could I say something?"

At the end, I said, "Racers have to see something to believe it. Somebody tells you, 'Put this spoiler on your car and you'll pick up a half-second,' and we'll say, 'We'll try it.' I haven't seen Jesus Christ. But I *know* what He's done in my life!"

—*Cliff Champion, shop foreman,*
#41 Kodiak Racing/
Larry Hedrick Motorsports team

Personal Challenge:

• *Have you lost the excitement and joy you had when you first knew Christ?*

Thought to Apply: If he has faith, the believer cannot be restrained. . . . He confesses and teaches this gospel to the people at the risk of life itself.

—MARTIN LUTHER (Reformer, 16th century)

Jimmy Carter's Bible Study

Key Bible Verse: But I have had God's help to this very day, and so I stand here and testify to small and great alike *(Acts 26:22a). Bonus Reading: Luke 24:45-53*

I attended a dinner in Colombia, South America, aimed at praying for the nation. For the first time in the history of Colombia, the president, his cabinet, and the senate attended an event hosted by evangelicals.

During the meal, the president said to me, "You know, Palau, the reason I'm here tonight is because of Jimmy Carter." He went on to explain that when the leaders of Latin America gathered to sign the Panama Canal treaty, President Carter invited every leader—radicals, conservatives and liberals—to a Bible study at the White House.

The next morning at the study, Carter asked each of the men to read a verse of Matthew 24. Carter then explained what he thought it meant and closed in prayer.

The president of Colombia said to me, "I was truly impressed that Carter cared that much for us. It isn't diplomatic to speak freely about spiritual things, but I realized that Carter really liked us and wanted us to know Jesus Christ."

When President Carter invited those men to a Bible study, he never knew what doors it would open. He just obeyed the Spirit's prompting.
—*Luis Palau*
in The Peter Promise

Personal Challenge:
• *With whom is the Holy Spirit prompting you to share?*

Thought to Apply: God will hold us responsible as to how well we fulfill our responsibilities to this age and take advantage of our opportunities.

—BILLY GRAHAM (evangelist)

Abnormal Consistency

Key Bible Verse: Whatever happens, conduct yourselves in a manner worthy of the gospel of Christ *(Philippians 1:27). Bonus Reading: 1 Peter 3:15-16*

The new Toronto Blue Jays rookie, Jesse Barfield, walks into the ballpark with his Walkman, sidles up to relief pitcher Roy Lee Jackson, and tells him, "Check out this new cut." Jackson asks, "What kind of music is that?"

"Confunction," says Barfield, proudly.

Jackson says, "I don't listen to that kind of music."

Barfield recalls thinking, "Well, you're black! What do you mean you don't listen to this kind?"

"I listen to Christian music." Barfield says, "I began to watch Roy to see if what he did was in line with what he said." That night, in a tight contest, Roy gave up the winning hit to the White Sox.

The next day Roy shut down the Sox. [Both nights] Jackson [calmly] showered, dressed, and walked out. Barfield noticed, *this guy doesn't get nasty when he loses; he doesn't go crazy when he wins.* "He simply showed me, through the way he walked with the Lord, how I could find inner peace. That's what I wanted."

Jesse attended a Bible study at Roy's home with his girlfriend. Afterward, Roy asked Jesse if he wanted to give his life to Christ. "We did it," Barfield says with a smile.

—*Dave Branon & Joe Pellegrino in* Safe at Home

Personal Challenge:
• *Does your life match your message?*

Thought to Apply: If Christ lives in us, controlling our personalities, he will leave glorious marks on the lives we touch.   —EUGENIA PRICE (writer)

Fishing for Dad

Key Bible Verse: "Come, follow me," Jesus said, "and I will make you fishers of men" *(Matthew 4:19).*
Bonus Reading: John 16:7-11

I was a lot like my dad. As a 17-year-old, I was well on my way to going into business with him—until two guys on my baseball team told me about Jesus. After two months trying to deny Him, I surrendered my life to Christ.

Naturally, I wanted my dad to embrace Jesus as well. At first, my approach was too strong. He disowned me the night after my baptism, calling me a "fanatic."

Over the years, I desperately wanted him to embrace Jesus. One weekend I flew to Minneapolis to fish with dad, convinced that was a pivotal time for witness. Although I made several attempts, I came back sorely disappointed. I believed my dad's salvation hinged on me.

After many trips like this, I realized my thinking was unbiblical. It is *God* who changes hearts. The *Holy Spirit* does the work of saving the lost. This realization relieved my guilt and frustration.

My dad's opposition began to soften. He began to show a deep love for God. My father died without me knowing for certain if he accepted Christ as his Savior. But I know I can trust the Lord with my father's destiny.

—Fritz Dale in
The Promise Keeper

Personal Challenge:
• *Pray for Christ's Spirit to begin the work of salvation in the life of someone you love.*

Thought to Apply: There is no expeditious road to pack and label men for God, and save them by the barrel-load.
—FRANCIS THOMPSON (English poet, 19th century)

Up Close & Personal with Alan Andrews

How to Build Friendships with Non-Christians

Q. What advice do you have for those of us struggling to share Christ with our neighbors and acquaintances?

A. While I am not the most effective natural evangelist, I would like to share some simple lessons I am learning:

1. **Know the value of prayer.** It is such a delight to get up each day and pray specifically for my friends who don't know Jesus. What a joy it is to pray God's blessing on their home and family. I also pray that God will fill them with encouragement in their work and relationships. In a world that is so destructive, it is a wonderful privilege, through prayer, to bring the love and grace of God into the lives and homes of my friends.

2. **Take time to relate to your friends.** I am, like you, very busy. It is so easy to fill my day with activities that seem urgent, but I've had to learn that loving people into a relationship with the Lord Jesus takes an investment of time.

3. **Wait on the Holy Spirit to lead.** As we pray for and take time with our friends, let the Holy Spirit be the leader. That takes patience on my part, as I've had to learn to listen to the Holy Spirit as God works in my friends' lives. I've had to learn to move at His speed and direction. He knows when it is right to say a word and when it is better to wait.

4. **Allow my relationship with Jesus to naturally flow into my relationships.** I don't need to preach or be overly urgent in sharing Jesus, but I do need to make certain that oth-

ers see my relationship with Him as central to who I am. I must not be ashamed of Him in any of my friendships.

5. **When the time is right, I must invite my friends to look at the Scriptures.** Ultimately, it will be the power of God's Word that

will do the work. The writer of Hebrews tells us that the Word of God is living and active (Hebrews 4:12). The power of the Word will melt the heart of an unbelieving friend.

Alan Andrews is the director of The Navigators in the U.S.

Sunday, Week 52   **Witness**

For Personal Study or Group Discussion

Real Life Application

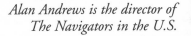

Key Bible Verse: I am not ashamed of the gospel, because it is the power of God for the salvation of everyone who believes *(Romans 1:16a). Bonus Reading: Mark 8:34-38*

Think and pray about these sentence starters on your own. Or, if you meet with other men, use them to trigger your discussion.

☐ One thing that helps me be an effective witness for Christ is . . .

☐ I want to pray for the salvation of these people: . . .

Credits: Adapted from—Monday: *The Lost Art of Disciple Making* (Zondervan/NavPress, 1978); Tuesday: P. J. Richardson & Robert Darden, *Wheels of Thunder* (Nelson, 1997); Wednesday: *The Peter Promise* (Discovery House, 1996); Thursday: *Safe at Home* (Moody Bible Institute of Chicago, Moody Press, 1992); Friday: *The Promise Keeper* (11-12/98); Saturday: *One-to-One: A Ministry Report from The Navigators*, a donor publication (Fall 98, issue 25)

Credits

Week 1 — Family

Monday	Bill McCartney, *Go the Distance* (Focus on the Family, 1996)
Tuesday	Gary Smalley, *Seven Promises of a Promise Keeper* (Focus on the Family, 1994)
Wednesday	Mark Moring, Editor
Thursday	Mike Singletary & Jerry B. Jenkins, *Singletary on Singletary* (Nelson, 1991)
Friday	John Trent, *The Making of a Godly Man* (Focus on the Family, 1997)
Saturday	From *Shoulder to Shoulder* by Rodney L. Cooper. © 1997 by Rodney L. Cooper. Used by permission of Zondervan Publishing House.

Week 2 — Honoring Christ

Monday	Mark Moring, Editor
Tuesday	Ken Walker, *Christian Reader* (Sept./Oct. 1995)
Wednesday	Jack Hayford, *Seven Promises of a Promise Keeper* (Focus on the Family, 1994)
Thursday	Wellington Boone, *Seven Promises of a Promise Keeper* (Focus on the Family, 1994)
Friday	Edwin Louis Cole, *Seven Promises of a Promise Keeper* (Focus on the Family, 1994)
Saturday	Randy Phillips, *Go the Distance* (Focus on the Family, 1996)

Week 3 — Friendship & Accountability

Monday	Louis McBurney, *Leadership* (Summer 1996). To subscribe, call 800-777-3136.
Tuesday	Mark Moring, *Campus Life* (Sept./Oct. 1996)
Wednesday	Howard Hendricks, *Seven Promises of a Promise Keeper* (Focus on the Family, 1994)
Thursday	Chris Lutes, *Campus Life* (Sept./Oct. 1996)
Friday	Stu Weber, *Go the Distance* (Focus on the Family, 1996)
Saturday	Chris Rice and the late Spencer Perkins, *Reconcilers* (Spring 1998)

Week 4 — Sexual Purity

Monday	Jerry Kirk, *Leadership* (Summer 1995). To subscribe, call 800-777-3136.
Tuesday	Gregg Lewis, *The Power of a Promise Kept* (Focus on the Family, 1995)
Wednesday	Steve Farrar, adapted from *What Makes a Man?* © 1992 by Promise

Keepers. Used by permission of NavPress, Colorado Springs, Colorado. All rights reserved. For copies call (800) 366-7788.

Thursday	Mark Moring, *Campus Life*
Friday	Gary Oliver, *Seven Promises of a Promise Keeper* (Focus on the Family, 1994)
Saturday	Jerry Kirk, *Leadership* (Summer 1995). To subscribe, call 800-777-3136.

Week 5 — Church

Monday	Bill McCartney, *Sold Out* (Word, 1997) Word Publishing, Nashville, Tennessee. All rights reserved.
Tuesday	Luis Palau, adapted from *What Makes a Man?* © 1992 by Promise Keepers. Used by permission of NavPress, Colorado Springs, Colorado. All rights reserved. For copies call (800) 366-7788.
Wednesday	Mark Moring, Editor
Thursday	John VanDyke, Product Development Manager, Bank Corp, Ionia, Michigan
Friday	Jesse Miranda, *Go the Distance* (Focus on the Family, 1996)
Saturday	Jesse Miranda, *Go the Distance* (Focus on the Family, 1996)

Week 6 — Marriage & Family

Monday	Haman Cross, Jr., *Urban Family* (Spring 1995)
Tuesday	Louise Ferrebee, "House of Cards," *Marriage Partnership* (Summer 1996)
Wednesday	Kevin A. Miller, "Coming in Second," *Marriage Partnership* (Fall 1996)
Thursday	Gary Smalley, *Go the Distance* (Focus on the Family, 1996)
Friday	John Yates, adapted from *What Makes a Man?* © 1992 by Promise Keepers. Used by permission of NavPress, Colorado Springs, Colorado. All rights reserved. For copies call (800) 366-7788.
Saturday	Gary Smalley, *Go the Distance* (Focus on the Family, 1996)

Week 7 — Sharing Faith

Monday	*Fresh Illustrations* (CTi/Baker, 1997)
Tuesday	Luis Palau, *Seven Promises of a Promise Keeper* (Focus on the Family, 1994)
Wednesday	Bill Bright, *Seven Promises of a Promise Keeper* (Focus on the Family, 1994)
Thursday	John Trent, *The Making of a Godly Man* (Focus on the Family, 1997)
Friday	Douglas R. Sword, *Christian Parenting Today* (May/June 1998)
Saturday	John Trent, *The Making of a Godly Man* (Focus on the Family, 1997)

Week 8 — Racial Reconciliation

Monday	Bill McCartney, *Seven Promises of a Promise Keeper* (Focus on the Family, 1994)
Tuesday	Dave Endrody, American Express account executive
Wednesday	Glen Kehrein, *Leadership* (Winter 1995). To subscribe, call 800-777-3136.
Thursday	From *WWJD Interactive Devotional* compiled by Dana Key. Copyright © 1997 by The Zondervan Corporation. Used by permission of Zondervan Publishing House.
Friday	John Perkins, *Go the Distance* (Focus on the Family, 1996)
Saturday	John Perkins, *Go the Distance* (Focus on the Family, 1996)

Week 9 — Courage

Monday	Marshall Shelley, *Leadership* (Summer 1995). To subscribe, call 800-777-3136.
Tuesday	Craig Brian Larson, *Contemporary Illustrations for Teachers, Preachers, and Writers* (Baker, 1996)
Wednesday	From *Shoulder to Shoulder* by Rodney L. Cooper. © 1997 by Rodney L. Cooper. Used by permission of Zondervan Publishing House.
Thursday	Joseph M. Stowell, *Preaching Today*, #178. To subscribe, call 800-806-7796 or go to http://st3.yahoo.com/cti/preac.html.
Friday	Craig Brian Larson, *Contemporary Illustrations for Teachers, Preachers, and Writers* (Baker, 1996)
Saturday	Steve Ruda, Promise Keepers' "Covenant Partner Profile"

Week 10 — Sacrifice

Monday	Jerry Bridges with Annette LaPlaca, "How to do the Undoable," *Marriage Partnership* (Summer 1996)
Tuesday	From *Better Men* by Phillip H. Porter, Jr. with W. Terry Whalin. Copyright © 1998 by Phillip H. Porter, Jr. and W. Terry Whalin. Used by permission of Zondervan Publishing House.
Wednesday	Joan Brasher, *Marriage Partnership* (Spring 1997)
Thursday	Robert Russell, *Preaching Today*, #176. To subscribe, call 800-806-7796 or go to http://st3.yahoo.com/cti/preac.html.
Friday	Kevin A. Miller, *Marriage Partnership* (Fall 1996)
Saturday	John Ashcroft, *Lessons from a Father to His Son* (Nelson, 1998)

Week 11 — Trust in God

Monday	Warren Wiersbe, *Being a Child of God* (Nelson, 1996)
Tuesday	David Biebel, *If God Is So Good, Why Do I Hurt So Bad?* (Spire, 1995)
Wednesday	From *Grace Walk* by Steve McVey. Copyright © 1995 by Harvest House Publishers, Eugene, Oregon 97402. Used by permission.
Thursday	Promise Keeper testimony, used with permission
Friday	*Decision* (October 1997)
Saturday	From *No More Excuses* by Tony Evans. Copyright © 1996. Used by permission of Good News Publishers/Crossway Books, Wheaton, Illinois 60187.

Week 12 — Fathering

Monday	Steve Farrar, *Anchor Man* (Nelson, 1998)
Tuesday	From *A Father for All Seasons* Copyright © 1998 by Bob Welch. Published by Harvest House Publishers, Eugene, Oregon 97402. Used by permission.
Wednesday	From *No More Excuses* by Tony Evans. Copyright © 1996. Used by permission of Good News Publishers/Crossway Books, Wheaton, Illinois 60187.
Thursday	From *The 7 Secrets of Effective Fathers*, Ken R. Canfield © 1992 Used by permission of Tyndale House Publishers, Inc. All rights reserved.
Friday	Kevin A. Miller, *Leadership* (Winter 1996) To subscribe, call 800-777-3136.
Saturday	Gary D. Chapman, *The Five Love Languages of Children* (Moody Bible Institute, Moody Press, 1997)

Week 13 — Coming Back

Monday	Evander Holyfield with Stephen Strang, *New Man* (Mar./Apr. 1998)
Tuesday	Adapted from *Dangers Men Face* © 1997 by Jerry White. Used by permission of NavPress, Colorado Springs, Colorado. All rights reserved. For copies call (800) 366-7788.
Wednesday	Tracey D. Lawrence, *The Promise Keeper* (May/June 1998)
Thursday	Gordon MacDonald, *When Men Think Private Thoughts* (Nelson, 1996)
Friday	Promise Keeper testimony, used with permission
Saturday	From *Better Men* by Phillip H. Porter, Jr. with W. Terry Whalin. Copyright © 1998 by Phillip H. Porter, Jr. and W. Terry Whalin. Used by permission of Zondervan Publishing House.

Week 14 — Meaningful Work

Monday	Stuart Briscoe, *Discipleship for Ordinary People* (Shaw, 1995)
Tuesday	From *Halftime* by Bob Buford. Copyright © 1994 by Robert P. Buford. Used by permission of Zondervan Publishing House.
Wednesday	From *No More Excuses* by Tony Evans. Copyright © 1996. Used by permission of Good News Publishers/Crossway Books, Wheaton, Illinois 60187.
Thursday	W. Terry Whalin, *Stand Firm* (May 1998)
Friday	From *The 7 Secrets of Effective Fathers*, Ken R. Canfield © 1992 Used by permission of Tyndale House Publishers, Inc. All rights reserved.
Saturday	Phil Downer with Chip MacGregor, *Stand Firm* (May 1998)

Week 15 — Meeting Challenges

Monday	Craig Brian Larson, editor, *Illustrations for Preaching & Teaching: from Leadership Journal* (Baker, 1993)
Tuesday	Bruce Watson, *Christian Reader* (Jul./Aug. 1998)
Wednesday	Craig Brian Larson, editor, *Illustrations for Preaching & Teaching: from Leadership Journal* (Baker, 1993)
Thursday	Gordon MacDonald, *When Men Think Private Thoughts* (Nelson, 1996)
Friday	Promise Keeper testimony, used with permission
Saturday	Dr. Benjamin Carson with Stephen Caldwell, *Life@Work* (Vol. 1, No. 1)

Week 16 — Money

Monday	Jerry and Ramona Tuma and Tim LaHaye, *Smart Money* (Multnomah, 1994)
Tuesday	From *No More Excuses* by Tony Evans. Copyright © 1996. Used by permission of Good News Publishers/Crossway Books, Wheaton, Illinois 60187.
Wednesday	Tom L. Eisenman, *Temptations Men Face* (InterVarsity, 1990)
Thursday	Craig Brian Larson, editor, *Illustrations for Preaching & Teaching: from Leadership Journal* (Baker, 1993)
Friday	James Dobson, *Life on the Edge* (Word, 1995) Word Publishing, Nashville, Tennessee. All rights reserved.
Saturday	Steve Farrar, *Anchor Man* (Nelson, 1998)

Week 17 — Integrity

Monday	Bill McCartney, *Sold Out* (Word, 1997) Word Publishing, Nashville, Tennessee. All rights reserved.

Tuesday	Frederica Mathewes-Green, *Christianity Today* (1997)
Wednesday	Jim Corley, *Christian Reader* (Jan./Feb. 1998)
Thursday	Ken Walker, *Christian Reader* (Jan./Feb. 1995)
Friday	Craig Brian Larson, editor, *Illustrations for Preaching & Teaching: from Leadership Journal* (Baker, 1993)
Saturday	Gordon MacDonald, *When Men Think Private Thoughts* (Nelson, 1996)

Week 18 — Beating Temptation

Monday	From *Better Men* by Phillip H. Porter, Jr. with W. Terry Whalin. Copyright © 1998 by Phillip H. Porter, Jr. and W. Terry Whalin. Used by permission of Zondervan Publishing House.
Tuesday	Craig Brian Larson, editor, *Contemporary Illustrations for Teachers, Preachers, and Writers* (Baker, 1996)
Wednesday	Promise Keepers Testimony, used with permission
Thursday	Adapted from *Dangers Men Face* © 1997 by Jerry White. Used by permission of NavPress, Colorado Springs, Colorado. All rights reserved. For copies call (800) 366-7788.
Friday	Craig Brian Larson, editor, *Illustrations for Preaching & Teaching: from Leadership Journal* (Baker, 1993)
Saturday	Edgar D. Barron, *The Promise Keeper* (May/June 1998)

Week 19 — Forgiveness

Monday	From *Eternal Impact*. © 1997 by Phil Downer. Published by Harvest House Publishers, Eugene, Oregon 97402. Used by permission.
Tuesday	From *The Worth of a Man* by Dave Dravecky with Connie Neal. Copyright © 1996 by David F. Dravecky. Used by permission of Zondervan Publishing House.
Wednesday	From *The Seven Seasons of a Man's Life* by Patrick M. Morley. Copyright © 1995 by Patrick M. Morley. Used by permission of Zondervan Publishing House.
Thursday	Chuck Colson, *A Life of Integrity* (Multnomah, 1997)
Friday	T. D. Jakes, *So You Call Yourself a Man?* (Albury, 1997)
Saturday	Mark Mittelberg, *Leadership* (Summer 1998) To subscribe, call 800-777-3136.

Week 20 — Boldness

Monday	Bill McCartney, *Sold Out* (Word, 1997) Word Publishing, Nashville, Tennessee. All rights reserved.
Tuesday	From *Fresh Wind, Fresh Fire* by Jim Cymbala with Dean Merrill. Copyright © 1997 by Jim Cymbala. Used by permission of Zondervan Publishing House.

Wednesday	Craig Brian Larson, editor, *Illustrations for Preaching & Teaching: from Leadership Journal* (Baker, 1993)
Thursday	Mark Mittelberg, *Leadership* (Summer 1998) To subscribe, call 800-777-3136.
Friday	Promise Keepers Testimony, used with permission
Saturday	T. D. Jakes, *So You Call Yourself a Man?* (Albury, 1997)

Week 21 — Hearing God

Monday	Tony Evans, *What a Way to Live!* (Word, 1997) Word Publishing, Nashville, Tennessee. All rights reserved.
Tuesday	From *The Worth of a Man* by Dave Dravecky with Connie Neal. © 1996 by David F. Dravecky. Used by permission of Zondervan Publishing House.
Wednesday	Gordon MacDonald, *Ordering Your Private World* (Oliver-Nelson, 1984)
Thursday	From *Better Men* by Phillip H. Porter, Jr. with W. Terry Whalin. Copyright © 1998 by Phillip H. Porter, Jr. and W. Terry Whalin. Used by permission of Zondervan Publishing House.
Friday	Henry Blackaby, *Experiencing God* (Broadman & Holman, 1994)
Saturday	Bill McCartney, *Sold Out* (Word, 1997) Word Publishing, Nashville, Tennessee. All rights reserved.

Week 22 — Handling Anger

Monday	Raymond McHenry, *Something to Think About* (Hendrickson, 1998)
Tuesday	David Stoop and Stephen Arterburn, *The Angry Man* (Word, 1991) Word Publishing, Nashville, Tennessee. All rights reserved.
Wednesday	Gene A. Getz, *The Measure of a Man*. Copyright © 1995. Regal Books, Ventura, CA 93003. Used by permission.
Thursday	Brian Weatherdon, *Leadership* (Winter 1998) To subscribe, call 800-777-3136.
Friday	T.D. Jakes, *So You Call Yourself a Man?* (Albury, 1997)
Saturday	From *The Worth of a Man by Dave Dravecky* with Connie Neal. Copyright © 1996 by David F. Dravecky. Used by permission of Zondervan Publishing House.

Week 23 — Loving Jesus

Monday	Henry Blackaby, *Experiencing God* (Broadman & Holman, 1994)
Tuesday	Chuck Colson, *A Life of Integrity* (Multnomah, 1997)
Wednesday	From *The Seven Seasons of a Man's Life* by Patrick M. Morley. Copyright © 1995 by Patrick M. Morley. Used by permission of Zondervan Publishing House.

Thursday	Promise Keepers Testimony, used with permission
Friday	Charles R. Swindoll, *David: A Man of Passion & Destiny* (Word, 1997) Word Publishing, Nashville, Tennessee. All rights reserved.
Saturday	David Robinson with Jay C. Grelen, *Christian Reader* (Mar./Apr. 1998)

Week 24 — Wise Decisions

Monday	From *Eternal Impact*. Copyright © 1997 by Phil Downer. Published by Harvest House Publishers, Eugene, Oregon 97402. Used by permission.
Tuesday	Bob Mumford, *Take Another Look at Guidance* (Lifechangers, 1993)
Wednesday	George O. Wood, *Pentecostal Evangel* (March 26, 1995)
Thursday	Henry Blackaby, *Experiencing God* (Broadman & Holman, 1994)
Friday	Taken from *Disappointment With God*. Copyright © 1988 by Philip Yancey. Used by permission of Zondervan Publishing House.
Saturday	Haddon Robinson, *Decision-Making by the Book* (Victor, 1991)

Week 25 — Commitment

Monday	John Trent, *Go the Distance* (Focus on the Family, 1996)
Tuesday	Craig Brian Larson, *Contemporary Illustrations for Preachers, Teachers, and Writers* (Baker, 1996)
Wednesday	Roger Palms, adapted from *What Makes a Man?* © 1992 by Promise Keepers. Used by permission of NavPress, Colorado Springs, Colorado. All rights reserved. For copies call (800) 366-7788.
Thursday	From *The 7 Secrets of Effective Fathers*, Ken R. Canfield © 1992 Used by permission of Tyndale House Publishers, Inc. All rights reserved.
Friday	Craig Brian Larson, editor, *Illustrations for Preaching & Teaching: from Leadership Journal* (Baker, 1993)
Saturday	Steve Farrar, *Anchor Man* (Nelson, 1998)

Week 26 — Truthfulness

Monday	Dave Endrody, American Express account executive
Tuesday	From *The Worth of a Man* by Dave Dravecky with Connie Neal. Copyright © 1996 by David F. Dravecky. Used by permission of Zondervan Publishing House.
Wednesday	From *Eternal Impact*. Copyright © 1997 by Phil Downer. Published by Harvest House Publishers, Eugene, Oregon 97402. Used by permission.
Thursday	Howard Hendricks, *A Life of Integrity* (Multnomah, 1997)

| Friday | Mark Galli, Editor |
| Saturday | From No More *Excuses* by Tony Evans. Copyright © 1996. Used by permission of Good News Publishers/Crossway Books, Wheaton, Illinois 60187. |

Week 27 — Enriching Your Wife

Monday	Dennis Rainey, *A Life of Integrity* (Multnomah, 1997)
Tuesday	From *The Seven Seasons of a Man's Life* by Patrick M. Morley. Copyright © 1995 by Patrick M. Morley. Used by permission of Zondervan Publishing House.
Wednesday	Gordon MacDonald, *When Men Think Private Thoughts* (Nelson, 1996)
Thursday	From *The 7 Secrets of Effective Fathers*, Ken R. Canfield © 1992 Used by permission of Tyndale House Publishers, Inc. All rights reserved.
Friday	Joan Brasher, *Marriage Partnership* (Summer 1998)
Saturday	Holly Phillips with Louise Ferrebee, *Marriage Partnership* (Summer 1997)

Week 28 — Work

Monday	Eugene H. Peterson, *Leap Over a Wall* (HarperCollins, 1997)
Tuesday	Steve Farrar, *Anchor Man* (Nelson, 1998)
Wednesday	Bill Nix, *The Promise Keeper* (Sept./Oct. 1998)
Thursday	Bill Nix, *The Promise Keeper* (Sept./Oct. 1998)
Friday	Stephen Caldwell, *Life@Work* (Vol. 1, No. 3)
Saturday	John Beckett with Dick Leggatt, *The Christian Businessman* (July/August 1998)

Week 29 — Trusting God

Monday	Tom Macklin, *Decision* (Dec. 1998)
Tuesday	Steve Brown, *Jumping Hurdles* (Baker, 1992)
Wednesday	Bruce Carroll with Jan Northington, *Christian Reader* (Sept./Oct. 1998)
Thursday	Steve Brown, *Jumping Hurdles* (Baker, 1992)
Friday	Bonne Steffen, *Christian Reader* (Nov./Dec. 1997)
Saturday	Charles R. Swindoll, *Three Steps Forward, Two Steps Back* (Nelson, 1980)

Week 30 — Commitment to Family

Monday	Steve Farrar, *Anchor Man* (Nelson, 1998)
Tuesday	Crawford W. Lorrits, Jr., *Never Walk Away* (Moody Bible Institute, Moody Press, 1997)
Wednesday	PK Net Testimony of the Week (September 4, 1997)
Thursday	PK Net Testimony of the Week (August 28, 1998)
Friday	J. Derek McNeil, *Men to Men* (Zondervan, 1996)
Saturday	Gary Smalley with John Trent, *Go the Distance* (Focus on the Family, 1996)

Week 31 — Serving

Monday	Laura Kellams, *Life@Work* (Vol. 1, No. 3)
Tuesday	Steve Brown, *Jumping Hurdles* (Baker, 1992)
Wednesday	Bill Hybels, *Preaching Today*, #164. To subscribe, call 800-806-7796 or go to http://st3.yahoo.com/cti/preac.html.
Thursday	PK Net Testimony of the Week (September 5, 1996)
Friday	Roger Barrier, *Preaching Today*, #164. To subscribe, call 800-806-7796 or go to http://st3.yahoo.com/cti/preac.html.
Saturday	Richard J. Foster, *Celebration of Discipline* (Harper & Row, 1978)

Week 32 — Connecting

Monday	Gordon MacDonald, *When Men Think Private Thoughts* (Nelson, 1996)
Tuesday	Gordon MacDonald, *When Men Think Private Thoughts* (Nelson, 1996)
Wednesday	PK Net Testimony of the Week (September 4, 1997)
Thursday	Johann Christoph Arnold, *A Plea for Purity* (1998) Plough Publishing, 800-521-8011; Spring Valley, Rte. 381 N, Farmington, PA 15437.
Friday	Crawford W. Lorrits, Jr., *Never Walk Away* (Moody Bible Institute, Moody Press, 1997)
Saturday	From *No More Excuses* by Tony Evans. Copyright © 1996. Used by permission of Good News Publishers/Crossway Books, Wheaton, Illinois 60187.

Week 33 — Encouragement

Monday	PK Net Testimony of the Week (March 5, 1998)
Tuesday	Stu Weber, *Locking Arms* (Multnomah, 1995)
Wednesday	Michelle Hayes, *Connection Newsletter* (July 17, 1998)
Thursday	William Hinson, *Preaching Today*, #114. To subscribe, call 800-806-7796 or go to http://st3.yahoo.com/cti/preac.html.

| Friday | From *The Worth of a Man* by Dave Dravecky with Connie Neal. Copyright © 1996 by David F. Dravecky. Used by permission of Zondervan Publishing House. |
| Saturday | John Trent, *Christian Parenting Today* (Jan./Feb. 1999) |

Week 34 — Resisting Evil

Monday	Gordon MacDonald, *When Men Think Private Thoughts* (Nelson, 1996)
Tuesday	Charles R. Swindoll, *Three Steps Forward, Two Steps Back* (Nelson, 1980)
Wednesday	Steve Farrar, *Anchor Man* (Nelson, 1998)
Thursday	Craig Stephen Smith, *Whiteman's Gospel* (Indian Life, 1997)
Friday	Cindy Crosby and Mark Sanborn, *Life@Work* (Vol. 1, No. 3)
Saturday	Bryan Chapell, *Preaching Today*, #181. To subscribe, call 800-806-7796 or go to http://st3.yahoo.com/cti/preac.html.

Week 35 — Racism

Monday	From *Disciplines of a Godly Man* by R. Kent Hughes. Copyright © 1991. Used by permission of Good News Publishers/Crossway Books, Wheaton, Illinois 60187.
Tuesday	From *The Character of God* © 1995 by R.C. Sproul. Published by Servant Publications, Box 8617, Ann Arbor, Michigan, 48107.
Wednesday	Luis Palau, *The Peter Promise* (Discovery House, 1996)
Thursday	James Line with Chuck Goldberg, *Decision* (October 1998)
Friday	James Line with Chuck Goldberg, *Decision* (October 1998)
Saturday	Joseph L. Garlington, *Right or Reconciled?* (Destiny Image, 1998)

Week 36 — Accountability

Monday	Adapted from *Dangers Men Face* © 1997 by Jerry White. Used by permission of NavPress, Colorado Springs, Colorado. All rights reserved. For copies call (800) 366-7788.
Tuesday	Wes Roberts with Stephen Caldwell and Sean Womack, *Life@Work* (Vol. 2, No. 2)
Wednesday	PK Net Testimony of the Week (March 19, 1998)
Thursday	From *Better Men* by Phillip H. Porter, Jr. with W. Terry Whalin. Copyright © 1998 by Phillip H. Porter, Jr. and W. Terry Whalin. Used by permission of Zondervan Publishing House.
Friday	Bill Hybels, *Preaching Today*, #57. To subscribe, call 800-806-7796 or go to http://st3.yahoo.com/cti/preac.html.
Saturday	From *Better Men* by Phillip H. Porter, Jr. with W. Terry Whalin. Copyright © 1998 by Phillip H. Porter, Jr. and W. Terry Whalin. Used by permission of Zondervan Publishing House.

Week 37 — Prayer

Monday	Leith Anderson, *Preaching Today*, #48. To subscribe, call 800-806-7796 or go to http://st3.yahoo.com/cti/preac.html.
Tuesday	Mike Lane, *Command* (December 1998)
Wednesday	Joseph Bernardin, *The Gift of Peace* (Loyola, 1997)
Thursday	Joseph Bernardin, *The Gift of Peace* (Loyola, 1997)
Friday	Charles R. Swindoll, *Preaching Today*, #50. To subscribe, call 800-806-7796 or go to http://st3.yahoo.com/cti/preac.html.
Saturday	Dick Eastman, *The Hour That Changes the World* (Baker, 1978)

Week 38 — Self-Discipline

Monday	John L. Moore, *Take the Reins* (Nelson, 1997)
Tuesday	From *Disciplines of a Godly Man* by R. Kent Hughes. Copyright © 1991. Used by permission of Good News Publishers/Crossway Books, Wheaton, Illinois 60187.
Wednesday	Calvin Miller, *Preaching Today*, #22. To subscribe, call 800-806-7796 or go to http://st3.yahoo.com/cti/preac.html.
Thursday	John L. Moore, *Take the Reins* (Nelson, 1997)
Friday	From *Disciplines of a Godly Man* by R. Kent Hughes. Copyright © 1991. Used by permission of Good News Publishers/Crossway Books, Wheaton, Illinois 60187.
Saturday	From *Daddy's Home at Last* by Mike Singletary with Russ Pate. Copyright © 1998 by Mike Singletary & Russ Pate. Used by permission of Zondervan Publishing House.

Week 39 — Sin & Forgiveness

Monday	Luis Palau, *The Peter Promise* (Discovery House, 1996)
Tuesday	Crawford W. Lorrits, Jr., *Never Walk Away* (Moody Bible Institute, Moody Press, 1997)
Wednesday	Adapted from *Dangers Men Face* © 1997 by Jerry White. Used by permission of NavPress, Colorado Springs, Colorado. All rights reserved. For copies call (800) 366-7788.
Thursday	Steve Brown, *Jumping Hurdles* (Baker, 1992)
Friday	Crawford W. Lorrits, Jr., *Never Walk Away* (Moody Bible Institute, Moody Press, 1997)
Saturday	Johann Christoph Arnold, *Seventy Times Seven* (1997) Plough Publishing, 800-521-8011; Spring Valley, Rte. 381 N, Farmington, PA 15437.

Week 40 — God's Love

Monday	Ian Pitt-Watson, *Preaching Today*, #40. To subscribe, call 800-806-7796 or go to http://st3.yahoo.com/cti/preac.html.
Tuesday	Don M. Aycock, from *God's Man*. Copyright © 1998. Kregel Publications, Grand Rapids, MI 49503.
Wednesday	Bill Hybels, *Preaching Today*, #43. To subscribe, call 800-806-7796 or go to http://st3.yahoo.com/cti/preac.html.
Thursday	Bruce Thielemann, *Preaching Today*, #48. To subscribe, call 800-806-7796 or go to http://st3.yahoo.com/cti/preac.html.
Friday	Hudson Armerding, *Command* (December 1998)
Saturday	From *Loving God* by Charles W. Colson. Copyright © 1983 by Charles W. Colson. Used by permission of Zondervan Publishing House.

Week 41 — Being an Example

Monday	Eugene H. Peterson, *Leap Over a Wall* (HarperCollins, 1997)
Tuesday	Timothy Jones, *Decision* (December, 1998)
Wednesday	Ken Canfield, *Spiritual Secrets of Faithful Fathers* (Beacon Hill, 1997)
Thursday	Steve Farrar, *Anchor Man* (Nelson, 1998)
Friday	Ken Canfield, *Spiritual Secrets of Faithful Fathers* (Beacon Hill, 1997)
Saturday	From *The 7 Secrets of Effective Fathers*, Ken R. Canfield © 1992 Used by permission of Tyndale House Publishers, Inc. All rights reserved.

Week 42 — Dealing with Failure

Monday	Steve Brown, *Jumping Hurdles* (Baker, 1992)
Tuesday	Adapted from *Dangers Men Face* © 1997 by Jerry White. Used by permission of NavPress, Colorado Springs, Colorado. All rights reserved. For copies call (800) 366-7788.
Wednesday	John Ashcroft, *Lessons from a Father to His Son* (Nelson, 1998)
Thursday	From *Leadership Prayers,* Richard Kriegbaum © 1998 Used by permission of Tyndale House Publishers, Inc. All rights reserved.
Friday	From *Loving God* by Charles W. Colson. Copyright © 1983 by Charles W. Colson. Used by permission of Zondervan Publishing House.
Saturday	John Block with Rosey Grier and Kathi Mills, *Winning* Copyright © 1990. Regal Books, Ventura, CA 93003. Used by permission.

Week 43 — Sexual Purity

Monday	Lew Gervais, director of Pressing Onward support groups
Tuesday	Adapted from *Dangers Men Face* © 1997 by Jerry White. Used by permission of NavPress, Colorado Springs, Colorado. All rights reserved. For copies call (800) 366-7788.

Wednesday	Lew Gervais, director of Pressing Onward support groups
Thursday	Charles R. Swindoll, *Three Steps Forward, Two Steps Back* (Nelson, 1980)
Friday	John Piper, *Future Grace* (Multnomah, 1995)
Saturday	Adapted from *Dangers Men Face* © 1997 by Jerry White. Used by permission of NavPress, Colorado Springs, Colorado. All rights reserved. For copies call (800) 366-7788.

Week 44 — Holiness

Monday	From *Loving God* by Charles W. Colson. Copyright © 1983 by Charles W. Colson. Used by permission of Zondervan Publishing House.
Tuesday	From *The Holiness of God,* R.C Sproul © 1985 Used by permission of Tyndale House Publishers, Inc. All rights reserved.
Wednesday	Adapted from *The Pursuit of Holiness* © 1978 by Jerry Bridges. Used by permission of NavPress, Colorado Springs, Colorado. All rights reserved. For copies call (800) 366-7788.
Thursday	Joseph M. Stowell, *Preaching Today,* #45. To subscribe, call 800-806-7796 or go to http://st3.yahoo.com/cti/preac.html.
Friday	Adapted from *The Pursuit of Holiness* © 1978 by Jerry Bridges. Used by permission of NavPress, Colorado Springs, Colorado. All rights reserved. For copies call (800) 366-7788.
Saturday	Adapted from *The Pursuit of Holiness* © 1978 by Jerry Bridges. Used by permission of NavPress, Colorado Springs, Colorado. All rights reserved. For copies call (800) 366-7788.

Week 45 — Marriage

Monday	Testimony from *The Promise Keeper*
Tuesday	Joseph L. Garlington, *Right or Reconciled?* (Destiny Image, 1998)
Wednesday	Adapted from *Dangers Men Face* © 1997 by Jerry White. Used by permission of NavPress, Colorado Springs, Colorado. All rights reserved. For copies call (800) 366-7788.
Thursday	From *Disciplines of a Godly Man* by R. Kent Hughes. Copyright © 1991. Used by permission of Good News Publishers/Crossway Books, Wheaton, Illinois 60187.
Friday	Robertson McQuilkin, *Christianity Today* (October 8, 1990)
Saturday	Louis and Melissa McBurney, *Marriage Partnership* (November/December 1987)

Week 46 — Anger

| Monday | Bruce Hennigan, from *God's Man,* edited by Don M. Aycock. Copyright © 1998. Kregel Publications, Grand Rapids, MI 49503. |
| Tuesday | Charles A. Ballard, "Prodigal Dad," *Say Amen* (Spring 1998) |

Wednesday	Adapted from *Dangers Men Face* © 1997 by Jerry White. Used by permission of NavPress, Colorado Springs, Colorado. All rights reserved. For copies call (800) 366-7788.
Thursday	From *Leadership Prayers*, Richard Kriegbaum © 1998 Used by permission of Tyndale House Publishers, Inc. All rights reserved.
Friday	Jackie Slater with Rosey Grier and Kathi Mills, *Winning* Copyright © 1990. Regal Books, Ventura, CA 93003. Used by permission.
Saturday	Jerry White, *Dangers Men Face.*

Week 47 — Character

Monday	Michael B. Brown, from *God's Man*, edited by Don M. Aycock. Copyright © 1998 Kregel Publications, Grand Rapids, MI 49503.
Tuesday	George Munzing, *Preaching Today*, #32. To subscribe, call 800-806-7796 or go to http://st3.yahoo.com/cti/preac.html.
Wednesday	Edwin Louis Cole, *Real Man* (Nelson, 1992)
Thursday	Larry Burkett, "True to Your Word," *The Christian Businessman* (Sept./Oct. 1998)
Friday	Wally Kroeker, *God's Week Has 7 Days* (Herald, 1998)
Saturday	Howard Hendricks, *A Life of Integrity* (Multnomah, 1997)

Week 48 — Spiritual Warfare

Monday	From *Spiritual Warfare*, Timothy M. Warner. Copyright © 1991. Used by permission of Good News Publishers/Crossway Books, Wheaton, Illinois 60187.
Tuesday	R. Arthur Mathews, *Born for Battle* (Shaw, 1978)
Wednesday	R. Arthur Mathews, *Born for Battle* (Shaw, 1978)
Thursday	Michael Green, *Exposing the Prince of Darkness* (Servant, 1981)
Friday	From *Spiritual Warfare* Timothy M. Warner. Copyright © 1991. Used by permission of Good News Publishers/Crossway Books, Wheaton, Illinois 60187.
Saturday	Roger Barrier, *Listening to the Voice of God* (Bethany, 1998)

Week 49 — Work

Monday	Dennis Hillman, from *God's Man*, edited by Don M. Aycock. Copyright © 1998. Kregel Publications, Grand Rapids, MI 49503.
Tuesday	From *God's Man*, edited by Don M. Aycock. Copyright © 1998. Kregel Publications, Grand Rapids, MI 49503.
Wednesday	Wally Kroeker, *God's Week Has 7 Days* (Herald, 1998)
Thursday	Harold Hawkins, from *God's Man*, edited by Don M. Aycock. Copyright © 1998. Kregel Publications, Grand Rapids, MI 49503.
Friday	Wally Kroeker, *God's Week Has 7 Days* (Herald, 1998)

| Saturday | Wally Kroeker with Ben Sprunger & Carol J. Suter, *Faith Dilemmas for Marketplace Christians* (Herald, 1997) |

Week 50 — Caring for Others

Monday	Calvin Miller, *Preaching Today*, #51. To subscribe, call 800-806-7796 or go to http://st3.yahoo.com/cti/preac.html.
Tuesday	Don Graham, *Leadership* (Vol. 9, No. 1). To subscribe, call 800-777-3136.
Wednesday	Larry A. Payne, *Fresh Illustrations for Preaching and Teaching* (Baker, 1997)
Thursday	Charles R. Swindoll, *Three Steps Forward, Two Steps Back* (Nelson, 1980)
Friday	Haddon Robinson, *Preaching Today*, #186. To subscribe, call 800-806-7796 or go to http://st3.yahoo.com/cti/preac.html.
Saturday	Haddon Robinson, *Preaching Today*, #102. To subscribe, call 800-806-7796 or go to http://st3.yahoo.com/cti/preac.html.

Week 51 — Fathering

Monday	PK Net Testimony of the Week (May 28, 1998)
Tuesday	Charlene Fain, *Say Amen* (Spring 1998)
Wednesday	Robert Leslie Holmes, from *God's Man*, edited by Don M. Aycock. Copyright © 1998. Kregel Publications, Grand Rapids, MI 49503.
Thursday	Jim Burton, from *God's Man*, edited by Don M. Aycock. Copyright © 1998. Kregel Publications, Grand Rapids, MI 49503.
Friday	Crawford W. Lorrits, Jr., *Never Walk Away* (Moody Bible Institute, Moody Press, 1997)
Saturday	Crawford W. Lorrits, Jr., *Never Walk Away* (Moody Bible Institute, Moody Press, 1997)

Week 52 — Witness

Monday	From *The Lost Art of Disciple Making* by Leroy Eims. Copyright © 1978 by Leroy Eims. Used by permission of Zondervan Publishing House.
Tuesday	P. J. Richardson & Robert Darden, *Wheels of Thunder* (Nelson, 1997)
Wednesday	Luis Palau, *The Peter Promise* (Discovery House, 1996)
Thursday	Dave Branon & Joe Pellegrino, *Safe at Home* (Moody Bible Institute, Moody Press, 1992)
Friday	Fritz Dale, *The Promise Keeper* (Nov./Dec. 1998)
Saturday	Alan Andrews, *One-to-One: A Ministry Report from The Navigators*, a donor publication (Fall 1998, issue 25)

Index

A

Accountability . . . . .Week 36

Anger . . . . .Week 46

B

Beating Temptation . . . . . . .Week 18

Being an Example . . . . .Week 41

Boldness . . . . .Week 20

C

Caring for Others . . . . .Week 50

Character . . . . .Week 47

Church . . . . Week 5

Coming Back . . . . .Week 13

Commitment . . . . .Week 25

Commitment to Family . . .Week 30

Connecting . . . . .Week 32

Courage . . . . Week 9

D

Dealing with Failure . . . . . . .Week 42

E

Encouragement . . . . .Week 33

Enriching Your Wife . . . . . .Week 27

F

Family .Week 1

Fathering . . . . .Weeks 12, 51

Friendship & Accountability . .Week 3

Forgiveness . . . . .Week 19

G

God's Love . . . . .Week 40

H

Handling Anger . . . . .Week 22

Hearing God . . . . .Week 21

Holiness . . . . .Week 44

Honoring Christ . . . . .Week 2

I

Integrity . . . . .Week 17

L

Loving Jesus . . . . .Week 23

M

Marriage . . . . .Week 45

Marriage & Family . . . . .Week 6

Meaningful Work . . . . .Week 14

Meeting Challenges . . . . . . .Week 15

Money . . . . .Week 16

P

Prayer . . . . .Week 37

R

Racial Reconciliation . . . . .Week 8

Racism . . . . .Week 35

Resisting Evil . . . . .Week 34

S

Sacrifice .Week 10

Self-Discipline . . . . .Week 38

Serving . . . . .Week 31

Sexual Purity . . . . .Weeks 4, 43

Sharing Faith . . . . .Week 7

Sin & Forgiveness . . . . .Week 39

Spiritual Warfare . . . . .Week 48

T

Trust in God . . . . .Weeks 11, 29

Truthfulness . . . . .Week 26

W

Wise Decisions . . . . .Week 24

Witness .Week 52

Work . . . . .Weeks 28, 49

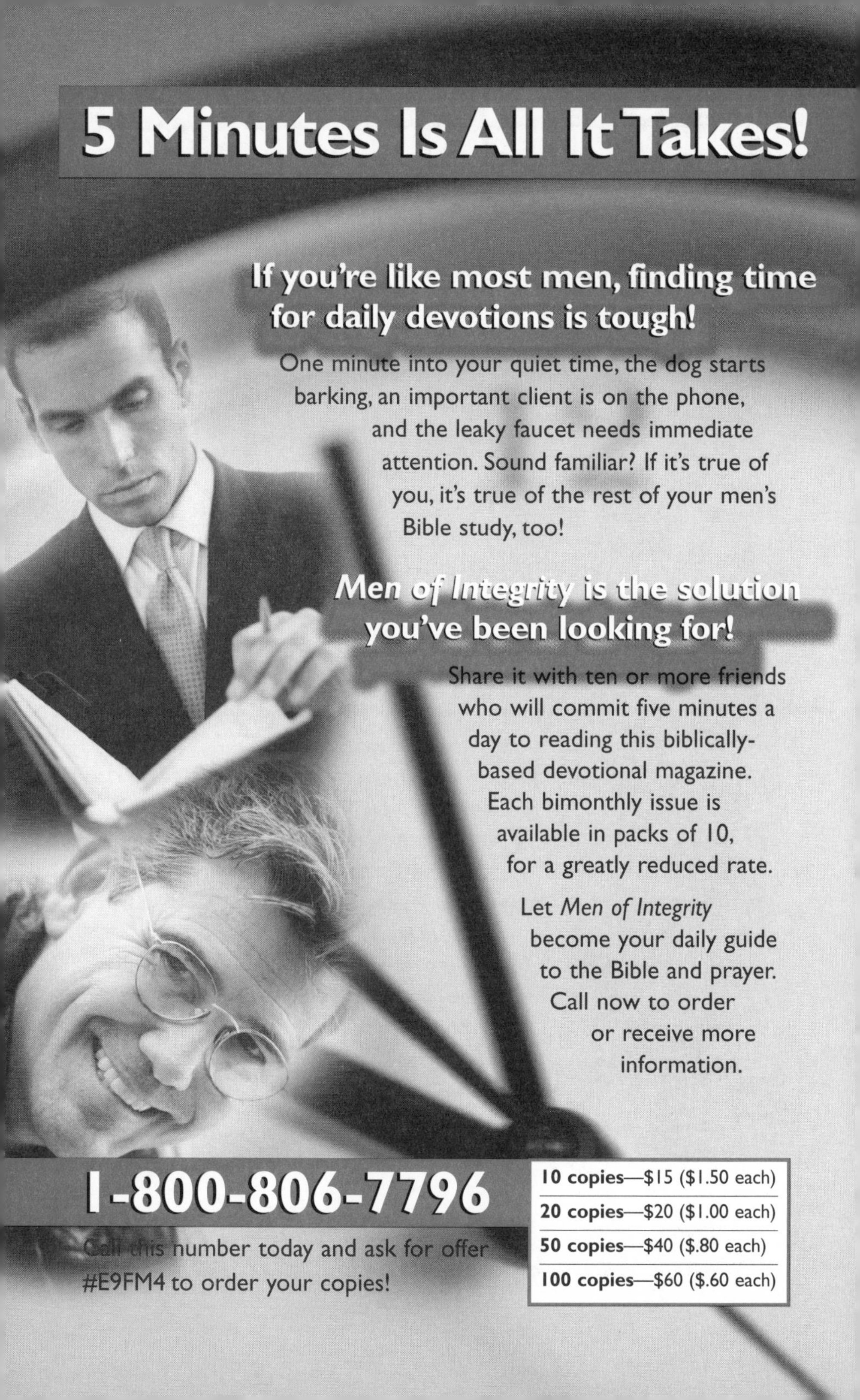
5 Minutes Is All It Takes!
If you're like most men, finding time for daily devotions is tough!
One minute into your quiet time, the dog starts barking, an important client is on the phone, and the leaky faucet needs immediate attention. Sound familiar? If it's true of you, it's true of the rest of your men's Bible study, too!
Men of Integrity is the solution you've been looking for!
Share it with ten or more friends who will commit five minutes a day to reading this biblically-based devotional magazine. Each bimonthly issue is available in packs of 10, for a greatly reduced rate.
Let Men of Integrity become your daily guide to the Bible and prayer. Call now to order or receive more information.
1-800-806-7796
Call this number today and ask for offer #E9FM4 to order your copies!
10 copies—$15 ($1.50 each)
20 copies—$20 ($1.00 each)
50 copies—$40 ($.80 each)
100 copies—$60 ($.60 each)

Additional Titles from Promise Keepers

APPLYING THE SEVEN PROMISES
Bob Horner, Ron Ralston, and David Sunde
These application studies encourage men to honor God and integrate his Word into all their relationships by incorporating the power of worship, prayer and mentoring to daily life. A key resource for men's small group study or for personal growth.

THE MAKING OF A GODLY MAN WORKBOOK
John Trent
Designed specifically to help men in their pursuit of a deeper, more abiding faith in God, this in-depth study offers a plan for integrating the seven promises of a Promise Keeper into everyday life. Insightful and practical, *The Making of a Godly Man* is a great tool for men's groups or individual study.

THE PROMISE KEEPER AT WORK
Bob Horner, Ron Ralston, and David Sunde
In 45 easy-to-use study sessions, *The Promise Keeper at Work* teaches men how to integrate their faith, as well as a higher ethical standard, into the workplace. With biblical guidelines and practical applications, this book is packed full of wisdom and insight that will give work and life new purpose.

SEVEN PROMISES OF A PROMISE KEEPER
Various Authors
This best-selling book has been completely revised and expanded with new author insights and stories on each of the Promise Keeper's seven promises. Men will find practical ways to deepen their Christian walk with encouraging chapters from Bill Bright, James Dobson, Gary Smalley, Luis Palau and many others.

SEVEN PROMISES PRACTICED
Various Authors

(Study Guide also available)

Based on the video series of the same title, *Seven Promises Practiced* offers a wealth of knowledge and insights outlining the Promise Keepers' seven promises for Christian men. With teaching from well-known leaders such as Jack Hayford, Gary Smalley, Charles Swindoll and Max Lucado, this seven-video series shows how to unlock the power and potential of men and how to cultivate life-changing relationships with family and friends.

SEVEN PROMISES PRACTICED,
VIDEO 1: A MAN AND HIS GOD
Jack Hayford

Pastor/author Jack Hayford teaches how Promise Keepers can honor Christ, with the help of the Holy Spirit, through worship, prayer and obedience to God's Word. A compelling beginning to the "Seven Promises Practiced" series.

SEVEN PROMISES PRACTICED,
VIDEO 2: A MAN AND HIS FRIENDS
Howard Hendricks

To keep their promises, men need accountability. In this video, distinguished professor and author Howard Hendricks shares how men can develop vital relationships with a few other brothers to help them be Promise Keepers.

SEVEN PROMISES PRACTICED,
VIDEO 3: A MAN AND HIS INTEGRITY
Crawford Loritts

A Promise Keeper is committed to practice spiritual, moral, ethical, and sexual purity. Crawford Loritts, pastor, author and Campus Crusade for Christ veteran, challenges men to make this commitment a consistent reality of life.

SEVEN PROMISES PRACTICED,
VIDEO 4: A MAN AND HIS FAMILY
Gary Smalley

A Promise Keeper is committed to building a strong marriage and family through love, protection and biblical values. Marriage and family expert Gary Smalley shows men how to demonstrate this value day-to-day, year-to-year.

SEVEN PROMISES PRACTICED,
VIDEO 5: A MAN AND HIS CHURCH
Charles R. Swindoll

The author of over 40 books, Dallas Seminary president Charles Swindoll examines the Promise Keepers commitment to support the mission of the local church through prayer, finances and service. A challenging, practical video of the "Seven Promises Practiced" series.

SEVEN PROMISES PRACTICED,
VIDEO 6: A MAN AND HIS BROTHERS
Max Lucado

Master storyteller Max Lucado challenges men to reach beyond racial and denominational barriers and embrace the brotherhood in Christ as a demonstration of the power of biblical unity.

SEVEN PROMISES PRACTICED,
VIDEO 7: A MAN AND HIS WORLD
Isaac Canales

Pastor/author Isaac Canales shares practical wisdom, showing how Promise Keepers can be obedient to the Great Commission and influence their world for Christ.